Much More Social Studies Through Children's Literature

Recent Titles in Through Children's Literature

Science Through Children's Literature: An Integrated Approach
Carol M. Butzow and John W. Butzow

Promoting a Global Community Through Multicultural Children's Literature
Stanley F. Steiner

Investigating Natural Disasters Through Children's Literature: An Integrated Approach
Anthony Fredericks

Math Links: Teaching the NCTM 2000 Standards Through Children's Literature
Caroline W. Evans, Anne J. Leija and Trina R. Falkner

Hobbies Through Children's Books and Activities
Nancy Allen Jurenka

The World of Work Through Children's Literature: An Integrated Approach
Carol M. Butzow and John W. Butzow

Integrating Art and Language Arts Through Children's Literature
Debi Englebaugh

Teaching Problem Solving Through Children's Literature
James W. Forgan

Technology Through Children's Literature
Holly Doe

Multicultural American History Through Children's Literature
Kay A. Chick and Deborah Ann Ellermeyer

Character Builders: Books and Activities for Character Education
Liz Knowles, EdD and Martha Smith

The Natural World Through Children's Literature: An Integrated Approach
Carol M. Butzow and John W. Butzow

Much More Social Studies Through Children's Literature

A Collaborative Approach

Anthony D. Fredericks

Illustrated by Judy Grupp

An imprint of Libraries Unlimited
Westport, Connecticut • London

Library of Congress Cataloging-in-Publication Data

Fredericks, Anthony D.
Much more social studies through children's literature : a collaborative approach / Anthony D. Fredericks ; illustrated by Judy Grupp.
p. cm. — (Through children's literature)
Includes bibliographical references and index.
ISBN-13: 978-1-59158-445-2 (alk. paper)
ISBN-10: 1-59158-445-0 (alk. paper)
1. Social sciences—Study and teaching (Elementary)—United States. 2. Children's literature—Study and teaching (Elementary)—United States. 3. Language experience approach in education—United States. I. Title.
LB1584.F6592 2007
372.83—dc22 2006037630

British Library Cataloguing in Publication Data is available.

Library of Congress Catalog Card Number: 2006037630
ISBN: 978-1-59158-445-2

First published in 2007

Libraries Unlimited/Teacher Ideas Press, 88 Post Road West, Westport, CT 06881
A Member of the Greenwood Publishing Group, Inc.
www.lu.com

Printed in the United States of America

The paper used in this book complies with the Permanent Paper Standard issued by the National Information Standards Organization (Z39.4.8–1984).

10 9 8 7 6 5 4 3 2 1

To Teri Puryear (aka "The World's Greatest Library/Media Specialist), for her dedication to children's literature, enthusiastic support, and endearing friendship. May they always be celebrated!

Contents

Preface xvii
Acknowledgments xix

Part I: Children's Literature in the Social Studies Curriculum

Chapter 1: Teaching Elementary Social Studies 3
Scope and Sequence 3
The National Council for the Social Studies 5
Rethinking the Social Studies Curriculum 8
Constructivism and Social Studies Instruction 9
Social Studies Teaching and Multiple Intelligences 10
Final Thought 12

Chapter 2: Social Studies and Children's Literature 13
Integrating Literature 13
The Literature-Based Approach to Social Studies Instruction 14
Advantages of Literature-Based Instruction 16

Chapter 3: Collaboration: The Name of the Game 19
Benefits 19
Forging the Partnership 20
Librarian ➔ Classroom Teacher 20
Classroom Teacher ➔ Librarian 22

Chapter 4: How to Use This Book 25
Book Selection 25
Hands-on, Minds-on Activities 26
Readers Theatre 27
Activity Sheets 28

Part II: Activities and Processes

Chapter 5: Child and Self 31
All the Colors of the Earth 31
Summary 31
Social Studies Disciplines 32
NCSS Thematic Strands 32
Critical Thinking Questions 32
Related Books 32
Activities 32
Giraffes Can't Dance 34
Summary 34
Social Studies Disciplines 34
NCSS Thematic Strands 34
Critical Thinking Questions 34
Related Books 35
Activities 35

Happy Birth Day! . . . 37
Summary . . . 37
Social Studies Disciplines . . . 37
NCSS Thematic Strands . . . 37
Critical Thinking Questions . . . 37
Related Books . . . 38
Activities . . . 38
I'm Gonna Like Me: Letting Off a Little Self-Esteem . . . 40
Summary . . . 40
Social Studies Disciplines . . . 40
NCSS Thematic Strands . . . 40
Critical Thinking Questions . . . 40
Related Books . . . 41
Activities . . . 41
Parts . . . 43
Summary . . . 43
Social Studies Disciplines . . . 43
NCSS Thematic Strands . . . 43
Critical Thinking Questions . . . 43
Related Books . . . 44
Activities . . . 44
The Secret of Saying Thanks . . . 46
Summary . . . 46
Social Studies Disciplines . . . 46
NCSS Thematic Strands . . . 46
Critical Thinking Questions . . . 46
Related Books . . . 47
Activities . . . 47

Chapter 6: Family . . . 49
Mama Loves Me from Away . . . 49
Summary . . . 49
Social Studies Disciplines . . . 49
NCSS Thematic Strands . . . 49
Critical Thinking Questions . . . 50
Related Books . . . 50
Activities . . . 50
So Far from the Sea . . . 52
Summary . . . 52
Social Studies Disciplines . . . 52
NCSS Thematic Strands . . . 52
Critical Thinking Questions . . . 53
Related Books . . . 53
Activities . . . 53

Star Blanket . . . 55
Summary . . . 55
Social Studies Disciplines . . . 55
NCSS Thematic Strands . . . 55
Critical Thinking Questions . . . 55
Related Books . . . 56
Activities . . . 56
The Star People: A Lakota Story . . . 58
Summary . . . 58
Social Studies Disciplines . . . 58
NCSS Thematic Strands . . . 58
Critical Thinking Questions . . . 58
Related Books . . . 59
Activities . . . 59
Tattered Sails . . . 61
Summary . . . 61
Social Studies Disciplines . . . 61
NCSS Thematic Strands . . . 61
Critical Thinking Questions . . . 61
Related Books . . . 62
Activities . . . 62
Chapter 7: Community and Neighborhood . . . 65
How Raven Stole the Sun . . . 65
Summary . . . 65
Social Studies Disciplines . . . 65
NCSS Thematic Strands . . . 65
Critical Thinking Questions . . . 66
Related Books . . . 66
Activities . . . 66
My Great-Aunt Arizona . . . 68
Summary . . . 68
Social Studies Disciplines . . . 68
NCSS Thematic Strands . . . 68
Critical Thinking Questions . . . 68
Related Books . . . 69
Activities . . . 69
On One Flower: Butterflies, Ticks and a Few More Icks . . . 71
Summary . . . 71
Social Studies Disciplines . . . 71
NCSS Thematic Strands . . . 71
Critical Thinking Questions . . . 71
Related Books . . . 72
Activities . . . 72

Chapter 7: Community and Neighborhood (*Cont.*)
The Other Side 74
Summary 74
Social Studies Disciplines 74
NCSS Thematic Strands 74
Critical Thinking Questions 74
Related Books 75
Activities 75
Quinito's Neighborhood: El Vecindario de Quinito 77
Summary 77
Social Studies Disciplines 77
NCSS Thematic Strands 77
Critical Thinking Questions 78
Related Books 78
Activities 78
Tomás and the Library Lady 80
Summary 80
Social Studies Disciplines 80
NCSS Thematic Strands 80
Critical Thinking Questions 80
Related Books 81
Activities 81
Wilfrid Gordon McDonald Partridge 83
Summary 83
Social Studies Disciplines 83
NCSS Thematic Strands 83
Critical Thinking Questions 83
Related Books 84
Activities 84

Chapter 8: City and Country 87
Fireboat: The Heroic Adventures of the John J. Harvey 87
Summary 87
Social Studies Disciplines 87
NCSS Thematic Strands 88
Critical Thinking Questions 88
Related Books 88
Activities 88
An Island Scrapbook: Dawn to Dusk on a Barrier Island 90
Summary 90
Social Studies Disciplines 90
NCSS Thematic Strands 90
Critical Thinking Questions 90
Related Books 91
Activities 91

Life on an Apple Orchard 93
Summary 93
Social Studies Disciplines 93
NCSS Thematic Strands 93
Critical Thinking Questions 94
Related Books 94
Activities 94
Mountain Town 96
Summary 96
Social Studies Disciplines 96
NCSS Thematic Strands 96
Critical Thinking Questions 96
Related Books 97
Activities 97
Near One Cattail: Turtles, Logs, and Leaping Frogs 99
Summary 99
Social Studies Disciplines 99
NCSS Thematic Strands 99
Critical Thinking Questions 99
Related Books 100
Activities 100
Rhyolite: The True Story of a Ghost Town 102
Summary 102
Social Studies Disciplines 102
NCSS Thematic Strands 102
Critical Thinking Questions 102
Related Books 103
Activities 103
Where Horses Run Free: A Dream for the American Mustang 106
Summary 106
Social Studies Disciplines 106
NCSS Thematic Strands 106
Critical Thinking Questions 106
Related Books 107
Activities 107

Chapter 9: States and Regions 109
Crab Moon 109
Summary 109
Social Studies Disciplines 109
NCSS Thematic Strands 109
Critical Thinking Questions 110
Related Books 110
Activities 110

Chapter 9: States and Regions (*Cont.*)

G Is for Golden: A California Alphabet. 112
Summary 112
Social Studies Disciplines 112
NCSS Thematic Strands 112
Critical Thinking Questions 112
Related Books 113
Activities 113
G Is for Grand Canyon: An Arizona Alphabet. 115
Summary 115
Social Studies Disciplines 115
NCSS Thematic Strands 115
Critical Thinking Questions 115
Related Books 116
Activities 116
High as a Hawk: A Brave Girl's Historic Climb 118
Summary 118
Social Studies Disciplines 118
NCSS Thematic Strands 118
Critical Thinking Questions 118
Related Books 119
Activities 119
I Have Heard of a Land 121
Summary 121
Social Studies Disciplines 121
NCSS Thematic Strands 121
Critical Thinking Questions 122
Related Books 122
Activities 122
Quilt of States: Piecing Together America 124
Summary 124
Social Studies Disciplines 124
NCSS Thematic Strands 124
Critical Thinking Questions 124
Related Books 125
Activities 125
The Tsunami Quilt: Grandfather's Story 127
Summary 127
Social Studies Disciplines 127
NCSS Thematic Strands 127
Critical Thinking Questions 127
Related Books 128
Activities 128

Chapter 10: Nation and Country 131
A Is for America: An American Alphabet. 131
Summary 131
Social Studies Disciplines 131
NCSS Thematic Strands 132
Critical Thinking Questions 132
Related Books 132
Activities 132
Coming to America: A Muslim Family's Story 134
Summary 134
Social Studies Disciplines 134
NCSS Thematic Strands 134
Critical Thinking Questions 134
Related Books 135
Activities 135
Martin's Big Words: The Life of Dr. Martin Luther King, Jr. 137
Summary 137
Social Studies Disciplines 137
NCSS Thematic Strands 137
Critical Thinking Questions 138
Related Books 138
Activities 138
Pearl Harbor Warriors: The Bugler, the Pilot, the Friendship 140
Summary 140
Social Studies Disciplines 140
NCSS Thematic Strands 140
Critical Thinking Questions 140
Related Books 141
Activities 141
So You Want to Be President? 143
Summary 143
Social Studies Disciplines 143
NCSS Thematic Strands 143
Critical Thinking Questions 144
Related Books 144
Activities 144
The Star-Spangled Banner 146
Summary 146
Social Studies Disciplines 146
NCSS Thematic Strands 146
Critical Thinking Questions 146
Related Books 147
Activities 147
Vote! 149
Summary 149
Social Studies Disciplines 149

NCSS Thematic Strands 149
Critical Thinking Questions 149
Related Books 150
Activities 150

Chapter 11: World 153
Antarctic Journal: Four Months at the Bottom of the World 153
Summary 153
Social Studies Disciplines 154
NCSS Thematic Strands 154
Critical Thinking Questions 154
Related Books 154
Activities 154
Beautiful Blackbird 156
Summary 156
Social Studies Disciplines 156
NCSS Thematic Strands 156
Critical Thinking Questions 156
Related Books 156
Activities 157
Horse Hooves and Chicken Feet: Mexican Folktales 159
Summary 159
Social Studies Disciplines 159
NCSS Thematic Strands 159
Critical Thinking Questions 159
Related Books 160
Activities 160
Jabuti the Tortoise: A Trickster Tale from the Amazon 162
Summary 162
Social Studies Disciplines 162
NCSS Thematic Strands 162
Critical Thinking Questions 162
Related Books 163
Activities 163
Lord of the Cranes 165
Summary 165
Social Studies Disciplines 165
NCSS Thematic Strands 165
Critical Thinking Questions 165
Related Books 166
Activities 166
This Place I Know: Poems of Comfort 168
Summary 168
Social Studies Disciplines 169
NCSS Thematic Strands 169
Critical Thinking Questions 169
Related Books 169
Activities 169

Part III: Readers Theatre

What Is the Value of Readers Theatre? . . . 171
Using Readers Theatre . . . 173
Presentation Suggestions . . . 174
References . . . 175
The First Thanksgiving (Nation) . . . 176
Social Studies Concept . . . 176
Summary . . . 176
Social Studies Disciplines . . . 176
NCSS Thematic Strands . . . 176
Critical Thinking Questions . . . 176
Three Ways of Living (City and Country) . . . 180
Social Studies Concept . . . 180
Summary . . . 180
Social Studies Disciplines . . . 180
NCSS Thematic Strands . . . 180
Critical Thinking Questions . . . 180
A Conversation with Thomas Jefferson (Nation) . . . 185
Social Studies Concept . . . 185
Summary . . . 185
Social Studies Disciplines . . . 185
NCSS Thematic Strands . . . 185
Critical Thinking Questions . . . 185
All Together Now (Community and Neighborhood) . . . 192
Social Studies Concept . . . 192
Summary . . . 192
Social Studies Disciplines . . . 192
NCSS Thematic Strands . . . 192
Critical Thinking Questions . . . 192
The Shapiros' New Adventure (World) . . . 196
Social Studies Concept . . . 196
Summary . . . 196
Social Studies Disciplines . . . 196
NCSS Thematic Strands . . . 196
Critical Thinking Questions . . . 196
Day of the Wave (States and Regions) . . . 203
Social Studies Concept . . . 203
Summary . . . 203
Social Studies Disciplines . . . 203
NCSS Thematic Strands . . . 203
Critical Thinking Questions . . . 203

Part IV: Activity Sheets

Literature Log I . . . 211
Literature Log II . . . 213
Story Map . . . 214
Story Pyramid . . . 215
Character Analysis Frame . . . 216
I Wonder 217
A Reader's Menu . . . 218
Author Study . . . 219
Word by Word . . . 220
Book by Book . . . 221

Appendix A: An Annotated Bibliography of Children's Literature . . . 223
The Concepts of Social Studies . . . 223
Self . . . 223
Family . . . 224
Communities and Neighborhoods . . . 225
City and County . . . 226
States and Regions . . . 227
Nation . . . 227
World . . . 228
The Disciplines of Social Studies . . . 229
Geography . . . 229
Anthropology . . . 230
Sociology . . . 231
Political Science . . . 232
Economics . . . 232
History . . . 233
Appendix B: Teacher Resources by Anthony D. Fredericks . . . 235
Index . . . 239

Preface

One of the first activities I share in my undergraduate methods course, "Teaching Elementary Social Studies," is to invite preservice teachers to make two lists. The first is of those social studies experiences they recall to be most memorable when they were elementary students. The other is a list of those experiences that were somewhat less than memorable. Not surprisingly, the "negative" lists are considerably longer than the "positive" lists. Typically, the lists look something like the following:

Negative Experiences	Positive Experiences
filling in workbook pages	constructing models
reading the chapter; answering the questions	taking field trips
watching old filmstrips/videos	interviewing people
taking true/false tests	dressing up as historical figures
listening to boring lectures (lots of them)	self-producing slide shows
round robin reading	designing posters
memorizing dates	making a diorama
memorizing capitals	putting together a mobile
memorizing presidents	writing a book
memorizing states	
memorizing the gross national product of Romania	
taking weekly quizzes	
using outdated textbooks	
using old handouts	
being asked too many questions	

We spend time analyzing the two lists and inevitably reach the conclusion that those events in which students had an active role (what I like to refer to as "hands-on, minds-on") are those that have the greatest instructional value and also consistently surface on the "positive" lists. On the other hand, and not surprisingly, those experiences in which students were *passive* observers are those that fostered negative attitudes toward social studies and often appear on the "negative" lists. Early in the semester it becomes clear that social studies instruction that *engages* rather than *dictates* has the most profound and significant influence in children's lives—both now and well after students leave elementary school.

This book, like its two predecessors—*Social Studies Through Children's Literature* (1991) and *More Social Studies Through Children's literature* (2000)—is designed to offer classroom teachers and school librarians a participatory approach to social studies education. In this "hands-on, minds-on" philosophy of learning, students are actively engaged in the dynamics of education—creating, manipulating, modeling, inventing, discussing, sharing, engaging, and *doing* social studies. This emphasis in this book, as it was in the others, is on the *processes* of learning more than on the *products*. It is my fervent philosophy (and the philosophy of this book) that learning is not the accumulation or memorization of "stuff"; rather, what we do with that "stuff" is intrinsically more valuable, more enjoyable, and more instructive.

The overwhelming success of those first two books and the enthusiastic response of educators throughout North America to a process orientation in elementary social studies education precipitated the creation of this latest edition. The energy and creativity of those first two books is maintained and extended in this edition. In addition, the standards issued by the National Council on the Social Studies are embedded in all the activities, projects, and experiences promulgated in these pages. Just as exciting is the inclusion of some of the best new trade books—each filled with breathtaking illustrations and magical text that engages children in the enthusiasm of authentic social studies education. New sections on readers theatre and participatory activity sheets round out this latest edition.

Whether you are a classroom teacher or school librarian, it is my hope that you will discover in these pages all the vibrancy, creativity, magic, and wonder of a hands-on, minds-on social studies program. I also hope that the youngsters with whom you work will discover a plethora of mind-expanding, concept-building, and real-world experiences that will engage and excite them for many years to come (and that they will create *extensive* "positive" lists and *vacant* "negative" lists).

We are about to begin a most incredible journey. Hop on board!

Tony Fredericks

Acknowledgments

This book would not have been possible without the support, encouragement, and contributions of several individuals.

I am particularly indebted to a most incredible and delightful research assistant—Stephanie Riley. She single-handedly combed the shelves of countless libraries, interviewed a host of teachers and librarians, doggedly tracked down trade books on the Internet and in bookstores, pursued numerous bibliographies, and generated a wealth of creative book extensions across all the dimensions of social studies. Her aid and assistance were instrumental in the design and completion of this book. Likewise, her energy and enthusiasm for this project are liberally sprinkled throughout the pages of this book and reflect her enormous passion and enthusiasm for the teaching profession. She is the crème de la crème of teachers and has earned special commendations, standing ovations, and a plethora of cheers for her dedication and professionalism on this project.

Thunderous accolades go to my longtime friend and colleague, Teri Puryear (aka "The World's Greatest Library/Media Specialist") at Lake Murray Elementary School in Lexington, South Carolina. Her commitment to children's literature and the role of trade books in the lives of students is unmatched and unparalleled. She is the consummate professional—providing resources, advice, and constant support in a multitude of ways. Her friendship and counsel are forever valued and celebrated.

I am equally indebted to Ceri Collins, librarian at the Montgomery Elementary School in North Wales, Pennsylvania, who provided important insights and pertinent ideas on the importance of a collaborative relationship between teachers and librarians. So, too, am I indebted to the many school librarians I interviewed in my travels as a children's author. Professionals from Colorado, California, Arizona, New Mexico, Michigan, Wisconsin, North Carolina, Florida, South Carolina, Virginia, New Hampshire, New Jersey, and Pennsylvania shared their insights and wisdom about books and activities critical in a literature-based social studies program. They all were instrumental in helping me address the collaborative methods that can make that process happen.

Ovations and praise are due to Judy Grupp for her marvelous illustrations throughout this book. Her attention to detail and ability to work under tight deadlines are truly appreciated.

Mahalo to Greenwell Farms (www.greenwellfarms.com) on the Big Island of Hawai'i for producing the finest Kona coffee in the world. That magic elixir sustained and nourished me throughout each and every stage of the writing process.

My wife, Phyllis, deserves special commendation for handling the idiosyncrasies and strange work habits of a writer-teacher-husband with love and patient understanding. Now, she can look forward to the cleaning of the attic, the clearing of the garage, and various other tasks still unchecked on the "honey-do" list.

Perhaps my cat, Tubby—a mass of gray fur and insatiable curiosity—deserves the highest accolades of all. He was an occasional visitor during early morning typing, afternoon research, and late evening editing. Requiring only an intermittent belly scratch and a warm place under my desk, he was both companion and comfort.

Part I

Children's Literature in the Social Studies Curriculum

CHAPTER 1

Teaching Elementary Social Studies

Much More Social Studies Through Children's Literature was born of a perceived and long-standing need to infuse children's literature into the entire elementary curriculum. It also grew out of many conversations with classroom teachers and school librarians around the country who were seeking to expand social studies education and make it part of a truly integrated curriculum. If one subscribes to the notion that books are vehicles by which students can explore every dimension of their world (and beyond), then we should also believe that we can facilitate those discoveries through an active, process-oriented, and literature-based social studies program. This book is designed to offer teachers and librarians a participatory approach to social studies education—an approach that says that when students are provided opportunities to make an investment of self in their education, that education will become both meaningful and relevant.

In essence, social studies is a broad-based exploration of people, how they live, and how they get along with one another. To that end, the social studies program encompasses all of the other disciplines of the elementary curriculum. For example, reading provides us with the tools to study and learn about people; science gives us opportunities to understand people and their interactions with the environment; language arts allows people to communicate with one another; and math provides us with the quantitative tools to measure and evaluate our world. In short, social studies is not an isolated subject, but rather one that can and should be integrated throughout all the academic experiences of children.

SCOPE AND SEQUENCE

The scope and sequence of most social studies programs is based on tradition as well as suggestions from the National Council for the Social Studies (NCSS). Typically, most elementary programs are designed according to the following hierarchy:

1. **CHILD/SELF**—At this stage, usually initiated at the kindergarten level, students are given opportunities to investigate topics most familiar to them, including their persons, going to school, rules for safe living, and working together.

2. **FAMILIES**—Here children are exposed to aspects of what families do, as well as the world beyond their own family. Topics at this level may include the relationship of the individual to the family, families and their needs, how families work, and families in neighborhoods.

3. **COMMUNITIES/NEIGHBORHOODS**—At this stage of the social studies program students are introduced to neighborhoods and communities. Typical topics include transportation and communication, community services, celebrating holidays, how neighborhoods change, and rural and urban communities.

4. **CITIES/COUNTRY**—At this level students are exposed to information on larger community concepts. Usually comparisons are made between communities and cities in terms of the parts of a city, life in early cities, local government, comparative cultures, and locations of cities.

5. **STATES/REGIONS**—This level of the social studies curriculum includes information on different sections of the United States as well as various geographical characteristics of selected states. Emphasis includes comparative studies on desert, mountain, plains, and forest regions of the United States and other selected areas within our country.

6. **NATION/UNITED STATES**—The primary emphasis at this level is on the United States, although it may include reference to Canada and/or Latin America. Topics include the founding of our country, historical facts, geographical data, chronology, and our cultural and ethnic heritage.

7. **WORLD**—This level often includes a large number of topics dealing with either the Western or Eastern Hemispheres or both. Areas covered include ancient civilizations, Asia, Europe, Africa, and the Middle East. At this level the curriculum is very crowded and diverse.

The curriculum above is usually referred to as the *widening horizons* or *expanding environments* curriculum. It is based on the idea that children first need to deal with concepts that are relative to their immediate environment (self) and systematically progress to concepts that move in concentric circles out and beyond that environment, as depicted in figure 1.1.

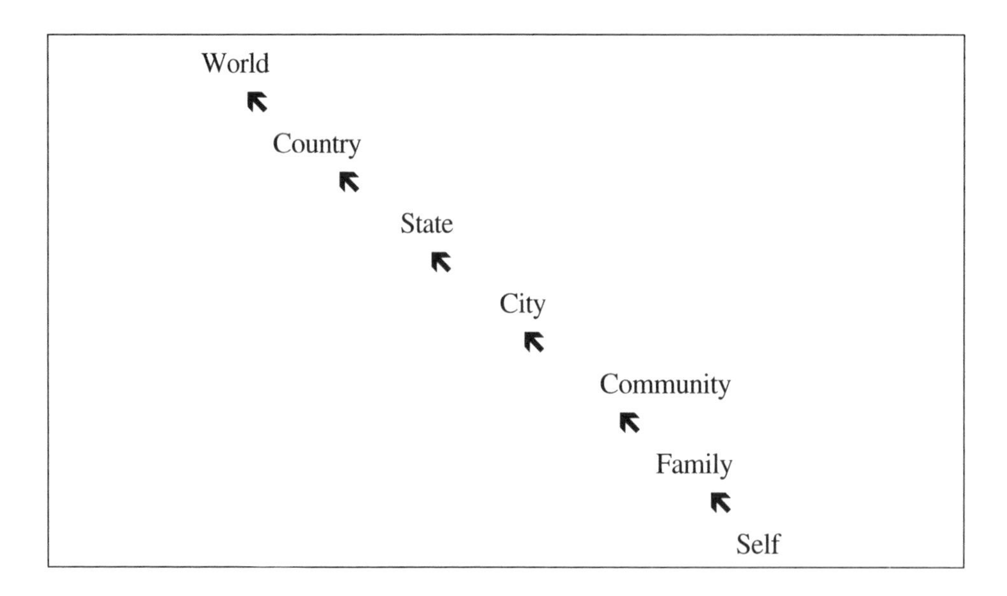

Figure 1.1. Systematic progression in the social studies curriculum.

While most social studies curricula are predicated on the *expanding environments* idea, teachers and librarians need to be cognizant of the interests, needs, and abilities of their students if they are to present a constantly evolving and dynamic social studies program. In short, good social studies programs allow for modification of the expanding environments plan; they begin with what children know, but they also include content that allows students to venture beyond their immediate environment.

THE NATIONAL COUNCIL FOR THE SOCIAL STUDIES

In response to a demand for a cohesive set of standards that address overall curriculum design and comprehensive student performance expectations in social studies education, the National Council for the Social Studies developed and promulgated the NCSS Standards. These standards are organized around broad themes and provide a focused outline of the essential components of a well-structured social studies curriculum.

Not only do the Standards provide an outline for the development of social studies instruction, they also bring coordination, consistency, and coherence to the improvement of social studies education. As such, the Standards are organized into 10 basic themes:

- Culture
- Time, Continuity, and Change
- People, Places, and Environment
- Individual Development and Identity
- Individuals, Groups, and Institutions
- Power, Authority, and Governance
- Production, Distribution, and Consumption
- Science, Technology, and Society
- Global Connections
- Civic Ideals and Practices

The NCSS Standards are intentionally integrative and multidisciplinary. That is, several traditional social studies disciplines (i.e., sociology, history, political science, geography, anthropology, economics) may be "blended" together to form a more cohesive look at a topic or theme. This does not diminish the import of those disciplines, but rather provides classroom teachers and school librarians with a plethora of extended teaching and learning opportunities throughout the entire social studies curriculum.

Following is an abridged version of the NCSS Standards.

I. Culture

The study of culture prepares students to answer questions such as: What are the common characteristics of different cultures? How do belief systems, such as religion and political ideals, influence other parts of the culture? What does language tell us about the culture? Relevant courses and disciplines include geography, history, sociology, and anthropology.

II. Time, Continuity, and Change

Human beings seek to understand their historical roots and to locate themselves in time. Knowing how to read and reconstruct the past allows one to develop a historical perspective and to answer questions such as: What happened in the past? How has the world changed? How might the world change in the future? Relevant courses and disciplines include history.

III. People, Places, and Environment

The study of people, places, and human-environment interactions assists students as they create their special views and geographic perspectives of the world. Students need to answer questions such as: Where are things located? Why are they located where they are? How do landforms change? Relevant courses and disciplines include geography and areas studies.

IV. Individual Development and Identity

Personal identity is shaped by one's culture, by groups, and by institutional influences. Students should consider such questions as: How do people learn? Why do people behave as they do? How do people meet their basic needs? How do individuals develop from youth to adulthood? Relevant courses and disciplines include psychology and anthropology.

V. Individuals, Groups, and Institutions

Institutions such as schools, churches, families, government agencies, and the courts play an integral role in people's lives. It is important that students learn how institutions are formed, what controls and influences them, and how they are maintained or changed. Students may address questions such as: What is the role of institutions in this and other societies? How am I influenced by institutions? What is my role in institutional change? Relevant courses and disciplines include sociology, anthropology, psychology, political science, and history.

VI. Power, Authority, and Governance

Understanding the historical development of structures of power, authority, and governance and their evolving functions in contemporary U.S. society and other parts of the world is essential for developing civic competence. Students need to confront questions such as: What is power? How is it gained? How are governments created? How can individual rights be protected? Relevant courses and disciplines include government, politics, political science, history, law, and other social sciences.

VII. Production, Distribution, and Consumption

Because people have wants that often exceed the resources available to them, a variety of ways have evolved to answer such questions as: What is to be produced? How is production organized? How are goods and services to be distributed? Relevant courses and disciplines include economics.

VIII. Science, Technology, and Society

Modern life as we know it would not be possible without technology and the science that supports it. But technology brings with it many questions such as: Is new technology better than old? How can we cope with the pace of technology? How can we manage technology so that the greatest number of people benefit from it? This theme draws upon the natural and physical sciences, social sciences, and the humanities. Relevant courses and disciplines include history, geography, economics, civics, and government.

IX. Global Connections

The realities of global interdependence require understanding the increasingly important and diverse global connections among world societies and the frequent tension between national interests and global priorities. Students need to be able to address such international issues as health care, the environment, human rights, economic competition, and political alliances. Relevant courses and disciplines include geography, culture, and economics. This theme may also draw upon the natural and physical sciences and the humanities.

X. Civic Ideals and Practices

An understanding of civic ideals and practices of citizenship is critical to full participation in society and is a central purpose of social studies. Students confront such questions as: What is civic participation and how can I be involved? What is the balance between rights and responsibilities? What is the role of the citizen in the community? How can I make a positive difference? Relevant courses and disciplines include history, political science, cultural anthropology, and fields such as global studies, law-related education, and the humanities.

Abridged from the Executive Summary of *Expect Excellence: Curriculum Standards for Social Studies Electronic Edition* (1996), 2–4.

When reviewing the standards above, it should become evident that many elements of those standards can be promoted in the philosophy and design of a literature-based approach to social studies education. Equally important is the fact that those standards assist teachers and librarians in defining the structural components of an effective social studies unit and the environment in which that instruction can take place.

RETHINKING THE SOCIAL STUDIES CURRICULUM

Whether you have been teaching for 1 year or 31 years, you undoubtedly have some assumptions, biases, and beliefs about what social studies is and how students learn this all-important subject. After more than 35 years of teaching, I, too, have some ideas and beliefs about teaching in general and about teaching social studies specifically. I'd like to invite you to take a few minutes to review these preconceptions, particularly in terms of how literature can and should be part of the teaching/learning cycle in social studies. It is not important that you agree with all of these statements, but rather that you evaluate them in terms of your own philosophy of how to teach social studies and how children can learn social studies.

1. The textbook should not be the entire social studies program. Instead, the program should be broad based, including a variety of materials and learning options.
2. Students have different learning styles, interests, and ability levels. The well-rounded curriculum is one that provides learning opportunities for each and every student, rather than one geared to the so-called average student (if there is such a creature).
3. Integrating social studies into the rest of the curriculum can be a positive experience for children. Students should be able to experience a broad definition of social studies as a positive dimension of all the other subject areas.
4. A child-centered curriculum is more meaningful and relevant than a teacher-directed one. In other words, when students are provided with opportunities to make their own decisions and select learning activities in keeping with their needs and interests, learning becomes much more productive.
5. Inquiry-based learning has powerful implications in any classroom or school library. Allowing students to chart their own paths of discovery and investigation can lead to the inculcation of valuable concepts.
6. Social studies instruction that relies on the memorization of dates, names, places, facts, and figures is boring! Placing this information in a context that has meaning for students helps them appreciate significant information as it relates to their lives.
7. Social studies should be taught all day, every day. This statement may be difficult to accept for most teachers and librarians, yet it is possible to infuse social studies into every aspect of the elementary curriculum without limiting other subjects or running out of time.

8. Teachers and librarians do not need to be repositories of all there is to know about social studies. When educators work with students to investigate and learn about areas of mutual interest, children are given a powerful message that one person does not need to know every fact and figure to be competent in social studies. Instead, individuals should be willing to share knowledge and information in mutually supportive ways.
9. Social studies is just as important as reading, math, science, and language arts! Social studies becomes important in children's lives when it is integrated into their life experiences and is used to extend those experiences.
10. Social studies is fun! Social studies can be one of the most dynamic, exciting, stimulating, and invigorating elements of any school day—particularly when it is taught by an enthusiastic teacher and an equally enthusiastic librarian!

CONSTRUCTIVISM AND SOCIAL STUDIES INSTRUCTION

One of the most exciting developments in elementary education is a shift away from a delivery system of teaching to a more constructivist model of education. Constructivism is not new—its theoretical underpinnings have been around for more than 70 years. However, it is a significant shift in teaching priorities. The traditional form of teaching relies on educators giving or delivering instruction to students. You may recognize this as a teacher lecturing students and students dutifully recording information or "attacking" skills sheets or endless workbook pages. In short, an expert tells novices what they need to know.

Psychologists have helped us look at the teaching-learning partnership in a new way. Through intensive research, we have learned that learning is not simply the accumulation of knowledge (which is passive), but rather how we make sense of knowledge. This is constructivism. Constructivism recognizes that knowledge is created in the mind of the learner. Teachers help students relate new content to the knowledge they already have. In addition, students have opportunities to process and apply that knowledge in meaningful situations (sometimes called "hands-on, minds-on" learning).

Educators who embrace a constructivist philosophy of teaching promote learning, especially the learning of social studies concepts and principles, through a multitude of actions and behaviors. These may include several of the following:

- linking background knowledge with textual knowledge
- asking lots of open-ended questions
- lots of hands-on learning opportunities
- relating concepts to the "real world" of students' lives
- assisting children in pursuing answers to their own self-initiated queries
- posing questions at higher levels of cognition (application, analysis, synthesis)
- using collaborative activities (student/student; student/teacher)
- engaging students in metacognitive thinking

- providing individual learning opportunities more than whole-class presentations
- promoting self-initiated investigations and discoveries

The most important consideration in any discussion of constructivism is that students need to know that knowledge is never a product; rather, it is a process. How we learn is intrinsically more important than what we learn. For social studies, this is a critical factor in the success children have within this subject as well as the success they can have as active, thinking, and participating members of society.

SOCIAL STUDIES TEACHING AND MULTIPLE INTELLIGENCES

Social studies offers a host of opportunities for students to actively engage in a constructivist approach to learning. It offers a variety of meaningful learning opportunities tailored to students' needs and interests. Children are given the chance to make important choices about *what* they learn as well as about *how* they learn it. Constructivism provides the means to integrate the social studies program with the rest of the elementary curriculum while involving students in a multiplicity of learning opportunities and ventures.

Incorporated into constructivist explorations are opportunities for students to take advantage of, hone, and build upon one or more of their multiple intelligences. According to Howard Gardner (*Frames of Mind: The Theory of Multiple Intelligences.* New York: Basic Books, HarperCollins, 1985), each individual possesses eight different intelligences (see "The Eight Human Intelligences," below) in varying degrees. These intelligences (as opposed to a single intelligence quotient as traditionally reported via many standardized intelligence tests) help determine how individuals learn and how they fare in their daily lives. Gardner defines an "intelligence" as consisting of three components:

- The ability to create an effective product or offer a service that is valuable in one's culture.
- A set of skills that enables an individual to solve problems encountered in life.
- The potential for finding or creating solutions for problems, which enables a person to acquire new knowledge.

Individuals differ in the strength (or weakness) of each of the eight intelligences in isolation as well as in combination. For example, whereas some individuals learn best through linguistic means, others are more kinesthetic learners, and still others are spatial learners. Suffice it to say that no two people learn in the same way, nor should they be taught in the same way.

The Eight Human Intelligences

According to Howard Gardner, individuals possess these eight intelligences in varying degrees.

1. *Verbal-Linguistic Intelligence* involves ease in producing language and sensitivity to the nuances, order, and rhythm of words. Individuals who are strong in verbal-linguistic intelligence love to read, write, and tell stories.

   Enhancement Activities: Writing, reading, storytelling, speaking, debating

2. *Logical-Mathematical Intelligence* relates to the ability to reason deductively or inductively and to recognize and manipulate abstract patterns and relationships. Individuals who excel in this intelligence have strong problem solving and reasoning skills and ask questions in a logical manner.

   Enhancement Activities: Problem solving, outlining, calculating, patterning, showing relationships

3. *Musical-Rhythmic Intelligence* encompasses sensitivity to the pitch, timbre, and rhythm of sounds as well as responsiveness to the emotional implications of these elements of music. Individuals who remember melodies or recognize pitch and rhythm exhibit musical intelligence.

   Enhancement Activities: Composing, singing, humming, making instrumental sounds, creating vibrations

4. *Visual-Spatial Intelligence* includes the ability to create visual-spatial representations of the world and to transfer them mentally or concretely. Individuals who exhibit spatial intelligence need a mental or physical picture to best understand new information. They are strong in drawing, designing, and creating things.

   Enhancement Activities: Painting, drawing, sculpting, pretending, imagining

5. *Bodily-Kinesthetic Intelligence* involves using the body to solve problems, make things, and convey ideas and emotions. Individuals who are strong in this intelligence are good at physical activities and eye-hand coordination, and have a tendency to move around, touch things, and gesture.

   Enhancement Activities: Dancing, miming, role playing, exercising, playing games

6. *Intrapersonal Intelligence* entails the ability to understand one's own emotions, goals, and intentions. Individuals strong in intrapersonal intelligence have a strong sense of self, are confident, and enjoy working alone.

   Enhancement Activities: Thinking strategies, focusing, metacognitive techniques, silent reflection, emotional processing

7. *Interpersonal Intelligence* refers to the ability to work effectively with other people and to understand them and recognize their goals and intentions. Individuals who exhibit this intelligence thrive on cooperative work, have strong leadership skills, and are skilled at organizing, communicating, and negotiating.

   Enhancement Activities: Communicating, receiving feedback, collaborating, cooperating, structured feedback

8. *Naturalist Intelligence* includes the capacity to recognize flora and fauna, to make distinctions in the natural world, and to use this ability productively in activities such as farming and biological science.

   Enhancement Activities: Planting, raising and tending, nurturing, observing, experimenting

The research on multiple intelligences has revealed that teaching aimed at sharpening one kind of intelligence will carry over to others. There is also mounting evidence that learning opportunities that involve a variety of intelligences allow students to take advantage of their preferred intelligence(s) as well as strengthen weaker intelligences.

FINAL THOUGHT

Social studies is much more than learning the names of all the state capitals, or the gross national product of Germany, or the different occupations that urban dwellers have. At the risk of repeating myself: social studies is a process—a process of discovery, investigation, exploration, and inquiry. It goes above and beyond the simple committing of random facts to memory. Instead, it offers students and educators innumerable opportunities to examine the world from a variety of angles and a variety of perspectives. It is not the reading of dull, dry, and pedantic textbooks (traditional), but rather academic participation and engagement of the highest order (current). Let's see how we can make that happen.

CHAPTER 2

Social Studies and Children's Literature

Melissa Gold has been teaching in a suburban school district outside Denver, Colorado, for the past six years. She began her teaching career in fourth grade, but has spent the last four years in third grade. ("I love their innocence, their silliness, and their positive outlooks on life. It is a true joy to teach eight-year-olds.") Melissa has crafted a vibrant and multilayered curriculum that focuses on the integration of children's literature throughout every subject and every topic. Her social studies curriculum provides students with a variety of stimulating activities, a classroom overflowing with books, opportunities to read those books in productive ways, and a program overflowing with meaningful social studies activities. In short, Melissa facilitates "active learning" and values the depth and breadth to which students can become immersed in their own academic endeavors.

In Melissa's classroom social studies comes alive—becoming an exciting and dynamic part of everyday classroom activities. Social studies is not separated from other subjects, but is naturally "blended" into a coherent curriculum that offers learning opportunities for each and every student. The obvious advantage is that students begin to see the natural relationships and interrelationships that exist between social studies and other subjects. Those subjects are an extension of the social studies program and are equally supported by that program. Melissa accomplishes this transformation through an integration of children's literature throughout every aspect of her social studies program.

INTEGRATING LITERATURE

Trying to teach social studies in an overactive and overburdened curriculum may seem daunting to many teachers, yet my own classroom experiences, as well as those of several colleagues, suggest that this need not be so. I have discovered that when good children's literature is integrated fully into the social studies curriculum, children have learning opportunities that extend far beyond the pages of the text and enhance their attitudes and aptitudes—not just in social studies, but across the curriculum.

The integration of literature into the social studies curriculum is timely in that there is a wealth of new and exciting children's books now being published that enhance social studies in intriguing and interesting ways. A variety of trade books, both old and new, adds immeasurably to the entire social studies program. Also, the integration of children's literature into the social studies program is supported by recent curricular changes in several states, each of which has implemented guidelines that underscore a strong relationship between literature and social studies teaching. Even more interesting is that many textbook publishers are now rushing to include literature selections as part of the lessons in their new text series. Although there is increasing interest and emphasis in making the "literature connection" in social studies, teachers often do not take advantage of these supplemental materials. Instead, they rely on the textbook as their primary source of information.

Much More Social Studies Through Children's Literature is based on the idea that incorporating trade books into the elementary social studies program provides students with extended learning opportunities going far beyond the facts and figures of social studies. New worlds of discovery and exploration open up for students through the magic of literature, worlds that expand the curriculum and enlarge students' appreciation of their environment and their place in it.

THE LITERATURE-BASED APPROACH TO SOCIAL STUDIES INSTRUCTION

Many social studies programs are designed to *give* children lots of information, have them *memorize* those data, and then ask them to *recall* the information on various assessment instruments. As discussed earlier, that may be a significant reason for students' less than enthusiastic response to social studies, because that type of instruction does not allow for the active involvement of students in their own learning, nor does it allow children opportunities to think creatively about what they are learning.

My own experiences as a teacher have taught me that when students, no matter what their abilities or interests, are provided with opportunities to manipulate information in productive ways, learning becomes much more meaningful. I refer to this as a *process approach to learning,* which provides students with an abundance of projects, activities, and instructional designs that allow them to make decisions and solve problems. In so doing, students get a sense that learning is much more than committing facts to memory. Rather, it is what children do with that knowledge that determines its impact on their attitudes and aptitudes.

A process approach to social studies is one in which children *do* something with the concepts and generalizations they learn. It implies that students can manipulate, decide, solve, predict, and structure the knowledge of social studies in ways that are meaningful to them. When teachers and librarians provide opportunities for students to actively process information, learning becomes more child centered and less text based. This results in a social studies program that is expansive, integrated, and dynamic.

A literature-based approach to social studies is a combination of activities, children's literature, "hands-on, minds-on" projects, and materials used to expand a social studies concept or idea. Literature-based social studies teaching and learning is multidisciplinary and multidimensional—it has no boundaries and no limits. In essence, a literature-based approach to social studies offers students a realistic arena within which they can learn and investigate social studies concepts for extended periods of time. It is a process approach to learning of the highest magnitude.

This approach to social studies instruction is built on the idea that learning can be integrative and multifaceted. A literature-based approach to social studies education provides children with a host of opportunities to become actively involved in the dynamics of their own learning. In so doing, they will be able to draw positive relationships between what "happens" in the classroom and what is happening outside the classroom. Literature-based teaching promotes social studies education as a sustaining and relevant venture.

Including children's literature within the social studies curriculum should be a natural and normal part of students' experiences with social studies. Doing so provides youngsters with valuable opportunities to extend and expand their knowledge of the world around as well as to develop a rich appreciation for the social studies concepts, values, and generalizations contained within good literature. By infusing books and literature into your social studies program, you are helping students understand that social studies is much more than a dry accumulation of facts and dates. Instead, you are helping your students explore and investigate their immediate and far-flung world in an arena that knows no limits.

The use of literature within social studies is based on several precepts:

1. Literature provides an ever-expanding array of information in a format that is welcome and familiar to students.
2. Literature extends the social studies curriculum beyond any textbook constraints.
3. Literature relates to children's lives in diverse and divergent ways.
4. Literature, both fiction and nonfiction, helps children understand their cultural, ethnic, and religious heritage.
5. Literature assists children in developing positive attitudes toward themselves, people in their immediate environment, and peoples from around the world.
6. Literature provides vicarious *and* firsthand experiences with all social studies disciplines.
7. Literature provides students with new information and knowledge unobtainable in any other format.
8. Literature stimulates creative thinking and problem-solving abilities in a variety of contexts.
9. Literature opens up the world and draws students in to make self-initiated discoveries.
10. Literature is fun!

When quality literature is made a significant part of the social studies program, children can become involved in activities and gain experiences that they may not be exposed to within a text-based program. In fact, literature-based instruction allows you to extend, expand, and take advantage of students' natural curiosity about how the world works. Literature-based instruction also provides you with many opportunities to combine the multiple intelligences of your students with the resources, information, and principles of your entire social studies curriculum. In short, literature-based teaching celebrates varied learning opportunities that provide students with a meaningful and balanced approach to social studies learning. Above all, literature-based instruction supports and emphasizes the many relationships that exist among social studies inquiry, a process approach to learning, and the exercise of constructivist teaching (and learning) in a positive and supportive environment.

ADVANTAGES OF LITERATURE-BASED INSTRUCTION

Literature-based instruction in social studies offers a plethora of advantages for both educators and students. Figure 2.1 synthesizes some of those benefits.

- It emphasizes and celebrates an individual's multiple intelligences in a supportive and creative learning environment.
- It focuses on the *processes* of social studies rather than the *products* of social studies.
- It reduces and/or eliminates the artificial barriers that often exist between curricular areas and provides an integrative approach to learning.
- It promotes a child-centered social studies curriculum—one in which children are encouraged to make their own decisions and assume a measure of responsibility for learning.
- It stimulates self-directed discovery and investigation both in and out of the classroom.
- It assists youngsters in developing relationships between social studies ideas and concepts, thus enhancing appreciation and comprehension.
- It stimulates the creation of important social studies concepts through firsthand experiences and self-initiated discoveries.
- More time is available for instructional purposes. Social studies instruction does not have to be crammed into limited, artificial time periods, but can be extended across the curriculum and throughout the day.
- The connections that can and do exist between social studies and other subjects, topics, and themes can be logically and naturally developed. Teachers and librarians can demonstrate relationships and assist students in comprehending those relationships.
- Social studies can be promoted as a continuous activity—one not restricted by textbook designs, time barriers, or even the four walls of the classroom. Educators can help students extend social studies learning into many aspects of their personal lives.
- Teachers and librarians are free to help students look at a social studies problem, situation, or topic from a variety of viewpoints, rather than the "right way" frequently demonstrated in a teacher's manual or curriculum guide.
- There is more emphasis on *teaching* students and less emphasis on *telling* students.
- Teachers and librarians can promote problem solving, creative thinking, and critical thinking processes within all dimensions of a topic.

Figure 2.1. Advantages of literature-based teaching.

Literature-based instruction facilitates the teaching of social studies as much as the learning of social studies. The entire social studies curriculum is broadened, strengthened, and made more attentive to the development of individual social studies competencies. The "marriage" of literature and social studies facilitates instruction (particularly for those who have had less-than-pleasurable experiences in their own educational background) and helps students view social studies as a process of discovery and exploration, rather than one of memorization and regurgitation.

We know that the use of quality trade books is generating some remarkable changes in the ways that social studies is taught and the ways in which students are learning. Literature-based instruction not only offers students unique opportunities to process and practice "hands-on, minds-on" social studies, but also provides teachers with integrative strategies and activities that enhance and promote social studies concepts in all curricular areas. In addition, students are assisted in drawing realistic parallels between classroom events and circumstances outside the classroom. In short, literature-based instruction can aid students in understanding the relevance of social studies to their everyday lives—certainly a major goal of any social studies curriculum.

CHAPTER 3

Collaboration: The Name of the Game

What both elementary teachers and school librarians have long known intuitively, and what has been validated with a significant body of research, is the fact that the literature shared in both classroom and library has wide-ranging and long-lasting implications for the educational and social development of children. More important, however, is the unassailable fact that when teachers and librarians join together to promote literature collaboratively, they are opening incredible windows that expand the influence of literature and extend learning opportunities for youngsters as never before.

In preparation for writing this book, I talked with school librarians and teachers throughout the United States. I discovered that the "collaboration factor" had a significant influence on the success of social studies programs—especially those in which children's literature played a major role. A substantial level of collaboration between the classroom teacher and the school librarian was essential if literature was to be made a successful element and a dynamic feature of any social studies curriculum. The partnership between teacher and librarian is, and continues to be, the crucial element in the success children enjoy within and throughout any academic endeavor.

As you might imagine, this partnership does not happen overnight. It involves a mutual sharing of ideas, possibilities, and projects. But when teachers and librarians band together, the curricular effect of literature in the social studies curriculum can be expanded exponentially. It involves trust and it involves coordination, but the overall effect is more than worth the effort.

BENEFITS

In my discussions with elementary school librarians and classroom teachers I discovered the following benefits in a collaborative partnership between these individuals:

- Instructional projects can be designed, developed, and taught over an extended period of time (days, weeks, months).
- Students can be exposed to a greater range of resources—both print and nonprint.
- The NCSS Standards can be promoted in a coordinated and systematic fashion.
- A constructivist philosophy of teaching and learning is promoted throughout the social studies curriculum.
- Teaching (and learning) can be individualized—the specific educational needs of selected students can be addressed and supported.

- More time is available for instructional purposes. In situations where social studies is being deemphasized (due to an increased attention to literacy skills), a partnership between teacher and librarian can expand the instructional possibilities.
- Social studies is promoted as a continuous activity, rather than an isolated subject taught on an intermittent basis.
- There is a greater emphasis on social studies as *problem solving* and *critical thinking* instead of the "traditional" view of it as simply the memorization of facts and figures.
- Social studies instruction becomes a mandate of the school rather than an instructional "add-on" to the curriculum.
- The "real lives" of students outside the school can be linked with social studies instruction taking place within the school.
- Cooperative teaching and cooperative learning can be promoted simultaneously.

FORGING THE PARTNERSHIP

When teachers and librarians work together, great things happen. When they do so as an essential ingredient of the social studies curriculum, then fantastic things happen—short term as well as long term. What follows is a listing of the ways in which teachers and librarians can develop a partnership that is mutually supportive, educationally sound, and dynamically oriented toward a literature-based approach to social studies instruction. The first list is a collection of strategies on how librarians can reach out to classroom teachers. The second list is an assembly of techniques on how classroom teachers can partner with their school librarian to effect a viable social studies program.

Consider these suggestions for your own school or educational setting. Share them with friends and colleagues, discuss them at in-service meetings or off-site conferences, post them in the faculty room, incorporate them into the school newsletter or other communiqués, and bring them up in your various conversations with colleagues. The more these ideas become a part of the conversation in school, the more they can become part of the process of an exciting social studies program.

Librarian → Classroom Teacher*

Here are some suggestions on how school librarians and/or media specialists can reach out to classroom teachers at the start of school and throughout the entire school year:

- Before the new school year begins, obtain the addresses of new staff members from the school principal. Send each new faculty member a welcoming note introducing yourself and your staff. Provide a brief description of your programs and services.
- Offer an orientation for new staff members. Show them where various materials are located, explain the procedures for checking them out, and answer any questions they may have.

* The author is deeply indebted to Ceri Collins and Teri Puryear for their suggestions and insights on this list.

- Present each new teacher with a book for her or his classroom bookshelf. Place a sticker in front to indicate who provided the book.
- Make a concentrated effort to visit each new staff member in her or his classroom during the opening weeks of school. Make sure staff have what they need in the way of materials, audiovisual equipment, or other resources.
- Establish a system whereby teachers can inform you (via e-mail) about the need for various books or resources in the library. Reach out and ask for suggestions on a regular and systematic basis.
- Each month, ask teachers about any forthcoming topics or units of study. Ask them about the materials or literature that you could provide them in designing any long-term projects.
- Make yourself available as much as possible by planning cooperatively for special events and library instruction, assisting with research projects, and helping students locate appropriate reading materials.
- Make yourself visible by participating on special committees outside the library.
- Keep track of what is being taught (or not being taught) within the social studies curriculum. Put together a relevant collection of materials and resources for specific components of the social studies program and promote those components to teachers on a regular basis.
- Lobby your administration on behalf of teachers for much-needed print and nonprint materials.
- Send teachers a monthly e-mail list of new materials and resources.
- Display new materials and resources during faculty meetings.
- Know the social studies curriculum and pay attention to special topics being studied so that you will be prepared to recommend resources that will enhance the teaching of those topics.
- Provide teachers with a variety of teaching tools beyond the print collection. These might include appropriate Web sites, videos, software, and the latest in technology.
- Solicit and entertain ideas from teachers relative to library services and materials.
- Plan for collaborative units to be taught together
- Offer to team teach units with teachers
- Offer to help in formative and summative assessments of student work.

Classroom Teacher → Librarian*

Here are some suggestions for how classroom teachers can reach out to school librarians or media specialists throughout the school year:

- Use the library regularly. This may seem simplistic, but many school librarians say that the library is often underused by teachers. However, nothing makes a librarian happier than having teachers (especially new teachers) utilizing the resources and services of the library on a regular basis throughout the school year.
- Encourage the school librarian to be your teaching partner by planning cooperatively for instruction in library and reference skills and working together to make those sessions successful for your students.
- Don't be afraid to make suggestions to the librarian about specific materials—both print and nonprint.
- Notify the librarian well ahead of time regarding forthcoming topics or upcoming units of study in your social studies program. Invite the librarian to partner with you in assembling relevant material.
- Make it a regular practice to stop by the library to search for new materials, books, literature, and other teaching resources.
- Provide your school librarian with a list of topics and assignments you will be tackling throughout the year. Invite the librarian to make suggestions regarding available resources.
- Work closely with the librarian to develop joint projects in which selected literature is introduced in the library and followed up with specific instructional activities in the classroom.
- Inform the librarian if there are insufficient materials or books on a forthcoming topic. Inquire about the possibility of obtaining more materials in time for the unit to be taught or for a successive school year.
- Stop by the library informally and take the time to chat and talk about suggested instructional plans and ideas for forthcoming units.
- Provide your librarian with a list of upcoming topics and ask for ideas on available literature.
- Make sure you are informed of any new materials obtained by the library.

* The author is deeply indebted to Ceri Collins and Teri Puryear for their suggestions and insights on this list.

Collaboration between teachers and the librarian is important so that kids aren't in the library just to look for something. If I know what teachers are doing in the classroom, then I can integrate it into what I'm doing in the library.

—Ceri Collins, Librarian, Montgomery Elementary School, North Wales, Pennsylvania

The cultivation of positive relationships between the library/media specialist and classroom teachers is the number one priority for the successful teaching of any subject, especially social studies.

—Teri Puryear, Library/Media Specialist, Lake Murray Elementary School, Lexington, South Carolina

This book is designed to help you create a dynamic and exciting social studies program through the integration of children's literature across that curriculum. It is also designed to expand and extend the school library's services and cement the influence of quality literature in any academic endeavor. Its success will depend on how eagerly literature is embraced as a teaching tool and how actively teachers and librarians work toward that goal.

The projects, activities, and suggestions offered in this book are designed to open up worlds of discovery for youngsters irrespective of grade level or program design. So, too, are they offered as a way for teachers and librarians to effect a cooperative relationship that enjoins them in a mutually beneficial and academically successful endeavor. The bonds of communication between teachers and librarians will ultimately determine the success of these ventures.

It is my sincere hope that you will discover a plethora of possibilities to expand and extend the *social studies + children's literature* equation into all aspects of your instructional program. By working collaboratively you are helping to "cement" a bond that will extend far beyond the walls of the school—a bond that can promote a lifelong love of reading, a deeper appreciation of social studies, and an enduring sense of appreciation for interrelated and coordinated learning ventures.

CHAPTER 4

How to Use This Book

Welcome aboard! Are you ready for some incredible teaching and learning experiences? I hope so. This book is designed to promote social studies concepts through exciting, dynamic, and fascinating children's literature. Whether you are a classroom teacher or a school librarian, you will discover a wealth of learning opportunities that will actively engage kids in a variety of "hands-on, minds-on" experiences. Let's take a look.

BOOK SELECTION

Chapters 5 through 11 contain a host of activities and processes designated for some of the best trade books in elementary social studies. These books have been selected because of their appropriateness to the social studies curriculum, their adaptability to all grades (K–6) and ability ranges (high-low), and their usefulness in promoting relevant social studies concepts. Included are

- Caldecott Award winners
- Caldecott Honor Books
- Reading Rainbow selections
- American Book Award medalists
- Recommendations from numerous children's librarians (school and public library)
- Recommendations from classroom teachers in a host of schools
- Recommendations profiled in *Book Links, Horn Book, The Reading Teacher, Social Education*, and other professional journals

In short, there's something for everyone!

The literature selections have been organized around the seven major areas of the elementary social studies curriculum—self and child, family, community and neighborhood, city and country, states and regions, nation and country, and world. The placement of a book within one of these categories may be arbitrary at best. It was my attempt to demonstrate the wide variety of children's literature available for every aspect of the social studies program—not to designate a particular book exclusively for a single division. Undoubtedly, you will discover that most of these books can be used across the length and breadth of the social studies curriculum.

The literature included within this book reflects a range of reading levels. You should feel free to select and use literature that best meets the needs and abilities of students in your classroom or library. An "energized" social studies curriculum will include literature selections throughout the entire academic year. You will discover innumerable opportunities for developing, expanding, and teaching all the social studies standards using the literature in these pages. In that regard, remember that the readability or difficulty level of a single book should not determine if or how it will be used; rather, the emphasis should be on whether students are interested and motivated to pursue literature-related activities that promote learning in a supportive and holistic social studies curriculum.

HANDS-ON, MINDS-ON ACTIVITIES

For each book there is a host of potential activities and processes. It is not necessary to use all of the activities. Rather, you and the students with whom you work should decide on those activities that best serve the needs of the social studies program and of the students themselves. Undoubtedly you will discover activities that can be used individually, in small groups, in large groups, or as a whole class. Providing students with opportunities to make activity selections within the context of a work of literature can be a powerful and energizing component of your program. When youngsters are given those opportunities, their appreciation of social studies and their interest in learning important social studies concepts grows tremendously.

As students become involved in the various trade books and their accompanying activities, I suggest that you guide them in researching and/or developing other activities based on classroom dynamics and teaching/learning styles. For learning to be meaningful, it must have relevance. I encourage you and your students to make these activities your own. Add to them, adapt them, and allow students to help you design additional activities, extensions, and projects that will challenge them, arouse their natural curiosity, and create a dynamic learning environment.

Teaching social studies via trade books is not necessarily an "all or nothing" proposition. That is, it is not necessary to use a single trade book for a full lesson or full day. What it does mean is that you have several options to consider in terms of how you can present a book or series of books to your class, how much you want them to dominate your daily curriculum, and how involved you and your students want to be. Here are some options to consider:

- Introduce a single book and provide students with a variety of selected activities (for that book) for one day.
- Teach a unit built on a combination of several related books.
- Design a thematic unit based on selected pieces of literature within a specific social studies standard (e.g., Culture; People, Places, and Environment; Global Connections).
- Design a thematic unit based on selected pieces of literature within a specific social studies discipline (e.g., history, geography, political science).
- Design a thematic unit based on selected pieces of literature within a specific social studies concept area (e.g., families, city and country, states and regions).

- Utilize the activities for one or two books during an entire day and follow up with the regular curriculum on succeeding days.
- Use a book or series of books as a follow up to information and data presented in a textbook or curriculum guide.
- Provide students with literature-related activities as independent work upon completion of lessons in the regular textbook.
- Teach cooperatively with a colleague and present a self-designed thematic unit to both classes at the same time (this can be done with two classes at the same grade level or two different classes, each at a different grade level).
- Use a book or group of books intermittently over the span of several weeks.

How you use these books (and their accompanying activities) may be determined by any number of factors. It is safe to say that there is no ideal way to implement literature into your classroom plans. The listing above is only a partial collection of ideas. The dictates of your own particular teaching situation, personal experience, and student needs may suggest other possibilities or other alternatives to this register of ideas.

READERS THEATRE

Part III of this book contains several readers theatre scripts for you to duplicate and use with students. These scripts have been coordinated with specific social studies literature selections and topics. Your are, however, free to use these scripts with whatever concepts and books you wish. Here are a few suggestions:

- Use a readers theatre script as part of a larger social studies unit.
- Use a readers theatre script as a classroom activity to be supplemented with literature obtained in the school library.
- Use a readers theatre script as a library activity to be followed up with selected classroom activities.
- After students have participated in several hands-on, minds-on activities, invite them to create their own readers theatre script.
- After students have participated in a readers theatre production in the library, invite them to identify related books and activities for classroom use.
- Invite students—in a classroom or library project—to create their own readers theatre production based on a single social studies book.

Presenting a readers theatre script need not be an elaborate or extensive production. As children become more familiar with and polished in using readers theatre, they will be able to suggest a multitude of presentation possibilities for future scripts. It is important to help children assume a measure of self-initiated responsibility in the delivery of any readers theatre. In so doing, you will be helping to ensure their personal engagement and active participation in this most valuable of social studies activities.

ACTIVITY SHEETS

Part IV of this book provides you with a collection of activity sheets to duplicate and use with children's literature in both the classroom and school library. The pages have been designed to be generic—that is, you will be able to use them with several different books throughout the school year; they are not specific to any single piece of literature or any single book. By the same token, you should feel free to modify or adapt these sheets in keeping with your classroom social studies curriculum or library program.

Each activity sheet is open-ended; that is to say, there are no right or wrong responses. Rather, children are afforded opportunities to investigate the dynamics of a book or the elements of a topic where the emphasis is more on the processes of learning rather than the products. Consider the following suggestions for using these sheets:

- Use a single activity sheet with multiple books within the same unit of study.
- Use an activity sheet as a regular feature of varying units throughout the school year.
- The activity sheets may be used in whatever sequence or order you deem appropriate. They are not arranged in any specific order, and you should feel free to distribute them as you see fit.
- Do not grade the activity sheets. Promote them as learning extensions rather than as homework assignments.
- Both teachers and librarians should be involved in selecting appropriate activity sheets for any book. That way a coordinated process is ensured—one that can be promoted and completed in both venues.
- As appropriate, encourage parents to work with their children in completing selected activity sheets. Again, this should be done not as a homework assignment, but rather as an opportunity for students and their parents to engage in a dialogue about what is taking place in the social studies program and the types of literature shared in that program.

Please keep in mind that it is not necessary to use an activity sheet for every book or every unit of study. They are but one item in your instructional repertoire. Used judiciously, they can provide an additional element of excitement and enthusiasm for the literature integrated into your social studies curriculum.

It is important to keep in mind that *Much More Social Studies Through Children's Literature* is designed to provide you with instructional options—options based on the best in children's literature. You should feel free to alter, modify, or adjust the more than 700 creative suggestions offered throughout the book in keeping with the interests, needs, and inclinations of the students with whom you work. If these ideas spark additional extensions or possibilities for your classroom or library, then so much the better! The result will be an incredible array of teaching possibilities and a fantastic plethora of learning possibilities.

Part II
Activities and Processes

CHAPTER 5

Child and Self

All the Colors of the Earth

Sheila Hamanaka

New York: Morrow Junior Books, 1994

SUMMARY

Run (don't walk) and get this book! Here is a celebration of the diversity of people—the comparisons of people to situations and events in nature. Beautifully told (with very simple language) and delightfully illustrated, this is a book to read aloud and discuss time and again. It is a wonderful introduction to who we are and how all humans are similar—one that needs to be read many times. Short and sweet, this is a book for all ages!

NOTE: This book is a celebration of similarities, not differences. It is a wonderful vehicle for talking about our shared commonalities—with each other and especially with elements of the natural world. You will find much to share, discuss, and celebrate with the simple text and engaging illustrations of this powerful book. For youngsters who may be confused or concerned about the misunderstandings, hatred, and invasions between and among countries, this book is a most appropriate instrument to honor and discuss the family of man.

SOCIAL STUDIES DISCIPLINES

Sociology

NCSS THEMATIC STRANDS

Individual Development and Identity

CRITICAL THINKING QUESTIONS

1. What did the author mean when she said that, "Children come in all the colors of the earth and sky and sea"?
2. What are some other things in nature that can be used to describe various shades of skin colors?
3. How are all humans alike?
4. What are the colors of nature that can be celebrated with your classmates?
5. What is your favorite "earth color"? Why?

RELATED BOOKS

Fox, Mem. *Whoever You Are*. New York: Voyager Books, 2001.

Kates, Bobbi. *We're Different, We're the Same*. New York: Random House Books for Young Readers, 1992.

Katz, Karen. *The Colors of Us*. New York: Owlet Paperbacks, 2002.

ACTIVITIES

1. Encourage students to create a collage of all the different colors of the earth, sky, and sea. Then place a picture of each student throughout the collage. This can be displayed on a bulletin board or wall.
2. Invite students to bring in various things from home and/or the outside that represent the colors of their skin, eyes, and hair. Invite students to then create a sequel to the story about the various colors that make each of them unique using the various items they brought to describe themselves.
3. Encourage students to look at various colors in nature. Have students bring in various plants and pictures of various animals. Discuss with students the differences in color among the varying items. Discuss how all of nature is beautiful because each item in nature is different, just like each person is unique because of our different colors.
4. Invite students to describe the members of their class in terms of "earth colors." What are some of the "earth colors" mentioned in the book that can be found among the students in a single class? What are some of the "earth colors" mentioned in the book that could be found among all the students in the school?

5. Invite students to take a nature walk around the school or their neighborhood and search for plants or plant parts that are represented in the book. Encourage students to create a collage of all the plant parts and to label each color as it is depicted in the book (e.g., "whispering gold," "tinkling pink") .
6. Invite students to discuss some colors that may not have been included in the book. Using the same language as the author, invite students to create their own original colors for people. They may wish to start with individuals in their class, then move to people in the school, and then to folks in the community or town where they live. What new colors can they create for those with whom they work and live every day?
7. Create a "word wall" in the classroom or library. Invite youngsters to select some of their favorite phrases, terms, and color descriptions from the book to post on the wall. Encourage students to be aware of other color descriptions in the books they read or listen to that could be added to the word wall.
8. Ask students to write a letter of appreciation to the author of this book indicating why they enjoyed the story. This can be done as an individual activity or a group project.
9. A small group of students may wish to create an audiorecording of the book. Various individuals can each read different pages of the book. Other students may wish to set up a special display in the classroom or library for others to listen to the recording and write down their impressions or interpretations of the text.
10. Invite students to create an advertisement for the book. What could they say that would entice more people (adults as well as children) to read this book? Students may wish to construct posters for display throughout the library or school.
11. Ask individual students to describe a friend in terms of her or his various "earth colors." How many different colors are represented in the friend? How many of those colors can be found in nature?

Giraffes Can't Dance

Giles Andreae

New York: Orchard Books, 2001

SUMMARY

Gerald has two left feet, and he was sure to be ridiculed at the annual Jungle Dance. But then a tiny cricket teaches him an important lesson—that is, sometimes you just need a different song. With that new song Gerald becomes the hit of the dance—I mean, he could really boogie! Told in rhyme, this timeless story speaks to all kids (and a lot of adults) about the value of just being you. Here's a book filled with imagination and color that will inspire lots of delightful discussion in classrooms and libraries.

SOCIAL STUDIES DISCIPLINES

Sociology

NCSS THEMATIC STRANDS

Individual Development and Identity

CRITICAL THINKING QUESTIONS

1. Why do you think that each type of animal in the story was able to dance differently than the other types of animals?

2. What did the cricket mean when he said "sometimes when you're different you just need a different song"?
3. What made Gerald realize that he too could dance?
4. What is something special that you can do?

RELATED BOOKS

Mitton, Tony. *Down by the Cool of the Pool*. New York: Orchard, 2002.

ACTIVITIES

1. Invite the students to write down their most positive attributes or characteristics and draw a picture of themselves taking part in, or doing something that highlights, these attributes or characteristics. Afterward, create a "We Are Special" bulletin board.
2. Invite children to make puppets of each of the animals in the story using paper bags and construction paper. Students can then write scripts for each character based on the story's plot. They can then perform a puppet show of the story for other students in the school.
3. Encourage students to discuss how they feel about the way that Gerald was treated by the other animals when he first tried to dance. Invite students to write about an experience that they had in which they were made fun of or embarrassed, or about how it would feel if they were put in that situation. As appropriate, ask selected students to orally share their experiences.
4. Invite children to cut out an outline of their faces using construction paper. Have students write down qualities or characteristics that they possess, and have them decorate their faces. Discuss with students that all people have similarities and differences, and that these differences make each of us unique.
5. Encourage students to write a poem or lyrics to a song discussing acceptance of others. Have the students draw a picture to go along with their poem or a CD cover to go along with their lyrics, illustrating groups of people getting along and accepting individual differences.
6. As appropriate, take time to share with students some of the skills or attributes that are challenging for you. Perhaps you're not a fast runner, or you cannot draw very well, or you're "all thumbs" when it comes to constructing things. Let students know that you are O.K. with those deficiencies. Perhaps you're working on improving them. But the bottom line is that you are who you are because you also take time to celebrate the abilities and attributes at which you excel.

7. Invite students to interview their parents, relatives, or neighbors about skills or attributes they feel (through self-assessment) they could use some assistance, training, or help in improving. Invite students to create a master list of those "deficiencies." Talk about ways in which they are able to maintain happy lives in spite of those shortcomings.

8. Invite students to create a series of true or false questions about themselves. Print these statements on sheets of paper and duplicate them. Pass out one sheet each day and invite students to see how much they know about their classmates. When a sheet is completed, the designated person can stand and explain each of the statements on her or his sheet to the other students.

9. Encourage students to write a sequel to *Giraffes Can't Dance* from the perspective of Gerald. What other "adventures" does he get himself into? What else does he learn about himself? Students may wish to post these along one wall or create a special Web page for other students to read.

10. Invite each child to create a portrait of herself or himself in the role of a character from a popular book. What characters do the children choose? What traits make the character an appropriate choice? Plan time for students to post their characters and discuss their selections.

Happy Birth Day!

Robie H. Harris

Cambridge, MA: Candlewick Press, 2002

SUMMARY

This book is a touching and moving account of the birth of a newborn baby girl. With inviting text and colorful illustrations, young readers are introduced to the miracle of birth. This is a story to be shared again and again—one that students of any age can relate to and that will spark lots of personal connections and active discussion.

SOCIAL STUDIES DISCIPLINES

Anthropology, sociology

NCSS THEMATIC STRANDS

Time, Continuity, and Change; People, Places, and Environment; Individual Development and Identity; Individuals, Groups, and Institutions

CRITICAL THINKING QUESTIONS

1. What was so special about the day you were born?
2. What would you like to say to the author of this book?
3. Why did the newborn baby cry as soon as she was born?
4. What kinds of things do babies need to get accustomed to when they are first born?
5. What do you think are some of the many challenges of taking care of a newborn?

RELATED BOOKS

Bowen, Anne. *I Loved You Before You Were Born.* New York: HarperCollins, 2001.

Costanzo, Charlene. *The Twelve Gifts of Birth.* New York: HarperCollins, 2001.

Crystal, Billy. *I Already Know I Love You.* New York: HarperCollins, 2004.

Harris, Robie H. *Hi New Baby!* Cambridge, MA: Candlewick Press, 2000.

ACTIVITIES

1. Invite students to interview their parents and other relatives about their recollections of the students' birth. Students may be interested in obtaining more than one retelling about their birth to determine if different people remember it in the same way. When completed, students may wish to gather their data together into an indexed directory of important events or occurrences surrounding their birth.

2. Encourage students to record important events from their own lives, putting one event on each of several index cards. Hang some strings along one wall of your classroom or library. Provide students with several clothespins and ask each one to select a string and hang her or his card along the string in the proper sequential order. Provide opportunities for each student to describe his or her personal "time line."

3. Invite students to visit www.kidsparties.com/traditions.htm. Here they can discover various traditions around the world for celebrating birthdays. Students can see how birthday parties got started, birthday celebrations in various countries, famous people's birthdays, and special family traditions. Invite students to add their own family-related information to that obtained from this site.

4. Students may wish to create personal "time lines" using photographs brought in from home. Encourage students to bring in several photos of themselves. The series of photos can be posted on an appropriate bulletin board in sequential order. Students can also write a short caption for each picture describing what the picture portrays, the approximate date, and what it means to the individual child.

5. Invite students to interview friends, family, and other acquaintances. Encourage each student to ask each person for a list of single adjectives that best describe the child's birth or the first few days after her or his birth. After students have collected an adequate sampling of adjectives, invite them to sort the adjectives into several categories (e.g., adjectives related to size, adjectives related to personality, adjectives related to temperament, or adjectives from family, adjectives from friends, and "adjectives from myself"). Provide students with an opportunity to decide on the categories they would like to use. Each student's list can be collected in a large scrapbook decorated with photos of all the children.

6. Invite students to create family alphabet books. Provide each student with 26 sheets of paper. Encourage students to write one letter of the alphabet on each sheet of paper. For each letter, invite each student to choose a word or phrase that describes something about her or his early life. When they are done, students may wish to bind their sheets between two sheets of cardboard to create a personal alphabet book.
7. Invite each child to imagine that he or she is a newborn baby in a hospital nursery. What would the child like to say to the other infants in the nursery? What kinds of things or people does he or she see? What kinds of experiences does she or he have?
8. Share several newspaper ads with your students. Then ask students to create an original ad about themselves (as though they were an item for sale). What qualities would they want to emphasize in a limited amount of space? What special features do they have that others would enjoy? Students may wish to emphasize physical or personality characteristics, or both. Post these in a prominent location in the room.
9. Invite students to create an original and special birth announcement for themselves. Share "regular" birth announcements and invite students to design their own that herald and joyfully announce their arrival in the world. What, specifically, would they like to have celebrated?

I'm Gonna Like Me: Letting Off a Little Self-Esteem

Jamie Lee Curtis; Laura Cornell (illus.)

New York: Joanna Cotler Books, 2002

SUMMARY

Developing self-esteem is an important part of growing up, and this author and illustrator team shows young readers how to do that—even when life has a couple of bumps in the road. Humorous text in concert with imaginative illustrations makes this book one to share with kids no matter what their age. The message is simple and never overbearing. It is done with craft and skill and a recognition that kids respond to an engaging rhyme pattern that keeps the action flowing.

SOCIAL STUDIES DISCIPLINES

Anthropology, sociology

NCSS THEMATIC STRANDS

People, Places, and Environment; Individual Development and Identity

CRITICAL THINKING QUESTIONS

1. Can you relate to any of the issues that the author discusses in the story, and if so, which ones?
2. What is the main message that the author is trying to convey to her readers?
3. Why is building self-esteem so important?
4. What do you do when something doesn't go the way you wanted it to?
5. How can people like themselves more?

RELATED BOOKS

Adams, Christine, and Robert J. Butch. *Happy to Be Me!: A Kid Book About Self-Esteem.* New York: Abbey Press, 2001.

ACTIVITIES

1. Invite students to create a sequel to the story by answering the question that the author posed on the last page of the book. Have students create illustrations to go along with each page.
2. Encourage students to write one thing that they do not like about themselves. Then have students make a list of some of the reasons why they should appreciate this attribute or physical appearance.
3. Invite students to keep a diary or journal of some of the various things that they do throughout a week that are nice, caring, or help them feel good about themselves. As appropriate, invite students to share these journals.
4. Invite students to form pairs. Ask each pair of students to answer the following question, "What do you like about your partner?" Partners should answer this question to each other. Student pairs may wish to create a special display or poster for posting in the classroom or library.
5. Invite students to take a lollipop from a bag and count how many letters are in the name of the lollipop's flavor. For example, if the flavor was grape, there would be five letters. Encourage students to come up with that many attributes or characteristics that they like about themselves, each of which starts with each letter from the flavor's name. Here's an example that the author of *Much More Social Studies . . .* created:

   G—grandfather

   R—reads a lot

   A—always tries new things

   P—paddles a kayak

   E—eats way too much Ben and Jerry's ice cream
6. Invite students to record several important features or characteristics of their own lives—one on each of several index cards. Hang some strings along one wall of the classroom or library. Provide students with several paper clips or clothespins and ask each one to select a string and hang her or his card along the string. Take time to share and discuss all the positive attributes that are in the group.
7. Invite students to interview their parents, caregivers, or relatives about their (the children's) personal attributes, features, or characteristics. What are some things that other people like about them? Students may wish to assemble their collections into personal collages (using words, phrases, and sentences cut from old magazines and newspapers). Individual collages can be posted along one wall of a classroom or library.

8. Invite students to imagine themselves 10 years in the future. What will they be doing? What will they be like? Ask students to project the features and characteristics that they will most admire about themselves a decade from now. What are some characteristics (those they have now or plan on having later) that they will be celebrating in 10 years?
9. Invite each student to create a song about herself or himself. Using the tune to a popular song, students may wish to create their own personal lyrics. Help each student focus on her or his positive attributes and characteristics.
10. Just for fun, invite youngsters to create a commercial or advertisement about themselves. That is, if they were being "sold" as a product, what would they want the world to know about them? What characteristics or features would they like to promote that would get someone to purchase them? Keep this activity light and fun and you may see an interesting array of ads and commercials.

Parts

Tedd Arnold

New York: Puffin Books, 2000

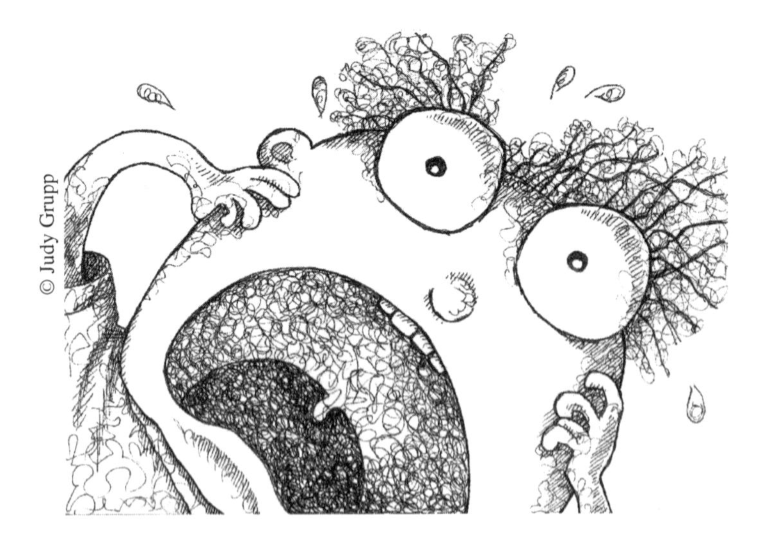

SUMMARY

This book will have students rolling in the aisles with laughter. It is a genuinely funny book that looks at our body parts through the innocent eyes of a young child. With a delightful rhyming pattern and an infectious dose of creativity, this is a read-aloud book that will beg to be told over and over again. Be sure to get the follow-up books in the series (see below) so that students get a "well-rounded" perspective on the humor evident in their own bodies.

SOCIAL STUDIES DISCIPLINES

Anthropology, sociology

NCSS THEMATIC STRANDS

Individual Development and Identity

CRITICAL THINKING QUESTIONS

1. Do you think that the style of writing that the author used in the book helped to make the story more effective?
2. What events that the main character went through in the story can you relate to?
3. If you were a parent, how would you explain that the various things that are happening to your child's body are normal?
4. What was the funniest part of *Parts*?
5. Has something funny happened to your body in the last year? If so, what was it?

RELATED BOOKS

Arnold, Tedd. *Even More Parts*. New York: Dial, 2004.

Arnold, Tedd. *More Parts*. New York: Puffin Books, 2003.

ACTIVITIES

1. Invite students to write additional pages for the story, using the same figurative language that Arnold used. These additional pages can include other things that students have noticed that change about people throughout their lives. Have students create illustrations to go along with their additional pages.
2. Encourage students to study the specific body parts that the main character notices throughout the story. Afterward invite students to assemble their information into appropriate pamphlets, brochures, or booklets for display in the classroom or library.
3. Encourage students to create a time line of normal things that will change and happen to their bodies throughout their lives. They may wish to interview the school nurse or their family doctor to collect the necessary information.
4. Give students a picture of an outline of a body. Invite students to label and circle the different parts that the main character noticed throughout the story.
5. You may wish to share the following information with students. Inform them that most of these measurements apply to adults—simply because children's bodies are still growing and developing (students may wish to "test" these measurements on adult family members—parents, relatives, neighbors, etc.):
   - A person's height should equal about 6 to 7.5 times the length of the head (from the chin to the top of the head).
   - For most adults, the distance from fingertip to fingertip (with arms outstretched side to side) is roughly equal to one's height.
   - The distance around a closed fist (over the knuckles) and the length of a foot (from end of heel to end of big toe) is approximately equal.
   - The distance from the shoulder to the elbow and the elbow and the wrist are about equal.
   - The bottom of one's ears line up with the base of the nose.
   - The width of an adult's mouth (from corner to corner) is the same as the distance between the middle of one eyeball and the middle of the other eyeball.
   - The length of a human hand (including the wrist) is approximately equal to the height of the person's head.
6. Pour 3 tablespoons of milk into each of three small plastic cups. In the first cup put 2 tablespoons of water. Cover the cup with plastic wrap, using a rubber band to hold the wrap in place. In the second cup put 2 tablespoons of lemon juice or vinegar and cover as above. In the third cup put 2 tablespoons of meat tenderizer and cover as above.

After one or two hours, invite students to observe the changes that have occurred in each cup. The changes that take place in cups two and three are similar to the digestive process in the human stomach.

7. Inform students that the human tongue has four types of taste buds (sour, bitter, salty, and sweet). Students can "map out" portions of their tongues as follows: Obtain several cotton swabs and invite students to dip each swab into the following solutions and then touch those swabs to various portions of their tongues:

    – lemon juice (sour)

    – salt water (salty)

    – sugar water or corn syrup (sweet)

    – tonic water (bitter)

    Students may wish to draw an oversized illustration of a human tongue and "plot" the location of the four major types of taste buds.

8. Push a wooden kitchen match into a small piece of modeling clay. Flatten the bottom of the clay. Lay your wrist, palm side up, on a table. Place the clay on your wrist near the thumb side. The match will begin vibrating with your heartbeat (you may need to adjust the location of the clay). Invite students to count your heartbeat in beats per minute. Repeat this activity with students and invite them to calculate their own personal heartbeats. Afterward invite them to participate in some form of physical activity (e.g., jumping jacks for 1 minute) and then repeat the activity. What do they notice?

9. Invite students to read all the books in this series. Ask them to evaluate each one in terms of the "funny factor." Which one was the funniest? Which one made them laugh the most? Students may wish to rank order the books in terms of the "funny factor."

10. Students may wish to obtain some props for a retelling of the story. For example, cotton for belly button stuffing, marbles for eyeballs, string for pieces of hair, and Chiclets™ gum for teeth. Retell the story and invite students to act it out using the selected props.

The Secret of Saying Thanks

Douglas Wood

New York: Simon & Schuster, 2005

© Judy Grupp

SUMMARY

We often take things for granted in our lives. In this inspirational book, the author points out to children some of the many things we are thankful for—things we begin to appreciate if we just stop for a moment to examine them more closely. This book will inspire spirited discussion at school and at home.

SOCIAL STUDIES DISCIPLINES

Sociology, economics

NCSS THEMATIC STRANDS

Culture; People, Places, and Environment; Individual Development and Identity

CRITICAL THINKING QUESTIONS

1. What is one secret that you would like to share?
2. What is something new that you recently discovered?
3. What do you like most about flowers?
4. What are some things that animals might teach us?

5. If you could wish upon a star, what would you wish for?
6. What makes you especially happy?

RELATED BOOKS

Ehlert, Lois. *Leaf Man.* Orlando, FL: Harcourt, 2005.

Wood, Douglas. *Making the World.* New York: Simon & Schuster, 1998.

ACTIVITIES

1. As appropriate, invite youngsters to maintain a "Secret Diary." In this diary (which nobody may view), they may want to record some of the secrets they have. What are some special things, events, or people in their lives? What is some piece of knowledge that they would rather not share with anyone else? You may wish to take time to discuss the value of secrets in people's lives.
2. Create a "Thanks" poster or sheet of newsprint in the classroom or library. Every so often, invite students to record things that they are thankful for. Or, you may wish to initiate a discussion on a regular basis (once a week for example) and record student ideas on a continuing poster.
3. Invite students to ask their parents or caregivers about items or events they are thankful for. Students may wish to collect this information into a master list or display.
4. Take youngsters for a brief walk around the school grounds. Invite each of them to look for something new—something they have never noticed before. It may be as simple as a stone or something more complex, such as a bird singing in a tree. Plan time afterward to discuss the new discoveries children make.
5. Ask children to talk about why flowers are so special in their lives. What are some of their favorite flowers? What does a flower or group of flowers do for them? If they could be any flower in the world, which one would they be? Why?
6. Plan a discussion time for children to talk about pets. What are some of the different kinds of pets that people have? Why do people have pets? What are the benefits of having a pet? What does a student's pet do for her or him? How can we show our appreciation of our pets?
7. Invite students to brainstorm all the different kinds of sounds in nature. You may wish to "get the ball rolling" by talking about some recent sounds you have heard: a bird chirping, the buzzing of a bee, the wind whispering through the trees. If necessary, take children outside and invite them to stand still for a few moments and just listen to the sounds of nature. What do they hear?

8. On a cloudless night, invite parents and children to spend some time outside and observe the stars. Ask students to look for stars that are together as well as stars that are far apart. Invite them to talk about why people like looking at stars. If stars could speak, what do students think they would tell us? Students may wish to construct a poster or display of some of their favorite stars or constellations.

9. Make every day "Thanksgiving." Start the day by asking each child to indicate one thing in her or his life for which he or she is thankful. What's one thing the child appreciates? If he or she could say "thanks" to one thing or one person in his or her life, what (or who) would it be?

10. Invite youngsters to write a letter of thanks to the author of this book. What would they like to say? What page or event in the book are they most thankful for? Why did they especially enjoy this book? You may wish to collect these letters into a special publication or send them to the author in care of his publisher.

CHAPTER 6

Family

Mama Loves Me from Away

Pat Brisson

Honesdale, PA: Boyds Mills Press, 2004

SUMMARY

A young girl and her mother share a special, if not unusual, relationship. They have the same birthday. The young girl loves to hear stories about the day she was born, but there are no presents for her on her birthday because her mother is in prison. But Mama makes a very special gift—one that cannot be bought—and one that will help them stay a little bit closer.

SOCIAL STUDIES DISCIPLINES

Sociology, economics

NCSS THEMATIC STRANDS

Individual Development and Identity; Civic Ideals and Practices

CRITICAL THINKING QUESTIONS

1. How did you feel when you learned that the mother was in prison?
2. How do you think she got in prison?
3. Why do you think the young girl loves her mother's stories so much?
4. If you could change any part of the story, what would you change?
5. What would you like to say to the young girl at the end of the book?
6. What would you like to say to the mother?

RELATED BOOKS

Bunting, Eve. *Fly Away Home*. New York: Clarion, 1991.

Bunting, Eve. *Smoky Night*. San Diego: Harcourt Brace, 1994.

ACTIVITIES

1. Invite children to create a sequel to the story. What happens to the girl and her mother in a month? In a year? In five years? Be sure to plan time for all students to share their stories.
2. If possible, invite a criminal justice expert (a local judge, a police officer, a college professor) to visit your classroom or library to talk about reasons people go to jail. As appropriate, the individual may wish to discuss the major reasons why women go to jail, including some references to the "average" length of incarceration for females.
3. Encourage students to write a fictitious letter to the young girl in the story. What words of support can students share with the girl that would give her hope for a better future?
4. Invite students to create a collage (pictures and words cut from old magazines and glued to a sheet of poster board) of the most important things in family life (e.g., love, sharing, conversation, listening, caring). Invite students to discuss the parent-child bond, as appropriate.
5. Students may enjoy developing the story into a readers theatre script (see part III of this book). Using the events of this story, a narrator, and selected characters, students may wish to reenact the book for class members or another class.
6. Provide students with other examples of Pat Brisson's books. If you wish, read excerpts from those books and invite students to note any similarities between the stories. What types of events or themes does she write about most often? Students may wish to assemble a collage of Pat Brisson's books, characters, or themes.

7. Plan time to talk about what makes a family a family. What are the essential ingredients? What are the necessary components? What are the primary elements? Invite students (in small groups) to assemble a "Guide to the Family." Provide opportunities for them to share their respective guides.
8. Invite students to discuss and share family adventures, outings, or traditions. You may wish to create a special bulletin board display on which students can regularly post significant occurrences. You may wish to label the bulletin board "Our Family of the Week" and invite each student to contribute memorable photos, artifacts, or other mementos every week for posting on the board. Plan time for students to share their families regularly.
9. Invite students to interview people in their households, neighborhoods, or communities about what it takes to be a good mother. Encourage students to meet in small groups, share the collected information, and then create an informative brochure; they can distribute the brochure through a local community agency.
10. Invite students to create posters on the importance of mothers (and fathers) reading with their children. If possible, obtain permission from several local businesses to display the posters in store windows or near cash registers. Every so often, students may wish to create new posters and rotate them.
11. Encourage students to create Mother's Day greeting cards that could be sent on a special day of the year (not necessarily on the third Sunday in May). Students may wish to designate a day in the fall or spring as Mother's Day and celebrate the accomplishments of their respective mothers.

So Far from the Sea

Eve Bunting

New York: Clarion Books, 1998

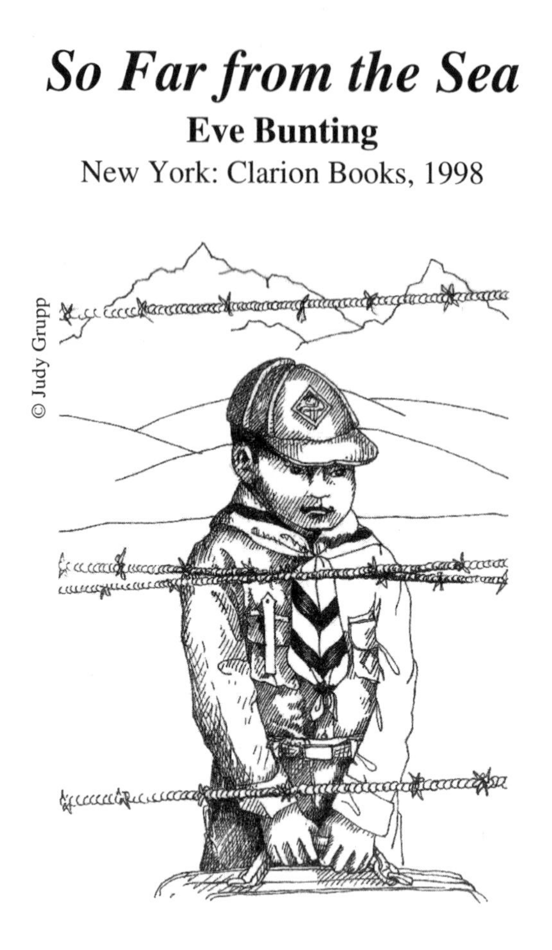
© Judy Grupp

SUMMARY

Laura Iwasaki and her family visit the Japanese internment camp of Manzanar. They are on their way to live in Massachusetts, and this is the last time they will be able to visit Laura's grandfather's grave. Her father remembers the war years and all that went on in the camp. One of his stories provides Laura with an idea—something she can leave forever with her grandfather. This book resonates on two levels—it is the story of how families survive together and is also a brief history lesson on a sad chapter in American history. Read it to children, but have some tissues nearby.

SOCIAL STUDIES DISCIPLINES

History, anthropology, geography, political science, sociology

NCSS THEMATIC STRANDS

Culture; Time, Continuity, and Change; People, Places, and Environment; Individual Development and Identity; Power, Authority, and Governance; Civic Ideals and Practices

CRITICAL THINKING QUESTIONS

1. Why do you think the illustrations in the story continuously change from black and white to color?
2. How would you feel if you were taken away from your family and your home?
3. Do you think that it was fair that persons of Japanese descent were taken away to internment camps?
4. Why would you like to have Laura as a friend?
5. How is Laura's family similar to or different from your family?

RELATED BOOKS

Mazer, Harry. *A Boy at War: A Novel of Pearl Harbor*. New York: Simon & Schuster, 2001.

Tanaka, Shelley. *Attack on Pearl Harbor*. New York: Hyperion Books, 2001.

ACTIVITIES

1. Invite students to write about something or someplace that has meaning to their families. Have students draw illustrations to go along with their writing, and allow time for students to share their work.
2. Invite students to interview family members or neighbors who have been in a war either as a member of the armed services or as a volunteer worker. What are some of their memories? Does war or conflict engender any pleasant memories for people?
3. If possible, contact the local VFW or Veterans Affairs office in your local area. Invite a former serviceman or servicewoman to speak to students about what war is like. The visitor may wish to address some of the restrictions that war brings. What are some personal sacrifices that people have to endure as a result of war? Are some groups of people treated differently than other groups?
4. Invite students to create a memorial in honor of a family member who is alive or who has passed away. Have students write a sentence explaining their memorial. As appropriate, students may wish to share these memorials in a supportive and nonjudgmental group setting.
5. Plan time to discuss the use of both color and black and white illustrations throughout this book. Why did the illustrator choose to depict some scenes in color and others in black and white? What is the overall effect? How does color (or lack of color) affect your interpretation or understanding of the story?
6. Invite students to read other books by this very popular author. Eve Bunting is known for tackling social issues and problems with compassion, sensitivity, and concern. Encourage students to record the various themes that she seems to address in most of her

books. Students may wish to construct a collage of items representing the author's life, a sampling of her books, predominant themes, and noteworthy characters.

7. Ask students to obtain information about various Japanese internment camps erected during World War II. Here are a few Web sites to get them started:

   http://www.pbs.org/childofcamp/

   http://www.infoplease.com/spot/internment1.html

   http://en.wikipedia.org/wiki/Japanese_internment

   http://www.teacheroz.com/Japanese_Internment.htm

   http://www.children-of-the-camps.org/

   After obtaining information from these sites, students may wish to develop their own PowerPoint™ presentation about life in the camps or about their impact on the lives of families.

8. One of the most complete Web sites about Japanese Americans is the Japanese American National Museum in Los Angeles (http://www.janm.org/). Invite students to log on to this site to view the Museum's offerings, exhibits, and artifacts. Students may wish to assemble a report on the museum and its goals. As an educator, you will discover a wide range of instructional resources for purchase and use in your classroom or library.

9. Invite students to organize themselves into two or three groups. Ask each group to mime some of the events in the story for their classmates. Which events are the most significant? Which ones present the greatest challenges for mime? Plan time to talk about the presentations and how they realistically portrayed the story's events or those in an actual internment camp.

10. What are some of the sacrifices that families had to make while in an internment camp? Discuss this question with students and ask them (in small groups) to make lists of those sacrifices. As appropriate, ask students about the sacrifices they would have to make if their families were relocated to an internment camp. How would their lives change? What would they have to do without?

11. Invite students to participate in a debate. Was putting people of Japanese descent into internment camps fair? Divide students into two groups—1 in favor of internment, 1 opposed to internment. After a period of debate, invite students to reach a conclusion or resolution about the need to intern Japanese Americans in various camps throughout the United States.

Star Blanket

Pat Brisson

Honesdale, PA: Boyds Mills Press, 2003

SUMMARY

The Star Blanket has 41 white stars and is deep dark blue—but it carries special memories of a little girl's family. Each star on that blanket represents one person in the girl's family, and she is told that if she can name them all she'll never have any trouble falling asleep. This book is a touching story of a family ritual—not unlike the rituals that are part of every family. It is a celebration of and homage to the closeness of families and the traditions they share with each other. You'll read this book again and again.

SOCIAL STUDIES DISCIPLINES

Sociology, history

NCSS THEMATIC STRANDS

Time, Continuity, and Change; People, Places, and Environment; Individual Development and Identity

CRITICAL THINKING QUESTIONS

1. Do you have anything that you use, or used to use, to help you fall asleep at night?
2. Is there a bedtime story that is special to you that someone tells or used to tell you?
3. Do you have anything that symbolizes your family, like the stars on Laura's blanket?
4. What was the most special gift that you ever received?
5. What are some of the traditions, customs, or celebrations in your family?

RELATED BOOKS

Flournoy, Valerie. *The Patchwork Quilt*. New York: Dial Books, 1985.

ACTIVITIES

1. Encourage students to draw a star like one of the stars on Laura's blanket. Invite students to write five statements, one on each point of the star, explaining what makes their family unique. Invite students to share their stars with the rest of the class.
2. Invite students to draw a picture of the most memorable gift that they have received from a family member or loved one. Encourage them to write a sentence explaining why it was so meaningful. Plan time for students to share their work in small supportive groups.
3. Encourage students to create a whole-class "blanket" like Laura's blanket. This blanket can be drawn, or students can use any other materials that are available. Instead of using stars to represent each family member or loved one, have students create different symbols (of their own choosing) that represent each person.
4. Encourage students to work together to create a whole-class "Family Scrapbook." They can look through old magazines and newspapers to select photos and articles about families or individual family members. As appropriate, students may wish to bring in photographs from home to add (temporarily) to this scrapbook.
5. As a variation of the activity above, invite students (in small groups) to create a family alphabet book. Provide each group with 26 sheets of paper. Ask students to write one letter of the alphabet on each sheet of paper. For each letter, invite students to select a word or phrase that describes something about themselves or their families and record it on the appropriate sheet. When this task is completed, each group may wish to bind their respective sheets between two pieces of cardboard to create a complete family alphabet book.
6. Just for fun, share several magazine or newspaper display ads with students. Then invite students to create original ads for their families (as though they were putting them up for sale). What would they choose to emphasize in a limited space? Which special features of the family do they think others would enjoy or appreciate? Students can emphasize family dynamics more than physical or personality characteristics. Post the "ads" prominently in the classroom or library.
7. Invite students to bring in photographs of various family members. Encourage students to use pushpins on a large world map to indicate where each family member has lived. Post the photographs next to those cities or countries.
8. Discuss different kinds of families with students. This book presents a very traditional American family. In a comfortable environment, invite students to share the different types of families of which they are a part. Discuss the varieties of families that exist today (e.g., single-parent families, extended families, adoptive families). Students may

wish to create a large collage of the various family types represented in their class. These can be posted on a classroom or library wall.

9. Invite students to create a story map, semantic web, or other graphic organizer for the story. Students may wish to work alone or in small groups. Post all the organizers along one wall of the classroom or library and provide opportunities for students to share their renditions of the book. Which one best captures the mood or intent of the book?

10. Ask students to survey other students, teachers, staff, and parents in the local community about their definitions of a family. Students may wish to ask both children and adults to complete the following sentence stem: "Families are . . . ." Provide opportunities for students to summarize the results of their survey and its implications.

The Star People: A Lakota Story

S. D. Nelson

New York: Harry N. Abrams, 2003

SUMMARY

Sister Girl and Young Wolf wander away from their village and soon find themselves lost on the prairie. Suddenly, animals race by them as a fire sweeps across the land. They save themselves by jumping into a stream, but soon miss their parents. They find comfort (and their way) from the Star People overhead. The illustrations in this book draw upon traditional Lakota art, and the story celebrates a timeless Lakota/Sioux story.

SOCIAL STUDIES DISCIPLINES

Anthropology, sociology, history

NCSS THEMATIC STRANDS

Culture; Time, Continuity, and Change; People, Places, and Environment; Individual Development and Identity

CRITICAL THINKING QUESTIONS

1. Why do you think Sister Girl and Young Wolf first wandered out into the prairie?
2. How would the fire have started?
3. Young Wolf and Sister Girl always seem to be helping each other. Why?
4. What kinds of things do you see when you look up at the stars?
5. Have you ever been scared in your life?
6. How did Elk Tooth Woman help the children find their way back to the village?

RELATED BOOKS

Keams, Geri. *Grandmother Spider Brings the Sun*. Flagstaff, AZ: Rising Moon, 1995.

ACTIVITIES

1. Students can learn about the history and customs of the Lakota Indians by accessing the following Web sites:

   http://library.thinkquest.org/CR0212101/

   http://www.windows.ucar.edu/tour/link=/mythology/northamerican_culture.html

   http://www.carnegiemuseums.org/cmnh/exhib-
   its/north-south-east-west/lakota/index.html

   http://wintercounts.si.edu/

   After they have had an opportunity to learn about the Lakota/Sioux, encourage students to create a display or mobile of some of the information they have aquired.

2. Invite students to write or illustrate an event in their lives in which they were away from their parents for a significant amount of time. Establish a time in which students can share these experiences as well as the attendant feelings. Plan time to discuss how their feelings may or may not have been similar to those expressed by the two characters in the book.

3. Invite students to create a bulletin board display of the various constellations illustrated in this book. They may wish to use a star map to identify constellations that the author or illustrator depicted.

4. If possible, borrow some costumes from the local high school or community little theater. Invite students to create an original skit about a day in the life of a Lakota Indian boy or girl. What activities, games, or chores would that individual participate in during the course of a typical day?

5. In the Author's Note in the back of the book, he talks about the significance of Cloud People and Star People. After sharing this information with students, invite them to go outside and locate imaginary Cloud People in the clouds overhead. They may wish to locate imaginary Star People at night when they are home. Invite students to create illustrations of the "people" they see in the clouds or stars.

6. As an extension of the activity above, invite students to select one of the illustrations and to create an imaginary story about that "person" or those "people." Ask students to invent their own legend or story that incorporates the "individual" or "individuals" into the plot of the story.

7. Encourage students to pretend that they are newspaper reporters assigned to cover the events depicted in this book. Which facts or details would they include in a TV broadcast? Which ones would be appropriate for newspaper articles? Ask students to defend their choices.
8. Invite students to interview their parents, grandparents, or relatives about family stories, folktales, or legends they learned as children. If some families have recently immigrated to this country, you may wish to invite children's relatives to share stories and legends from their countries of origin.
9. Invite students to search through the school library and assemble a collection of literature focused on Native American legends. Students may wish to create a special display in the library or put together an annotated bibliography of books to be shared with other classes throughout the school.

Tattered Sails

Verla Kay

New York: G. P. Putnam's Sons, 2001

© Judy Grupp

SUMMARY

Thomas, Edward, Mary Jane, and their parents leave London bound for America in the early 1600s. The trip is not pleasant or joyful, but there is much waiting for them when they reach their new homeland. In Verla Kay's distinctive rhyming pattern, students are introduced to some of the hardships Pilgrims had to face on the long voyage across the Atlantic Ocean. This is an excellent read-aloud book with some interesting historical notes at the end to share and discuss.

SOCIAL STUDIES DISCIPLINES

History, anthropology, sociology, geography, economics

NCSS THEMATIC STRANDS

Time, Continuity, and Change; Individuals, Groups, and Institutions; Civic Ideals and Practices

CRITICAL THINKING QUESTIONS

1. Why do you think the author goes from using negative words to positive words as the story unfolds?
2. How do you think the children felt when they had to leave the only home they ever knew?

3. Why do you think Thomas, Edward, and Mary Jane's parents decided to move?
4. Do you think that the characters were happier once they moved?
5. Can you remember a time when you had to move?

RELATED BOOKS

Kay, Verla. *Covered Wagons, Bumpy Trails*. New York: G. P. Putnam's Sons, 2000.

ACTIVITIES

1. Invite students to write about a time when they had to move away and how they felt, adapted to, and handled the situation. If students have never experienced this, have them write about how they think they would feel if they had to move away.
2. Allow time for students to research the 1600s, and the various reasons people came to America. Invite students to work in groups, and have each group choose one of the reasons people came to America. Have students create a rhyming story with illustrations, like Kay did, about a fictitious family moving to America.
3. Invite students to interview family members about who was the first family member to come to America, and when this occurred. Create a class time line of students' family members' coming to America.
4. One of the customs the Pilgrims had was that children spoke only when spoken to. Structure a classroom or library simulation in which students may speak only when you tell them to or ask them a question. After a preselected length of time (an hour, half a day), discuss with children their feelings about this custom.
5. Invite students to pretend that they are moving to America in the 1600s. Encourage students to write a postcard about their life in America to a family member who stayed behind.
6. Invite students to work in small groups to create various travel brochures for the New World. What aspects should be emphasized? What features of the New World should be depicted in the brochures? What elements should not be included in the brochures? Students may wish to include drawings or photos in their brochures.
7. One of the tasks selected members of a Pilgrim family had to do was to make butter. Students may enjoy making their own homemade butter, too. Here are simple directions:
   - Pour heavy cream into small jars with tight-fitting lids (baby food jars work best).
   - Shake the jars until the cream separates into a solid and a liquid.
   - Allow the solid to drain in a strainer for a few minutes.
   - Stir in a little salt and spread on bread or muffins.

8. Invite students to consult various library holdings for the different types of ships that were used in the early 1600s. They may wish to create a scrapbook or bulletin board display of their findings. You may wish to obtain one or two models from a local craft or hobby store and work with students in constructing sample vessels.

9. Students may enjoy making cornbread in much the same manner as the Pilgrims did. Here's a simple recipe:

   - Boil 3 cups of water and stir in 1 cup of cornmeal grits.
   - Simmer until all the water is absorbed.
   - Allow to cool and turn onto a work surface which has been floured with a cup of fine cornmeal flour.
   - Work the mixture into two round, flat cakes.
   - Bake on a floured cookie sheet at 400 degrees F for about 45 minutes.

10. Log on to the Web site for Plimoth Plantation, the living history museum of the seventeenth century: http://www.plimoth.org/. Provide opportunities for students to access the information on this site and to arrange it into an attractive display, bulletin board, or poster. Plan time to discuss what they learn on this site and how it compares to the information in the book.

11. Sailing across the Atlantic Ocean took a long time in the early 1600s. Invite students to research the games and other activities ship passengers might have engaged in during their voyage. What games or activities would students take with them if they were to embark on a long and perilous journey across the ocean?

CHAPTER 7

Community and Neighborhood

How Raven Stole the Sun

Maria Williams

New York: Abbeville Press, 2001

SUMMARY

Many, many years ago, long before there was a sun and a moon, the people of the world lived in complete darkness. Campfires provided the only light they had. But the trickster Raven set out one day to transform himself and to steal the sun for the people. This traditional Tlingit story tells of what happened to him and his snow-white feathers. The book is a celebration of traditional Native American folktales and stories that are part of this country's rich heritage. These stories are cultural expressions and remembrances of communities, tribes, and indigenous people in the Western Hemisphere.

SOCIAL STUDIES DISCIPLINES

Anthropology, sociology, history

NCSS THEMATIC STRANDS

Culture; Time, Continuity, and Change; People, Places, and Environment

CRITICAL THINKING QUESTIONS

1. Is this story similar to any other stories you know?
2. Why do you think the Raven is such an important character in Native American stories?
3. Does the Raven remind you of any historical figures in American history?
4. Why do you think the Tlingit created this story?

RELATED BOOKS

Bial, Raymond. *The Tlingit*. New York: Benchmark Books, 2002.

McDermott, Gerald. *Raven: A Trickster Tale from the Pacific Northwest*. New York: Harcourt, 1993.

Staub, Frank. *Children of the Tlingit*. Minneapolis, MN: Carolrhoda Books, 1999.

ACTIVITIES

1. The Author's Note on page 26 of the book explains the legend of the Raven in Native American folklore. Invite students to collect other Raven stories and books. They may wish to search through the holdings of the school library or public library. Afterward they may wish to develop an annotated bibliography of Raven books to share with other classes or grades.
2. Students may be interested in learning more about the Tlingit people. There is some information on page 28 of the book. Students may also wish to log on to the following Web sites for additional data:

   http://www.carnegiemuseums.org/cmnh/exhibits/north-south-east-west/tlingit/

   http://www.alaskanative.net/

   Students may wish to create a Tlingit blanket or bib (as illustrated on pages 28 and 29 of the book) with sheets of construction paper, on which they can display their accumulated information.
3. The Tlingit celebrate through potlatch memorial ceremonies. These are great feasts and dances where several clans get together for several days. Using illustrations from the book, invite students to create a series of masks that could be used at a potlatch. The masks can be constructed from brown paper lunch bags and decorated with tempera paints, beads, and yarn.
4. This story is an example of a *pourquoi* story—one that has been created to explain an act of nature or a natural phenomenon. Invite students to create their own original *pourquoi* stories to "explain" events in the natural world. For example, how would they explain the rising and falling tides, or why snow is white, or why volcanoes happen? Students may wish to assemble their collection of self-made folktales into a book to be donated to the school library.

5. This book is part of a series of folktales and legends written and illustrated by Native American writers and artists. Invite students to search for other Native American stories in which the author and/or artist is a Native American. Are there a lot of these books? Or, are books authored or illustrated by Indians relatively few? What reasons can students offer for their discoveries?

6. Invite students to create "Before" and "After" illustrations or models of Raven. "Before" illustrations would have Raven totally white; "After" illustrations would have him all black. Students may wish to create a wide variety of two-dimensional and three-dimensional representations of Raven for display in the classroom or library.

7. The stars were an important part of Native American stories and culture. Students may enjoy investigating the role of stars and constellations in Native American folktales and legends at the following Web sites:

   http://www.kstrom.net/isk/stars/starmenu.html

   http://www.windows.ucar.edu/tour/link=/the_universe/uts/amtribes.html

   http://www.ancientx.com/nm/anmviewer.asp?a=51&z=1

   http://eev2.liu.edu/e3/stargazer/native.htm

   As a follow-up, invite students to create informative brochures or leaflets on the roles of stars and constellations for various Native American cultures.

8. Invite students to write a sequel to the story that focuses on another of Raven's escapades. What other kind of trouble does Raven get himself into? What else does he do to or for the Tlingit people? Is he adored or hated?

9. This book is co-published in cooperation with the National Museum of the American Indian (www.nmai.si.edu). Invite students to learn as much as they can about the museum's efforts to preserve, protect, and foster Native American cultures. Encourage them to create a PowerPoint™ presentation or slide show about the work of the museum.

10. If possible, invite a local storyteller to visit your classroom or library. Names of individuals can be obtained through the local phone book, the children's librarian at a local public library, an independent bookstore in your area, or a local storytelling troupe. Ask if someone could share one or more Native American legends or folktales with students. Students may be interested in learning about the origin of a particular story and its various renditions.

My Great-Aunt Arizona

Gloria Houston

New York: Scholastic, 1992

SUMMARY

This book is a celebration of teachers and teaching. It is a wonderful tale of a wonderful lady who made a lasting impression on the children she taught for 57 years. It is also about a life and a community that are far removed from those many students have experienced. But it is a close-knit community in which one young lady is able to realize her dreams and foster the dreams of others.

SOCIAL STUDIES DISCIPLINES

Geography, history, sociology

NCSS THEMATIC STRANDS

Culture; Time, Continuity, and Change; People, Places, and Environment; Individual Development and Identity; Individuals, Groups, and Institutions

CRITICAL THINKING QUESTIONS

1. Why do you think that Arizona never visited the faraway places that she taught her students about?
2. Why do you think the school buildings only consisted of one classroom?

3. How would you feel if all the students in your school were in one classroom, and you had children of all different ages and abilities in your class?
4. What would be some of the advantages of learning in a one-room schoolhouse?
5. What are some of the things that teachers do to influence their students?

RELATED BOOKS

Rathbun, Frankie Beathard. *Ten Kids and a Teacher: Memories from a One Room School.* Enumclaw, WA: Pleasant Word, 2006.

ACTIVITIES

1. Have students research and look at pictures of one-room schoolhouses. Then invite them to create a diorama, out of a shoebox, of a one-room schoolhouse, based on the pictures they saw and the information they read.
2. Encourage students to look at some of the similarities and differences between the one-room schoolhouses and their own school building. Have students create a Venn diagram illustrating those comparisons.
3. Have students think about a faraway place that they would like to visit one day. Invite students to draw a picture of this place, and write why they would like to go there. Allow time for students to share their work.
4. Encourage students to write about someone in their community who has had a positive impact on their lives, like Arizona had on her many students. Allow students to send or give these writings to that specific person.
5. Throughout each season, Arizona used to play with her brother and enjoy the outdoors of her neighborhood. Allow students to discuss different things that they can do in their own neighborhoods throughout each season.
6. Discuss with students the benefits of planting and conserving trees. Invite students to plant trees on the school grounds, just like Arizona did with her students each year.
7. Invite students to create a readers theatre script from this book. Share one or more readers theatre scripts (from part III of this book) and then ask students to develop an original script using the characters and scenes from this story.
8. Invite children to discuss how their lives are different from those of the students in this story. How are their lives similar to the lives of these children? Students may wish to construct a mobile or large poster illustrating the similarities and differences.

9. One of the favorite foods (one not mentioned in the book) children of this time period ate at lunch was homemade cornbread. Here's a recipe you may wish to share with youngsters:

   Mix and sift 1 cup enriched flour, 3 teaspoons baking powder, ½ teaspoon salt, and ½ cup sugar.

   Stir in ½ cup yellow corn meal.

   Add 1 cup milk to one well-beaten egg and stir into first mixture.

   Add 1 tablespoon melted shortening and blend.

   Pour mixture into a greased 8-inch pan and bake in a hot oven (400 degrees F) for about 20 minutes.

   Cut into squares and serve.

10. Invite youngsters to interview older relatives or residents of a local senior center. Encourage them to obtain information from these older citizens about some of their school memories. Did any attend a one-room schoolhouse? Who were some of their memorable teachers? Students may wish to assemble their research into a series (by time period) of informative brochures or newsletters.

On One Flower: Butterflies, Ticks and a Few More Icks

Anthony D. Fredericks

Nevada City, CA: Dawn Publications, 2006

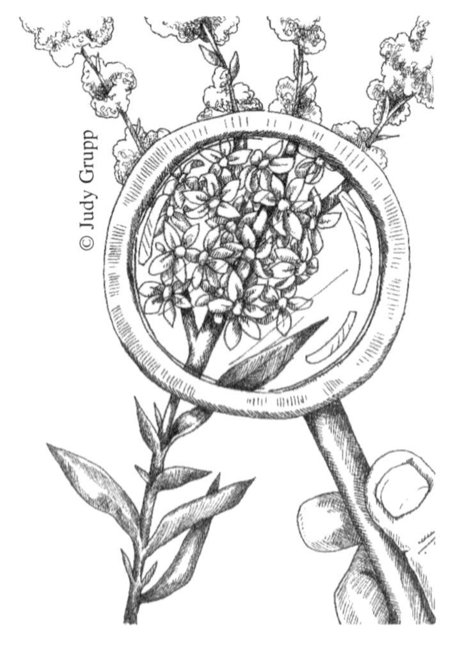

SUMMARY

Two boys set out to discover the amazing variety of creatures that live on and around a goldenrod flower. In the process they learn about how a community works, the interactions that take place in that community, and the benefits (and hazards) of community living. Colorful illustrations and a rhyming text provide readers with an engaging look into the busy world of insects.

SOCIAL STUDIES DISCIPLINES

Sociology

NCSS THEMATIC STRANDS

People, Places, and Environment

CRITICAL THINKING QUESTIONS

1. How is the community in the book similar to the community in which you live?
2. What was the most amazing thing you learned in this book?
3. What do you think the two boys will do after making their discoveries?

4. What other kinds of animal communities do you think might exist near where you live?
5. How are insects similar to people?

RELATED BOOKS

Fredericks, Anthony D. *Under One Rock: Bugs, Slugs and Other Ughs*. Nevada City, CA: Dawn Publications, 2001.

Nolan, Jerdine. *Plantzilla*. San Diego: Silver Whistle, 2002.

Wood, Douglas. *Making the World*. New York: Simon & Schuster, 1998.

ACTIVITIES

1. Invite students to check out the Web site of the Young Entomologist's Society (www.members.aol.com/yesbugs). Encourage youngsters to obtain information about one or more of the critters profiled in this book. What information does this site have that would be useful to young explorers? Encourage them to put together an informational brochure.
2. After reading the book invite students to participate in a "mini-field trip" to a flower somewhere on the school grounds. Ask them to spend some time carefully observing the flower (quietly and without moving). What types of creatures visit the flower? What types of creatures live near the flower? Are any of the creatures illustrated in the book visitors to their flower?
3. Ask an entomologist from a local high school or college to visit your classroom. Invite the person to share some additional information about each of the creatures in the book with your students. Afterwards, ask students to create posters or some other type of visual display informing people about the special characteristics or features of the selected animals.
4. Invite students to create a brief PowerPoint™ presentation about the book or about one of the animals featured in the book. They may wish to share their presentations with students in another class or grade level. Your students may wish to arrange for a special presentation in the school library or some other suitable venue.
5. After students have read the "Field Notes" section of this book, invite them to assemble their own lists of "Fantastic Facts" about the insects and other creatures featured in these pages. Small groups of students may each wish to work with a single critter and gather as many facts as possible about that specific animal. Plan opportunities for students to share their information (via posters, brochures, newspaper, or some other form of visual display).

6. Invite students to read some of the "insect poetry" listed in the "How to Learn More" section of the book. After reading some of that poetry, invite them to create and assemble their own book of poetry about the insects that live in and around their own neighborhoods. They may wish to give a poetry reading to share their work.
7. After students have read the book, visit a nearby toy store or hobby store and obtain plastic models of the creatures featured. Ask students to use these models to create three-dimensional dioramas of various scenes (using old shoeboxes, construction paper, pipe cleaners, and other props). Be sure these are prominently displayed throughout the classroom.
8. The book begins with a letter from the stinkbug. After students have read this letter, invite them to create alternate "beginning letters" that might be penned by some of the other critters profiled in the book. For example, what might the tick say? How would the butterfly start off this book? What "words of wisdom" would the ambush bug offer?
9. After students have read this book, invite them to discuss some of the similarities and/or differences between the community of animals on the flower and the community in which they live. Students may be interested in creating a large poster that illustrates those differences and/or similarities.
10. Students may want to learn more about butterflies after reading this book. Invite them to log on to the Web site of "Friends of the Monarchs" (http://www.pgmonarchs.org/fomu.html), which is the site of a nationwide volunteer group dedicated to preserving the declining populations of monarch butterflies. Students may wish to publicize the efforts of this group, create an informational display, or contact them for additional information and resources.
11. After reading the book, ask students to survey other youngsters in the school about their favorite insects. Which are the most "popular?" Which are the least "popular?" Ask students to assemble their findings into various charts and graphs. What is the most "popular" insect of all? Is it one of the insects in this book?

The Other Side

Jacqueline Woodson

New York: G. P. Putnam's Sons, 2001

SUMMARY

This is an incredibly touching book about racial segregation and how the innocence of childhood finds a way through this social barrier. Two girls—one white, one black—meet over an old wooden fence. They long to play with each and get to know one another, but there are traditions to uphold. But childhood is not about traditions, it is about discoveries. This story demonstrates how a simple act can make a world of difference. The book will spark rich and wonderful discussions about the importance of community, long summer days, and the commonalities we all share.

SOCIAL STUDIES DISCIPLINES

Sociology, political science, history

NCSS THEMATIC STRANDS

Culture; Time, Continuity, and Change; Individual Development and Identity; Individuals, Groups, and Institutions; Civic Ideals and Practices

CRITICAL THINKING QUESTIONS

1. Why was there a fence "that stretched through our town"?
2. Why didn't Clover's mother want her to climb over the fence?

3. Why did Clover's mother tell her, "Because that's the way things have always been"?
4. What does the word "friendship" mean to you?
5. What does the last page in the book mean to you?

RELATED BOOKS

Edwards, Pamela Duncan. *The Bus Ride That Changed History: The Story of Rosa Parks.* Boston: Houghton Mifflin, 2005.

Haskins, Jim. *Separate But Not Equal.* New York: Scholastic, 2002.

ACTIVITIES

1. Invite students to think about how they could make their community a more positive and peaceful place. Encourage students to write a letter to a local newspaper discussing those issues.
2. Invite students to write a sequel to the story. What will the girls do? How will their lives be different in 10 years; in 20 years? Will the fence ever be "knocked down?" Will the girls all remain friends?
3. Students may wish to obtain some historical information about racial segregation in this country. They can do so by logging on to one or more of the following Web sites:

   http://www.pbs.org/wgbh/pages/frontline/shows/secret/oral/

   http://www.nps.gov/malu/documents/jim_crow_laws.htm

   http://www.americanhistory.si.edu/brown/

   http://www.jimcrowhistory.org/

   Invite students to create an informational newsletter about racial segregation in this country. What are the events, laws, or beliefs that promoted racial segregation? Are any of the laws still in place today?
4. Invite one student to take on the role of Annie in the story. Encourage other students to pose questions to "Annie" about her experiences in the story. Questions such as the following may be used: Why did you sit on the fence in the first place? What did you see that you didn't see before? Were you afraid at any time? Is Clover your best friend now?
5. Invite students to write a series of imaginary diary entries as though they were taking on the persona of one of the following story characters: Annie, Clover, or Clover's mother. How would they have recorded their views or impressions of the first "fence-sitting" episode? How did they feel? Encourage students to share their various diary entries with each other.
6. Invite students to discuss any "fences" that may be in their town. Is there anything (e.g., customs, beliefs, traditions) that might perpetuate a "fence" in the town—an arti-

ficial (or real) barrier between groups of people? Students may wish to interview their parents or other adults about potential or real town "fences."

7. Schedule a "Neighborhood of the Week." Each week, invite students to bring in photographs of their neighborhoods, listings of neighborhood events, special attractions, or unusual buildings. They can prepare descriptions and captions for each of these and then post them on a classroom or library bulletin board.

8. Invite students to write journal entries about one thing in their own neighborhoods they would like to change. Why did they select that particular item? How would they change it? How would that change benefit other neighborhood residents?

9. Invite students to take an imaginary trip to the town mentioned in the book. Encourage them to keep a journal about their visit. They may wish to include information such as people met, places visited, restaurants eaten in, and houses seen. Invite students to note the similarities and differences between Clover and Annie's town and their own hometown.

10. Invite students to create a "Recipe for Friendship." Following is a list of incomplete ingredients. Duplicate this list and invite students to work in small groups to identify the information that could fill in the various blanks. Let students know that there are no right or wrong responses and that there will be many variations. (Note: The first one has been done for you.)

    - 1 cup __happiness__
    - 2 tablespoons __________
    - ½ cup __________
    - 3 teaspoons __________
    - pinch of __________
    - 2 pints of __________
    - large helping of __________

Quinito's Neighborhood: El Vecindario de Quinito

Ina Cumpiano

San Francisco: Children's Book Press, 2005

SUMMARY

Quinito knows that his neighborhood is made up of much more than just buildings, stores, and streets. It is also made up of all the people in his family and all the people who live and work in those buildings and stores. It is the people who make a community come alive and pulsate with their special personalities and unique contributions. This book is a celebration not only of Hispanic communities, but of all communities and the people who bring them to life. The text is in both English and Spanish.

SOCIAL STUDIES DISCIPLINES

Anthropology, sociology, economics

NCSS THEMATIC STRANDS

Culture; People, Places, and Environment; Individuals, Groups, and Institutions; Civic Ideals and Practices

CRITICAL THINKING QUESTIONS

1. What are some of the jobs that are needed to make a community run effectively?
2. Do you think that most jobs depend on other jobs, or do you think that every job can be done individually without the help of other professions?
3. What did you enjoy most about Quinito's neighborhood?
4. How did the illustrations contribute to your enjoyment of this story?
5. Which of the individuals in this book would you like to meet? Why?

RELATED BOOKS

Kiefer, Jeanne. *Jobs for Kids*. Brookfield, CT: Millbrook Press, 2003.

Rosa-Mendoza, Gladys. *Jobs Around My Neighborhood.* Wheaton, IL: Metmi Publishing, 2002.

ACTIVITIES

1. Invite students to create some type of graphic organizer showing the connections between themselves and some of the individuals in their community. Once the graphic organizers are complete, discuss with students how we rely on others in our community, and how community members rely on us.
2. Encourage students to create a mural, like Quinito's aunt did, of their own neighborhood or of their community. Display these murals on the wall or bulletin board.
3. Invite students to think about different jobs that they may be interested in doing when they get older. Invite students to write a few sentences describing the job and why they are interested in this job. Students may draw an illustration of themselves doing this job.
4. Invite students to design a neighborhood questionnaire. Students may wish to interview their neighbors about what they think makes a good neighborhood. How are the perceptions of adults different from (or similar to) the perceptions of students? Encourage students to create a chart, graph, or mural that defines the essential ingredients of a good neighborhood.
5. Invite students to talk about the roles and responsibilities of neighbors. What is a good neighbor? What does a neighbor do for others in her or his community? What makes a neighborhood a neighborhood? What do students like (or dislike) about their neighborhoods?
6. Invite students to construct their own English/Spanish dictionary based on the words in this book. They may wish to title their production "An English/Spanish Community Dictionary." Invite someone from the school or neighborhood to contribute the Spanish equivalents for other "community words" that students wish to include in the dictionary.

7. Students may wish to do some research in other literature sources on the Internet about celebrations that take place in Hispanic communities and neighborhoods. These may include (but aren't limited to) Los Dias de Los Muertos (Days of the Dead) and Cinco de Mayo (May 5—The Mexican Independence Day). Invite students to construct descriptive posters that illustrate the history and elements of these special celebrations.

8. Celebrate a Neighborhood Day in the classroom or library. Invite various people from your community to visit and share information about their occupations. You may choose to invite the mayor, the fire chief, the postmaster, a doctor, a dentist, a nurse, the owner of a lumber store, a sanitation worker, a seamstress, an insurance salesperson, or representatives of other occupational groups. Provide a forum in which students can interview each of the visitors and collect the data in the form of a scrapbook or a series of brochures.

9. Invite students to conduct an imaginary interview with Quinito. Invite one student to take on the role of Quinito. Encourage other students to interview Quinito about his perceptions or discoveries in his neighborhood. What does he enjoy most about the neighborhood? Who are some other special people not mentioned in the book? If possible, you may wish to videotape the interview.

10. Provide students with the yellow pages of your local phone book. Invite them to look at the various listings, the display ads, and the variety of goods and services offered. Then encourage students to create a special set of "yellow pages" for Quinito's neighborhood. How might some of the businesses advertise their services in the yellow pages? Students may wish to assemble their display ads into a scrapbook or some other published format to include with a copy of this book.

Tomás and the Library Lady

Pat Mora

New York: Dragonfly Books, 1997

© Judy Grupp

SUMMARY

Tomás and his family are migrant workers who travel from one state to another picking crops. One summer the family arrives in Iowa and, to escape the scorching heat, Tomás discovers the local public library. There he also discovers the wonder of books and the joy of reading. His imagination takes flight due to the efforts of the town librarian—an individual who makes a lifelong impression on the young boy. This is a true story that achieves its greatest poignancy when you share the Author's Note at the end of the book.

SOCIAL STUDIES DISCIPLINES

Anthropology, sociology, geography, economics

NCSS THEMATIC STRANDS

Culture; Time, Continuity, and Change; People, Places, and Environment; Individuals, Groups, and Institutions; Civic Ideals and Practices

CRITICAL THINKING QUESTIONS

1. How would you feel if you had to keep moving and leaving your home?
2. What types of stories hold your attention so much that you forget about everything else around you, like Tomás did?

3. What kind of schooling do you think Tomás got?
4. What did the Author's Note at the end of the book mean to you?
5. Why do you think Tomás would be a good friend?

RELATED BOOKS

Altman, Linda Jacobs. *Amelia's Road.* New York: Lee & Low Books, 1993.

Atkin, Beth S. *Voices from the Fields: Children of Migrant Farmworkers Tell Their Stories.* Boston: Little, Brown, 2000.

ACTIVITIES

1. Have students write a sequel to the story. What do you think Tomás did with his new book once he went back home? Do you think he got new books? Do you think he visits a library near his house in Texas? Do you think he tells stories to others?
2. Invite the local public librarian to visit your classroom or school library. Invite that individual to share some of the features and services of the local public library. Be sure students have an opportunity to sign up for their own personal library cards.
3. Invite students to gather information about migrant workers in this country. They can begin their search with the following Web site: http://www.weedpatchcamp.com/. Also, encourage students to obtain information from school and public library resources on migrant workers. Invite students to put together their own PowerPoint™ presentation on migrant workers—their lifestyle, their daily life, their travels, and their housing.
4. Invite students to assemble a collection of books that feature libraries or librarians. How many books talk about the work that librarians do? How many books celebrate a local public library?
5. Students may be interested in reading some of the other books by this author. What themes does she include in most of her stories? Are her stories only about Hispanic figures, or do they have universal themes? What do readers (and critics) enjoy most about her books?
6. Students may wish to put together an annotated bibliography of Hispanic children's literature for their grade level. How many books are available in the school library? How many are available in the public library? Are there sufficient books about Mexicans and other Hispanic groups? Do they receive fair and equitable treatment in children's literature?
7. A number of Spanish words are used throughout this book. Invite students to assemble a small brochure that has both English and Spanish words from the book. The brochure could be made available in concert with the book.

8. Invite students to design a poster declaring the importance of reading. Students may wish to create an English/Spanish poster on the virtues of reading for every citizen. Selected posters can be displayed in the school or public library.
9. Invite students to conduct an imaginary interview with Papá Grande. What questions would they like to ask him? Encourage one student to take on the role of Papá Grande and to respond to the questions posed by her or his classmates. How would Papá Grande's responses differ from those that Tomás might make?
10. Invite students to complete some of the sentence stems below:

    "If I was a migrant worker I would ___________."

    "If my family moved around a lot, we would ___________."

    "If I were Tomás, I would ___________."

    "If I was in a library for the first time, I would ___________."

    "If I never learned to read, I would ___________."

Wilfrid Gordon McDonald Partridge

Mem Fox

La Jolla, CA: Kane/Miller Book Publishers, 1989

SUMMARY

Wilfrid Gordon McDonald Partridge is a most inquisitive boy—he's always asking questions. He especially asks questions of all the residents of an old folks home next door to his house. He wants to know what a "memory" is, and he's somewhat perplexed by the answers he receives. But he makes a most interesting discovery when he inadvertently shares some memories with his friend, Miss Nancy. With simple text and delightful illustrations, children will quickly grasp the value of both young and old in any community.

SOCIAL STUDIES DISCIPLINES

Sociology

NCSS THEMATIC STRANDS

Time, Continuity, and Change; People, Places, and Environment; Individual Development and Identity

CRITICAL THINKING QUESTIONS

1. What do you think a memory is?
2. What are some other ways that Wilfred Gordon could have helped Miss Nancy get her memory back?

3. Is there anyone in your neighborhood who has helped you, or whom you have helped, in a time of need? If so, what did you do or what did someone do for you?
4. What are some memorable times in your life? In the lives of your family members?
5. Why is it sometimes difficult for older people to remember things?

RELATED BOOKS

Drake, Jane, and Ann Love. *My Vacation Place: A Memory Book.* Toronto: Kids Can Press, 2001.

ACTIVITIES

1. Invite students to write about and illustrate their favorite memory. Allow time for students to share their work.
2. Encourage students to "adopt" senior citizens from a neighboring senior citizen's home. Have students write letters back and forth to their "adopted" senior. One day, take a trip to the senior citizens' home so that students and seniors can talk about some of their favorite memories.
3. Encourage students to create a list of items that would help them remember things, if they ever lost their memory. Have students include something warm, something from long ago, something that makes them cry, something that makes them laugh, and something as precious as gold. Allow time for students to share their lists and to explain why these items would help bring back their memory.
4. Invite students to think about their favorite memory concerning their neighborhood or community. Have students share these memories with each other.
5. Ask students to gather different items or pictures that represent each student's neighborhood. Invite students to place these items in a box labeled "Time Capsule." Have students pretend that this box has just been rediscovered years later. Encourage students to share their items with the class, discussing what memories these items evoke.
6. Invite students to keep an eye on the local newspaper for stories or articles about senior citizens. Ask them to create a collection of those articles in a box or large envelope. When approximately 20 stories have been collected, invite students to sort the articles into various categories. The categories may include "Health," "Income," "Housing," etc. Ask students to determine the theme that is represented most in the articles. What reasons can they offer for the prevalence of that theme?
7. Invite students to search through the pages (white or yellow) of the local phone book. How many listings are there for senior citizens? For example, how many senior citizen centers are in your local community? How many attorneys specialize in work for senior citizens? Are there specific recreation facilities or opportunities for senior citi-

zens? Students may wish to estimate how many services in their local community are directed at senior citizens. If there is a paucity of resources, invite students to write a letter to the mayor, town council, county commissioners, or the editor of the local newspaper to voice their concern.

8. Invite students to conduct an imaginary interview with Wilfrid Gordon McDonald Partridge. Invite one student to take on the role of Wilfrid. Encourage other students to interview "Wilfrid" about his role in this story. What did he learn about memories? Does he still need to do some more "research?" Whom else would he like to talk to?

9. Invite youngsters to interview older relatives. What are some of the pleasant memories they recall? Why are some events easier to remember than others? Students may wish to make audiorecordings of their interview and share them with a class or group. As appropriate, one of those interviews might be developed into a book similar in focus to *Wilfrid Gordon McDonald Partridge*.

10. Invite students to write journal entries about one thing they would like to change regarding older citizens. It might be the availability of public transportation or the recreational resources in the community. Take time to share these concerns in small groups or whole class sessions.

CHAPTER 8

City and Country

Fireboat: The Heroic Adventures of the John J. Harvey

Maira Kalman

New York: G. P. Putnam's Sons, 2002

SUMMARY

The *John J. Harvey* was an old fireboat that had seen better days. However, a group of people got together and offered to buy this ancient boat and refit it. It was fixed up almost like new. Then, on one horrific day in September 2001, the world was changed forever. A call came from the New York City fire department that they needed help. And the *John J. Harvey* responded. It helped fight the fires and extinguish the flames of that disastrous day. The *John J. Harvey,* although just an ancient fireboat, was a hero.

SOCIAL STUDIES DISCIPLINES

Economics, history, geography, sociology, anthropology

NCSS THEMATIC STRANDS

People, Places, and Environment; Individuals, Groups, and Institutions; Power, Authority, and Governance; Civic Ideals and Practices

CRITICAL THINKING QUESTIONS

1. What do you think would have happened if the *John J. Harvey* had never been repaired?
2. In what ways do you think the attack affected New York City and its citizens?
3. How would you feel if your city was attacked and on fire?
4. Why was the *John J. Harvey* considered a hero?
5. Read the last page again. Why did the author end the book this way?

RELATED BOOKS

Block, Evelyn B. *September 11, 2001: A Day in History*. Philadelphia: Xlibris Corp., 2003.

Poffenberger, Nancy. *September 11, 2001: A Simple Account for Children*. Cincinnati, OH: Fun Publishing, 2001.

Wheeler, Jill C. *September 11, 2001: The Day That Changed America*. Edina, MN: Abdo & Daughters Publishing, 2002.

Winter, Jeanette. *September Roses*. New York: Farrar, Straus & Giroux, 2004.

ACTIVITIES

1. At the beginning of the story, the author discusses various things that occurred in 1931 in New York City. Invite students to research and find a year in which many amazing things occurred in their own city.
2. Encourage students to find out how many lives were lost in the attacks on September 11, 2001. Invite students to collect that amount of a specific object, such as M&Ms, paperclips, or pennies to be able to visualize how many lives were really lost.
3. Invite students to write a story using their own city as the setting. Have students develop a fictitious plot that discusses something happening in their city that requires many members in their area to cooperate to solve the problem. Provide opportunities for students to display their work.
4. Encourage students to use construction paper and other materials to create their own replica of the *John J. Harvey* fireboat. Invite some students to retell the story while others manipulate the construction paper replicas.
5. Invite students to write a letter to family members and friends pretending that they were one of the crew members on the *John J. Harvey* the day of the attacks. Encourage

students to write about how they would have felt if they were in New York City on September 11, 2001, and took part in putting out the fire.

6. Invite students to write an imaginary letter to New York City students who were affected by the events that took place on September 11, 2001. Encourage students to ask questions that they would like answered about the students' feelings and the impact that it had on their lives, etc.

7. Invite students to consult books and other printed materials in the library to obtain background information about New York City. They may wish to access selected Web sites, such as the following, to obtain relevant information:

   http://www.nytimes.com/specials/nyc100/

   http://www.pbs.org/wnet/newyork/

   http://www.lib.utexas.edu/maps/new_york.html

   http://newyorkinphotos.com/wtc/

   http://www.pbs.org/wnet/newyork/series/interview/interview.html

   After youngsters have obtained sufficient data, invite them to construct a large wall mural of life in New York. They may wish to indicate points of interest, historical locations, famous streets, and other special features. Be sure to have them plot one or more of the locations profiled in the book, too.

8. Encourage students to create a record book about New York City. They may want to look up and provide information on the following:

   What is the tallest building?

   What is the longest bridge?

   How many people live in the city?

   How many schools are in New York?

   How many people work in New York?

   How many people ride the subway system each day?

9. Invite students to create a time line of events in the history of New York. Beginning with examples cited in the book, invite students to post illustrations and descriptions of various sites and events throughout the city's history. This information can be displayed on a very long sheet of newsprint posted along one wall of the classroom or library. It could also be displayed on a strip of adding machine tape posted along a hallway in the school.

10. Invite students to create their own memorial for September 11, 2001. They may wish to honor the firefighters, police officers, or everyday citizens who worked to save lives and property. Students may also elect to write imaginary letters of support and praise to individuals involved in the various rescue efforts. Be sure these products are appropriately displayed in the classroom or library.

An Island Scrapbook: Dawn to Dusk on a Barrier Island

Virginia Wright-Frierson

New York: Simon & Schuster, 1998

SUMMARY

Sketch pads and paintbrushes in hand, an artist and her daughter explore every inch of a North Carolina barrier island. They find some amazing creatures, observe a wide variety of wildlife, sketch and paint dozens of scenes, and learn more than they ever thought possible about this exciting ecosystem. This book is a wonderful marriage of art and literature and will captivate youngsters with both sight and sound. An excellent choice for read-aloud and sharing.

SOCIAL STUDIES DISCIPLINES

Geography, anthropology, sociology

NCSS THEMATIC STRANDS

Time, Continuity, and Change; People, Places, and Environment; Science, Technology, and Society

CRITICAL THINKING QUESTIONS

1. What islands and beaches have you visited, and how do they compare to the island in the story?

2. What are some of the reasons that the characters in the story sketched and painted pictures and wrote about the various things that they saw while they visited the island?
3. Are the environmental issues that the island and its living organisms faced similar to those in the area in which you live in? How are they similar, and how do they differ?
4. How is this book different from other books you have read?

RELATED BOOKS

Jauck, Andrea, and Larry Points. *Barrier Islands Are for the Birds*. Mariposa, CA: Sierra Press, 2000.

ACTIVITIES

1. Invite students to find various library or Internet resources discussing various birds and plants in your area. Encourage them to assemble the information into "Field Guides." Afterward you may wish to take them on a local nature walk. While on their walk, encourage students to identify the various birds and plants they see in their environment, just as the characters did in the story.
2. Encourage students to write about and draw pictures of their favorite vacation places. Gather these illustrations into a classroom vacation scrapbook, which can be placed in the classroom library. Discuss the similarities and differences between the students' vacation places and the one depicted in the book.
3. Invite students to contact one or more local environmental groups in your area (addresses can be found in the telephone book) and invite them to share information on their efforts to preserve the environment in your part of the country. Students may wish to ask how they and other citizens can become active in the groups' efforts.
4. Encourage students to conduct library investigations of the seashores of the United States. In which states are they located? Do they all experience the challenges referred to in this book? What are some of the differing environmental concerns in various parts of the country?
5. Divide students into several small groups. Invite each group to create an environmental protection plan for the local community. Which local agencies or groups will give information? What response would students get from the local chamber of commerce or from city hall? Invite students to investigate the resources available and how those resources could be used to develop a long-range plan.
6. Provide each of several groups of students with topographical maps of the barrier islands (these can be obtained online or through the geography department of a local college or university). Invite each group to investigate the annual weather conditions for the barrier islands and the impact of weather on the shoreline and on the creatures that live there.

7. Invite students to create a readers theatre script (see part III) in which they are members of a barrier island community. What would some of their responsibilities be? How would they participate in the community's efforts to preserve the local environment? Invite students to present answers to these questions (after sufficient library research) in a script. You may wish to assign roles and invite students to perform the play for another class. Be sure to solicit reactions from that other class.
8. As a corollary to the activity above, invite students to discuss the advantages of people working together to preserve a part of the environment. What can a group of people do that one person cannot? What does the phrase "strength in numbers" mean?
9. Invite students to create an imaginary newscast about the events that took place in this book. Two students could take on the roles of the mother and daughter, while other students report on the discoveries, events, and sightings made throughout the day. Students may enjoy videotaping the newscast for later viewing.
10. Invite students to emulate the characters in the book. Take them on a sketching nature tour of the school grounds. What do they notice that they haven't seen before? What would they like to draw or sketch? Later, you may wish to collect their descriptions and drawings into a scrapbook patterned after the one in this book.

Life on an Apple Orchard

Judy Wolfman

Minneapolis, MN: Carolrhoda Books, 2004

SUMMARY

Living on a farm and harvesting apples for a living is something most children have never experienced. This insightful book looks at a year in the life of an "apple family" as seen through the eyes of Emily. It provides readers with an interesting view of farming and the responsibilities of all family members. Children will have a greater respect for farming (and the apples they eat) after reading this book with its wonderful photographs.

SOCIAL STUDIES DISCIPLINES

Anthropology, economics, geography, sociology

NCSS THEMATIC STRANDS

Production, Distribution, and Consumption; Science, Technology, and Society

CRITICAL THINKING QUESTIONS

1. Why is it important for the family in the story to take care of their apple orchard during all four seasons?
2. Would you want to live on a farm with an apple orchard? Why or why not?
3. What do you think are some of the major challenges about living on a farm with an apple orchard?
4. What do you know about apples (at the end of the story) that you didn't know before?
5. What is your favorite variety of apples?

RELATED BOOKS

Gibbons, Gail. *Apples*. New York: Holiday House, 2000.

Holub, Joan. *Who Was Johnny Appleseed?* New York: Grosset & Dunlap, 2005.

Landau, Elaine. *Apples*. New York: Children's Press, 2000.

Snyder, Inez. *Apples*. New York: Children's Press, 2004.

Wellington, Monica. *Apple Farmer Annie*. New York: Dutton Juvenile, 2001.

ACTIVITIES

1. If possible, locate an apple orchard in your area that gives tours to students. Take students on a field trip to this location to learn more about apple orchards and the work that goes into harvesting apples. Afterward invite students to create a brochure about the various things learned during the field trip.
2. Invite students to visit the Web site www.urbanext.uiuc.edu/apples. Here, students can learn fun apple facts, the lifecycle of an apple tree, and the different types of apples available, and they can participate in fun apple activities. Invite them to create a poster that lists some of the most interesting information.
3. Encourage students to write an imaginary letter to the family in the story (or to Emily) asking any questions the students still may have about living on a farm with an apple orchard. What else would they like to know about this lifestyle?
4. Invite students to participate in an apple tasting contest. Take several different types of apples and cut them into small pieces. Invite each student to sample a variety of apples. Invite students to describe the various tastes (bitter, sweet, sour, etc.). Students may wish to create a chart listing the variety of tastes that can be found in the apples purchased in a local supermarket.
5. Invite each student to cut out a construction paper apple. After appropriate library research, each student can record a list of reasons (for his or her respective "apples") why apples are healthful. Place these "apples" on an apple bulletin board.

6. Encourage students to search through books in the school library, public library, or at home for apple recipes. Ask each student to bring in one apple recipe. Share the recipes with students and ask them to vote for their favorite. If possible, use school facilities to cook or bake the selected recipe and share it with the students.
7. There are a number of American "apple stories"—the most popular of which is the legend of Johnny Appleseed. Collect several different books about Johnny Appleseed as well as other apple legends and share them with the students. Invite students to assemble an annotated bibliography of apple books to share with other classes and other grades.
8. Ask students to create a two-sided poster. Invite them to conduct appropriate library research about city life and about farm life. Afterward invite them to record several facts and figures about life in a city on one side of the poster. On the other side they can record facts and figures about life on a farm. Invite them to discuss any similarities and differences.
9. Encourage students to create an "Apple Farm Newspaper" that includes all the happenings and events that take place on an apple farm. Invite students to look at the design and set-up of the local newspaper in designing their own. Students may wish to take on the roles of reporters and describe daily events, special occurrences, family news, work schedules, and other similar news.
10. If possible, invite a farmer to visit and discuss her or his daily schedule (it doesn't have to be an apple farmer). Invite students to collect information that could be developed into a PowerPoint™ presentation or Web page that could be shared with other students throughout the school. Ask students to make verbal and written comparisons between the family in the book and how the presenter lives.

Mountain Town

Bonnie Geisert and Arthur Geisert

Boston: Houghton Mifflin, 2000

SUMMARY

Life in a mountain town is unlike life in any city. Here the living is a little more laid back and the residents have to deal with events and circumstances their friends in larger urban areas don't have to think about. This author and illustrator team has combined to create a view of city life that is both unique and singular. Plan to spend considerable time observing and discussing the small details in the illustrations that provide insights unavailable elsewhere. This is an excellent addition to any study of city life.

SOCIAL STUDIES DISCIPLINES

Geography, anthropology, history, economics

NCSS THEMATIC STRANDS

Time, Continuity, and Change; People, Places, and Environment; Power, Authority and Governance; Civic Ideals and Practices

CRITICAL THINKING QUESTIONS

1. How is the mountain town similar to and different from your own town?
2. What are some ways that the people who lived in the town in the story have adapted to their environment?

3. Would you want to live in the mountains? Why or why not?
4. If you lived in a mountain town, what would you miss most?
5. What is something you would like to ask the residents of a mountain town?

RELATED BOOKS

Mader, Jan. *Rocky Mountains*. New York: Children's Press, 2004.

ACTIVITIES

1. Encourage students to create a Venn diagram comparing and contrasting their own town with the mountain town in the story.
2. Invite students to create their own three-dimensional mountain town. Students can use clay, modeling clay, or other available materials.
3. Divide students into four groups and assign each a season (spring, summer, fall, winter). Invite each group to pretend that they live in a mountain town. Encourage them to create a series of weather reports for their particular season.
4. Invite students to create a list of various items they would bring with them if they were taking a hike and having a picnic in the mountains. Encourage students to draw a picture of the view that they might see, or a photograph that they might take, while having a picnic in the mountains.
5. Invite students to prepare a short skit about the Fourth of July in the town. Students can take on the roles of various townspeople, each of whom is interviewed by a newspaper reporter.
6. Divide students into several groups and invite each group to create a song to the tune of a popular ditty. For example, using the tune for "Over the River and Through the Woods," students could create the following example:

   Up in the mountains where snow does fall

   We see the mountain town

   The trees are white, the hills are filled

   As snow keeps falling down.

   Students may also wish to create versions of the song using people and events in their own town.
7. Invite students to create a community newspaper for a fictitious mountain town. Students can create current event articles on local neighborhoods, school events, political elections, community celebrations, and the like. Using the events and descriptions in the book, invite youngsters to piece together a newspaper that represents a day in the life of a mountain town.

8. Invite students to create a telephone directory for an imaginary mountain town. Encourage them to focus on the "yellow pages"—that is, those services that would be specific and particular to life in a mountain town.

9. Students may wish to check out some of the mountain towns in Montana—specifically those that are promoted for films and movies. They can be found on the following Web site: http://montanafilm.com/cities.htm. Invite students to discuss the similarities and differences between these towns and the one featured in the book.

10. Invite students to rewrite the book as though they were living in the town. What specific features would they want to share with readers who had never visited that town? What would they like the "outside world" to know about? What misconceptions about living in a mountain town would they like to clear up?

Near One Cattail: Turtles, Logs and Leaping Frogs

Anthony D. Fredericks

Nevada City, CA: Dawn Publications, 2005

SUMMARY

This book introduces young readers to the wonders of a wetlands environment. Readers journey with the heroine as she discovers an incredible variety of wildlife in this dynamic community. Frogs with big bulging eyes, sunbathing turtles, zip-zipping dragonflies, paddling beetles, and brown-feathered ducks "swim, soar or crawl in this sog-soggy home." The emphasis is on the plants and animals that make this ecosystem such an incredible place to investigate and discover. This title won the 2006 Green Earth Book Award for the best environmentally themed children's book of the year.

SOCIAL STUDIES DISCIPLINES

Geography

NCSS THEMATIC STRANDS

People, Places, and Environment

CRITICAL THINKING QUESTIONS

1. Which of the animals did you find most interesting?
2. Which of the animals would you like to learn more about?

3. What would you like to discover in a wetlands environment?
4. How are all the animals able to live together?
5. What did you enjoy most about the book?
6. If you could ask the author one question, what would it be?

RELATED BOOKS

Cone, Molly. *Squishy, Misty, Damp & Muddy*. San Francisco: Sierra Club, 1996.

National Wildlife Federation. *Wading into Wetlands*. New York: Learning Triangle Press, 1997.

Silver, Donald. *One Small Square: Swamp*. New York: Learning Triangle Press, 1997.

Staub, Frank. *America's Wetlands*. Minneapolis, MN: Carolrhoda, 1995.

ACTIVITIES

1. Encourage students to write a letter to the girl in the story. What would they like to say to her? What would they like to know about her adventures in the wetland ecosystem profiled in the book? What else would they like to know about her?
2. Invite each student in the class to select one of the animals illustrated in this book. Encourage each child to conduct necessary research (e.g., in the library or on the Internet) on his or her identified species. Then invite students to write a series of diary entries told from the perspective of the creature. For example, "A Day in the Life of a Frog," or "My Life as a Dragonfly."
3. Provide students with an assortment of magazines that contain pictures of wetland creatures (e.g., *National Geographic, Ranger Rick, National Wildlife*). Encourage them to bring in old magazines from home. Invite students to make a class collage of a wetlands environment by pasting pictures of different critters on a large sheet of newsprint (to be displayed in the classroom).
4. Invite students to read one or more of the other books in this series: *Under One Rock: Bugs, Slugs and Other Ughs* (2001), *In One Tidepool: Crabs, Snails and Salty Tails* (2002), *Around One Cactus: Owls, Bats and Leaping Rats* (2003), and *On One Flower: Butterflies, Ticks and a Few More Icks* (2006). How are the books similar? How are the books different?
5. Invite students to contact several of the following groups and ask for information about the work they do and the types of printed information they have available for students: Ducks Unlimited (One Waterfowl Way, Memphis, TN 38120; www.ducks.org), Izaak Walton League of America (707 Conservation Lane, Gaithersburg, MD 20878; www.iwla.org), National Wildlife Federation (11100 Wildlife Center Drive, Reston, VA 20190; www.nwf.org), Wetlands International—North America (c/o USFWS, Division of International Affairs, 4401 North Fairfax Dr., Room 730-ARLSQ, Arlington, VA 22203-1622).

6. Invite students to look through the classified section of the local newspaper. Based on examples in the newspaper, challenge students to create an original classified advertisement based on information in the book. For example:

   > FOR RENT: Lily pad. Sometimes wet, sometimes dry. Lots of neighbors. Lots of plants. Waterfront property with great view. Reasonable rates. Available immediately. Call Freddy Frog at 123-4567 any time after bird migration.

7. Be sure to check out the following Web site: http://www.cln.org/themes/wetlands.html. Here, students and teachers will find a multitude of curricular resources (information, content, etc.) to help them learn about wetlands. In addition, there are lots of links to instructional materials (e.g., lesson plans) that will help you provide instruction in this theme. In a word, this site is SUPER!

8. Provide students with blank maps of North America. After appropriate research, invite them to color in the places in the United States and Canada where wetlands would be found. If more appropriate, consider providing youngsters with a blank map of your state and invite them to locate regional wetland areas.

9. Invite students to put together a "Wetlands Newspaper" that presents interesting facts and observations about wetland creatures. Invite students to use the same sections as the local newspaper (e.g., Sports—how fast some wetland animals can move; Fashion—the latest "colors" all the fashionable critters are wearing; Food and Health—the different diets of wetland creatures). Students can use a word processing program to assemble the newspaper and then print it for distribution to other classrooms.

10. Invite students to log onto the wildlife page of the National Wildlife Federation at http://www.nwf.org/wildlife/. Students may wish to locate various animals profiled in *Near One Cattail* and learn additional information about them through this all-inclusive site. This site is also appropriate for research on selected wetland and endangered animal species.

11. Discuss with students the similarities and/or differences between the community of animals in a wetlands environment and the community in which they live. Invite students to create an oversized Venn diagram illustrating those comparisons.

12. Here are three excellent videos (all VHS) about wetlands that you may wish to obtain for your classroom or library (all are available from Amazon.com): *Wetlands, Marshes and Swamps* (1996), *Conserving America: The Wetlands* (1994), and *Wild Wetlands (Animal Safari, Vol. 7)* (2000).

13. Invite students to discuss the similarities between human dwellings and animal homes. What are some of the things that determine where an animal lives? Are those conditions or features similar to the considerations of humans in selecting a living site? Do animals, particularly wetland animals, have more options for living spaces than humans?

Rhyolite: The True Story of a Ghost Town

Diane Siebert

New York: Clarion, 2003

SUMMARY

"In the desert, out of sight/Rests the town of Rhyolite." Thus begins this poetic history of the life and death of a mining town that once existed in the southwestern desert of Nevada. A colorful parade of characters and an equally delightful array of events and circumstances make this an ideal read-aloud book. It offers insight into the settlement of the American West—both the good and the bad.

SOCIAL STUDIES DISCIPLINES

Sociology, economics, geography, history

NCSS THEMATIC STRANDS

Culture; Time, Continuity, and Change; People, Places, and Environment; Production, Distribution, and Consumption; Civic Ideals and Practices

CRITICAL THINKING QUESTIONS

1. How did the illustrations add to your enjoyment of the story?
2. What did you learn about mining for gold that you didn't know before?

3. Would you have enjoyed being a miner in 1904?
4. How is Rhyolite different from where you live? How is it similar?
5. What would you find most amazing about Rhyolite today?

RELATED BOOKS

Fredericks, Anthony D. *Around One Cactus: Owls, Bats and Leaping Rats*. Nevada City, CA: Dawn Publications, 2003.

McDermott, Gerald. *Coyote: A Trickster Tale from the American Southwest*. San Diego: Voyager Books, 1994.

Siebert, Diane. *Mojave*. New York: Harper, 1988.

ACTIVITIES

1. Students may enjoy creating their own desert terrarium. The following directions will help them design a fully functioning terrarium:
   a. Fill the bottom of a large glass container with a layer of coarse sand or gravel. Combine one part fine sand with two parts potting soil and spread this over the top of the first layer.
   b. Sprinkle this lightly with water.
   c. Place several varieties of cactus in the terrarium (it might be a good idea to wear gloves). Most nurseries carry cacti, or they can be ordered through the mail from selected seed companies and mail order nursery houses.
   d. When planting the cacti, be sure that the roots are covered completely by the sandy mixture.
   e. Students may decide to place several desert animals such as lizards or horned toads in the terrarium. Be sure the animals have a sufficient quantity of food and water available.
   f. The desert terrarium can be left in the sun and does not need a glass cover. It should, however, be lightly sprinkled with water about once a week.
2. Invite students to write to one or more of the following national parks and request information about the flora and fauna that inhabit those special regions. When the brochures, flyers, leaflets, and descriptive information arrive, invite students to assemble them into an attractive display in the classroom or a school display case.

Death Valley National Park
P.O. Box 579
Death Valley, CA 92328

Joshua Tree National Park
74485 National Park Drive
Twentynine Palms, CA 92277

Great Basin National Park
Baker, NV 89311

3. Students may wish to visit a local gardening center or nursery. Invite them to purchase an inexpensive cactus plant. Ask them to carefully observe their own cactus. What shape is it? Does the shape change as it grows? What do the needles look like? Students may wish to observe cactus features with a magnifying lens and record their observations in a "Desert Journal."

4. Divide students into several small groups. Encourage each group to practice reading some pages. Invite the groups to record the entire book on audiotape (several practices may be necessary). Students may wish to suggest sound effects (e.g., coyotes). Encourage students to contribute the tape to the school library.

5. Students can keep up-to-date on the latest events, discoveries, and news about life in the deserts of the United States by accessing the Web site of *Desert USA Magazine* (www.desertusa.com). Here they can learn about the lives of the flora and fauna that inhabit U.S. deserts. They may wish to gather selected information together in the form of descriptive brochures or pamphlets for the classroom library.

6. Invite students to create their own original salt map deserts. Provide them with the following recipe and encourage them to work in teams to create an original depiction of a desert scene.

   1½ cups coarse salt (kosher salt works well)

   1 cup flour

   1½ cups water

   Have students mix the salt and flour together in a medium-sized mixing bowl. Add enough water to make a stiff dough. Students should form the mixture on top of a stiff piece of cardboard or small sheet of plywood (ask them to work quickly). Ask students to shape their mixture into hills, mountains, large flat areas, or other geographical features that represent the Sonoran Desert. Allow the mixture to dry for two to three days. After it dries, students can paint it with tempera paints.

7. Students may wish to make their own sand drawings. Obtain packages of colored sand from a local craft or hobby store. Provide each student with a square of stiff cardboard and a bottle of school glue. Encourage students to create an illustration of a desert scene by using the glue as though it were a paintbrush. Before the glue dries, students should sprinkle small amounts of colored sand on the glue to create interesting mosaics or motifs. Allow the paintings to dry for several days and display them in the classroom.

8. Divide the class into several groups and invite each group to plan a trip across the desert. Encourage each group to assemble a list of supplies and equipment they would need for their journey. What would be some essential items? What would they expect to see? Invite students to compare their information and post the lists on the bulletin board for whole-class discussions.

9. Invite students to talk about how life in Rhyolite would be different from the lives that they lead today. What would they have to do without? What would they miss? What hardships would they have to endure?
10. Invite students to discuss how the wood-cut illustrations contributed to their enjoyment of the book. How do those illustrations add to the starkness of life in a desert town? As appropriate, work with the art teacher to demonstrate wood cuts or invite students to create their own wood-cut blocks for printing.

Where Horses Run Free: A Dream for the American Mustang

Joy Cowley

Honesdale, PA: Boyds Mills Press, 2003

SUMMARY

A herd of wild horses runs free across the open prairie . . . free, that is, until they are captured and penned. Their fire and beauty is hemmed in by fences and wire until a sympathetic cowboy comes along to set them free. This is a fictional story based on true events—events that are as poignant today as they were a hundred years ago when these wild mustangs graced the American West. This book will open students' eyes to the majesty and beauty of the open plains.

SOCIAL STUDIES DISCIPLINES

Economics, geography, history

NCSS THEMATIC STRANDS

Time, Continuity, and Change; People, Places, and Environment

CRITICAL THINKING QUESTIONS

1. Why do you think the cowboy wanted to save the horses?
2. Why were the horses captured and penned in the first place?

3. Why should horses be allowed to run free across the open plains?
4. Why do horses get sick when they are in pens?
5. Why have people enjoyed horses over the years?

RELATED BOOKS

Kathrens, Ginger. *Cloud's Legacy: The Wild Stallion Returns*. Irvine, CA: Bowtie Press, 2004.

Peterson, Chris, and Alvis Upitis. *Wild Horses: Black Hills Sanctuary*. Honesdale, PA: Boyds Mills Press, 2003.

Vogel, Julia, and Michael Rowe. *Wild Horses*. (Our Wild World). Chanhassen, MN: NorthWord, 2004.

ACTIVITIES

1. Students may enjoy accessing the information about wild horses on the following Web sites:

   http://net.unl.edu/artsFeat/wildhorses/

   http://www.pbs.org/wnet/nature/cloud/

   http://www.pbs.org/wnet/nature/cloudslegacy/

   After students have accessed the information, invite them to construct an appropriate display (poster, collage, etc.) for the classroom or library. What are some specific facts they would like to share with other students?

2. Divide students into several small groups and invite each group to take either a pro or con position on the systematic round-up of wild horses throughout the American West. What are the advantages? What are the disadvantages? Provide each group with an opportunity to argue their position(s).

3. Invite students to put together a time line of significant events in the history of the horse in North America. Encourage students to work in small groups and post a large sheet of newsprint across one wall of a classroom or library. Students may wish to record important dates, personal illustrations, or milestones in the natural history of the horse on this continent. Plan time for students to share their creations.

4. Encourage students to create a shape book. Invite them to cut out an outline of a horse from two sheets of oak tag. Students may wish to staple several blank sheets of paper between the two outlines to form a book and then record significant facts, features, or characteristics about North American horses. These books can be arranged in an attractive display in the classroom or library.

5. Schedule a "Wild Horse Day" or "Mustang Day" in your classroom or library and invite other students to join the festivities. Students can present skits on the introduction

of horses to the North American continent, construct posters or dioramas about horses, share stories and folktales about life on the plains, and construct clay models of various breeds of horses. "Horse Day" can be a day to celebrate the significance and importance of the horse through books, stories, songs, and various activities.

6. Invite students to create an imaginary story about the life of the mustang as told from the perspective of the mustang. The narrator can outline her or his daily life or present details about her or his entire life. Students may wish to have the narrator reflect on how it was in "the good old days" when there were no fences on the prairies or plains.

7. Invite students to write letters to their congressional representatives on the value of free range wild horses. Invite them to ask about any current or pending legislation related to preserving wild horses, not in captivity, but in the wild. Some students may wish to write letters to the editor of the local newspaper.

8. Invite students to assemble various charts on the different breeds of horses in the United States. Which of the breeds has the most numbers? Which has the least? What human or environmental factors would affect those population numbers?

9. Students may wish to collect information about the "Adopt a Wild Horse" program from either of the following Web sites:

   http://www.wildhorseandburro.blm.gov/index.php

   http://www.mustangs4us.com/adopt_a_mustang.htm

10. As appropriate, students may wish to conduct a fund drive to collect money to be used for the adoption of a wild horse or mustang. This can be done as a class activity, grade-level project, or whole school venture.

CHAPTER 9

States and Regions

Crab Moon

Ruth Horowitz

Cambridge, MA: Candlewick Press, 2000

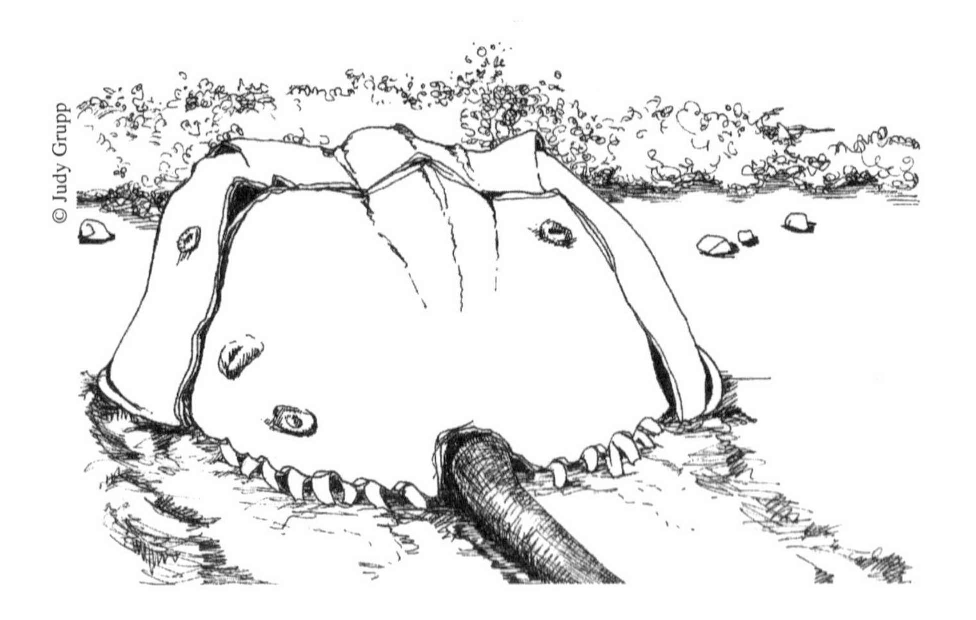

SUMMARY

Each spring thousands, no millions, of horseshoe crabs crawl from the waters of Delaware Bay to mate under the glare of a full moon. This annual ritual has been taking place for 350 million years and is truly one of nature's most incredible sights. This book tells the story of a young boy's discovery along a beach beside the Delaware Bay—a discovery that was both simple and poignant. This is a book that begs to be read aloud over and over again.

SOCIAL STUDIES DISCIPLINES

Geography, sociology

NCSS THEMATIC STRANDS

Time, Continuity, and Change; People, Places, and Environment; Individual Development and Identity; Science, Technology, and Society

CRITICAL THINKING QUESTIONS

1. Have you ever been to a place similar to the one Daniel and his family visited?
2. What did you find amazing about the horseshoe crabs?
3. Why did Daniel turn the crab over?
4. What was the most amazing fact on the last page of the book?
5. If you could say anything to Daniel, what would it be?

RELATED BOOKS

Crenson, Victoria. *Horseshoe Crabs and Shorebirds: The Story of a Food Web*. New York: Marshall Cavendish, 2003.

Dunlap, Julie. *Extraordinary Horseshoe Crabs*. Minneapolis, MN: Carolrhoda, 1999.

ACTIVITIES

1. The best Web site on horseshoe crabs is the one maintained by the Ecological Research and Development Group (www.horseshoecrab.org). Here students can obtain the latest information and up-to-the-minute reports on horseshoe crab research and their annual migration patterns. You may wish to invite students to collect information and facts from this site and compile it into an informational brochure or Webquest for other students.
2. Invite students to read the last page of this book. What was the most interesting fact they learned about horseshoe crabs? Students may wish to use information from this and other books and Web sites to create a "Top Ten" list of facts about horseshoe crabs. These lists can be developed into posters and hung in the classroom or library.
3. Delaware is this country's "First State," yet many people don't know very much about this Middle Atlantic State. That may be partly due to its size, but also due to a lack of resource materials. Students may wish to log on to one or more of the following Web sites to obtain information about Delaware:

   http://www.lib.utexas.edu/maps/delaware.html

   http://www.state.de.us/dedo/information/information.shtml

   http://www.enchantedlearning.com/usa/states/delaware/

   http://www.worldalmanacforkids.com/explore/states/delaware.html

   http://worldatlas.com/webimage/countrys/namerica/usstates/de.htm

   After students have obtained information about Delaware, they may wish to develop it into a readers theatre script (see the examples in part III of this book) for presentation to another class or grade level.

4. Students may wish to learn more about Delaware Bay. They can do so by logging on to the following Web sites;

    http://en.wikipedia.org/wiki/Delaware_Bay

    http://www.ajmeerwald.org/dbsp/html/meermus.html

    http://www.answers.com/topic/delaware-bay

    After they have researched this waterway, they may wish to invite a biologist or oceanographer from a local college or university to discuss the various types of flora and fauna that might be found in this unique ecosystem. After the scientist's visit, invite students to construct a poster or mobile of pertinent information about Delaware Bay.

5. Another state that borders Delaware Bay is New Jersey. Invite students to survey their friends and relatives to discover anyone who has lived in or visited New Jersey. Ask students to conduct interviews of these individuals and to collect the recorded information into a "living history" museum of photos, facts, travel information, highlights, sites, and historical data about the "Garden State."

6. Invite selected students to take on the role of Daniel in the story. Ask them to imagine that it is one year later (after the end of the story). Encourage students to write an imaginary letter (from Daniel) back to their classmates telling them of the adventures, discoveries, and sites encountered at the shore.

7. Horseshoe crabs have been around since before the time of the dinosaurs. Students may wish to create a lengthy time line of some important historical events that have occurred since the emergence of horseshoe crabs. Use a long strip of adding machine tape and post it along one wall of the classroom or library. Invite students to write significant events in earth or human history along the paper. These may include events such as the extinction of the dinosaurs, shifting of tectonic plates, cave people, invention of printing, manned landing on the moon, etc.

8. Divide the class into several groups. Invite each of the groups to research a state along the Atlantic Seaboard. For which ones is the most information available? How do the states compare in relation to size, population, natural resources, or length of shoreline? What are some of the distinctive environmental features of each of the states? Students may wish to present their information in self-created booklets or brochures.

9. Students may wish to write imaginary letters of appreciation to (1) the state of Delaware, (2) Delaware Bay, (3) the state of New Jersey, or (4) horseshoe crabs. These letters can be collected in the form of a scrapbook or journal.

10. Invite students to look through several old magazines and prepare collages about the state of Delaware or of Delaware Bay. What are some of the important geographical features? What are some of the most picturesque places? What are some special sites to see?

G Is for Golden: A California Alphabet

David Domeniconi

Chelsea, MI: Sleeping Bear Press, 2002

© Judy Grupp

SUMMARY

Everything you ever wanted to know about the Golden State can be found in the pages of this delightfully illustrated book. Part of the series of state alphabet books produced by Sleeping Bear Press, this edition looks into the history, customs, geographical features, and other features associated with California. From Hollywood to Yosemite and from Ishi to John Muir, this book has it all.

SOCIAL STUDIES DISCIPLINES

Geography, history, economics, sociology, political science

NCSS THEMATIC STRANDS

Time, Continuity, and Change; People, Places, and environment; Civic Ideals, and Practices

CRITICAL THINKING QUESTIONS

1. In what ways is California similar to your state?
2. What aspect of California did you find most interesting, and why?
3. If you were to visit California, what things from the book would you want to see?
4. If you were to live in California, where would you want to live?
5. If you could meet any historical figure in this book, who would it be?

RELATED BOOKS

Ferris, Julie. *California Gold Rush: A Guide to California in the 1850's.* New York: Kingfisher, 1999.

Pelta, Kathy. *California.* Minneapolis, MN: Lerner Publishing, 2001.

ACTIVITIES

1. Invite students to create their own state alphabet book. This can be done as a whole class exercise, or each student can receive a letter and create a page of the book. You may wish to check other state alphabet books in this series for examples and samples (www.sleepingbearpress.com).
2. Encourage students to explore their state symbols, such as their state flower and bird. Have students create some representation of their state displaying the various state symbols. This could include a poster or some other sort of visual display for the classroom or library.
3. Invite students to find the answers to the questions in the back of the book regarding the state of California. They may wish to quiz each other or set up a *Jeopardy!* type game in which they come up with questions for designated answers located throughout this book.
4. Invite students to create an alphabet book about the school. Can they locate at least one fact about the school for each letter of the alphabet? They may wish to interview teachers and administrators for pertinent information. Using a word processing program, they could turn their research into an attractive brochure for the community or for new families moving into the area.
5. Invite students to list the name of their state vertically down the left side of a sheet of paper. Ask them to list one fact or important piece of information for each letter, creating an anagram. Students may wish to develop this into a large poster for display on a wall or in the hallway.
6. Invite students to imagine that they are visiting California; encourage them to write imaginary postcards to their friends and relatives and describe the sites they are visiting. Students may wish to illustrate the fronts of several index cards and write their messages on the back. Completed cards can be posted on a classroom or library bulletin board.
7. Invite students to create individual or group mobiles about the state of California. Ask them to record pertinent facts on the first level of the mobile. On the second level, students can hang names of tourist spots and attractions from throughout the state. On the third level, they can record names and descriptions of selected historical sites. Display these in either the classroom or library.

8. Invite students to create an oversized book (a *big* book) on California to include specific facts and information about the state. The book can be cut from two sheets of stiff cardboard into the shape of California (staple several sheets of paper between the covers). Encourage students to contribute their book to the classroom or school library.

9. Students may wish to log on to several Web sites to obtain additional information about the Golden State. Here are a few to get them started:

   http://lcweb2.loc.gov/ammem/cbhtml/cbhome.html

   http://www.donaldlaird.com/landmarks/

   http://missions.bgmm.com/index.htm

   http://www.lib.utexas.edu/maps/california.html

   http://www.enchantedlearning.com/usa/states/california/

   After students have obtained sufficient information from these and other sites, they may wish to create their own Webquest or design their own Web page about California. They may wish to include some of the information in this book as part of their creation, too.

10. Invite students to create a salt map of California. Provide them with the following recipe and encourage them to work in teams to create one or more depictions of the state. (Note: You may need to adjust the quantities below according to the number of students with whom you are working.)

    Materials: 1½ cups coarse salt (kosher salt works best), 1 cup flour, 1½ cups water.

    Directions: Mix the salt and flour together in a medium-sized mixing bowl. Add enough water to make a stiff dough. Form the mixture on a piece of stiff cardboard or small sheet of plywood (work quickly). Shape the mixture into hills, mountains, large flat areas, or other geographical features that can be found in California. Allow the creation to dry for two or three days. When it is dry, paint it with tempera paint.

G Is for Grand Canyon: An Arizona Alphabet

Barbara Gowan

Chelsea, MI: Sleeping Bear Press, 2002

SUMMARY

From "Astronomy" to "Zanjero," this book provides readers with an inviting and extensive tour of the Grand Canyon state—Arizona. Students will learn about the history, traditions, sites, and people of this multifaceted state. There's a lot to learn in the pages of this delightful book, which combines poetic descriptions with narrative investigations that offer a rich and varied journey through the state.

SOCIAL STUDIES DISCIPLINES

History, geography, anthropology, sociology, political science, economics

NCSS THEMATIC STRANDS

Culture; Time, Continuity and Change; People, Places, and environment; Power, Authority and Governance; Production, Distribution, and Consumption

CRITICAL THINKING QUESTIONS

1. What was the most amazing thing you learned about Arizona?
2. If you could visit any part of Arizona, what part would you want to see?
3. What was the most unusual animal in the book?
4. How is Arizona similar to or different from your state?

RELATED BOOKS

Blashfield, Jean. *Arizona.* (America the Beautiful Second Series). Brookfield, CT: Children's Press, 2000.

Gowan, Barbara. *Desert Digits: An Arizona Number Book.* Chelsea, MI: Sleeping Bear Press, 2006.

ACTIVITIES

1. Divide students into several small groups. Encourage each group to practice reading some pages. Invite the groups to make an audiorecording of the entire book (several practices may be necessary). Students may wish to suggest sound effects (e.g., slithering snakes, swooping hawks, etc.), too. Invite students to contribute the tapes to the classroom or school library.
2. Students can stay up-to-date on the latest events, discoveries, and news about life in the desert by accessing the Web site of *Desert USA Magazine* at http://www.desertusa.com. Here they can learn about the lives of the flora and fauna that inhabit desert regions. They may wish to gather selected information in the form of descriptive brochures or pamphlets for the classroom or school library.
3. Students may wish to take a virtual tour of a desert at http://www.mbgnet.net/sets/desert/index.htm. Here they will learn what a desert is like, what causes deserts, desert of the world, desert plants and animals, and desert life at night. This is a wonderful site, chock-full of information.
4. Divide students into several groups and invite each group to plan a two-week visit to Arizona. Encourage each group to assemble a list of supplies and equipment they would need as well as a list of the sites they would plan to see. Provide each group with a road map of Arizona (available at large bookstores such as Border's and Barnes & Noble) and invite them to plan a driving tour of the state. The groups may wish to share and compare their respective lists.
5. Students may wish to visit a local gardening center or nursery. Invite them to purchase a cactus (these are typically inexpensive). Invite them to observe their cacti carefully—what shape are they? What do the needles look like? What are their dimensions? Students may wish to observe cactus features with a magnifying lens and record their observations in a journal.
6. Students may enjoy creating their own desert terrarium. The following instructions will help them design a fully functioning terrarium:
   - Fill the bottom of a large glass container with a layer of coarse sand or gravel. Combine one part fine sand with two parts potting soil and spread this over the first layer.
   - Sprinkle lightly with water.

– Place several varieties of cactus into the terrarium (it might be a good idea to wear gloves). Most nurseries carry cacti, or they can be ordered through the mail from selected seed companies and mail-order nursery houses.

– When planting the cacti, be sure the roots are covered completely with the sandy mixture.

– Students may wish to place desert animals (such as lizards and horned toads) in the terrarium. Be sure the animals have enough food and water available.

– The desert terrarium can be left in the sun and does not need a glass cover. It should, however, be lightly sprinkled with water about once a week.

7. Invite students to request an Official Visitor's Guide to Arizona from http://www.arizonaguide.com/. When the guide arrives, invite students to compare the information in the guide with that in the book. What areas are covered in the guide that are not mentioned in the book (and vice versa)? What did they learn in the book that wasn't included in the guide? What other information should be included in the book to make it more complete?

8. Students can learn all about Arizona's most famous landmark—the Grand Canyon—at these Web sites:

   http://www.kaibab.org/

   http://www.pbs.org/wgbh/amex/canyon/

   http://sunsite.nus.edu.sg/mw/iss06/canyon.html

   After students have obtained information from these sites, invite them to research materials in the school library about this natural wonder. Afterward students may wish to create a panoramic display or oversized wall poster of the Grand Canyon along with fascinating information and amazing facts.

9. Invite students to research the various Native American tribes that live in Arizona. How long have they lived there? How did they survive (or perish)? What were their lives like? Encourage students to gather information into a descriptive slide show or PowerPoint™ presentation for other classes.

10. Students may be interested in researching and then creating several "Top Ten" lists of Arizona information. Here are a few possibilities to get them started:

    – Top 10 largest cities according to population (Phoenix is number 1)

    – Top 10 species of animals according to population.

    – Top 10 plants according to number

    – Top 10 hottest days in history

    – Top 10 most visited sites

    – Top 10 highest points

    – Top 10 colleges or universities according to student population

    – Top 10 longest rivers.

    – Top 10 agricultural products

High as a Hawk: A Brave Girl's Historic Climb

T. A. Barron

New York: Philomel Books, 2004

SUMMARY

Eight-year-old Harriet wants to climb Longs Peak in Colorado. She wants to do it for herself, but especially for the mother she has lost. To get to the top she'll have to overcome a freezing blizzard, a steep slope, and her own insecurities. This story, based on an actual event in 1905, will provide youngsters with a view of the highest state in the union—Colorado—and the majesty of the Rocky Mountains.

SOCIAL STUDIES DISCIPLINES

Geography, history, sociology

NCSS THEMATIC STRANDS

Time, Continuity, and Change; People, Places, and Environment; Individual Development and Identity

CRITICAL THINKING QUESTIONS

1. If you could meet Harriet Peters, what character traits do you think she would possess?
2. What one question would you like to ask Harriet?

3. Why do you think Harriet was so determined to reach the top of the mountain?
4. Do you think that Harriet helped to inspire Enos to continue protecting the mountain and its surroundings, despite opposition? If so, how?
5. Why was Harriet was so determined to see a hawk when she reached the top of the mountain?

RELATED BOOKS

Blashfield, Jean. *Colorado.* (America the Beautiful Second Series). Brookfield, CT: Children's Press, 1999

Krudwig, Vickie. *Hiking Through Colorado History*. Golden, CO: Westcliffe Publishers, 1998.

Ogintz, Eileen. *A Kid's Book of Vacation Fun in the Rocky Mountains: Games, Stories, Fun Facts, and Much More*. New York: HarperCollins, 1996.

Whitney, Louise D. *C Is for Centennial: A Colorado Alphabet*. Chelsea, MI: Sleeping Bear Press, 2002.

ACTIVITIES

1. Encourage students to pretend that they have the opportunity to interview either Harriet Peters or Enos Mills. Invite students to create a list of interview questions that they would ask her or him. If you wish, you can take on the role of either Harriet or Enos and respond to the questions posed by youngsters.
2. Invite students to write about a time when they accomplished something that was difficult or that others did not think they could do. Encourage students to compare their feelings to Harriet's feelings. They may wish to develop a series of ongoing posters to display in the classroom or library.
3. Invite students to visit the Rocky Mountain National Park Web site at http://www.rocky.mountain.national-park.com to find out more about the mountain's history and the park today. After students have collected sufficient information, ask them to develop a brochure or Web page that introduced this exciting and dynamic park to other students.
4. Encourage students to research and find the highest point of elevation in their own state. Invite students to create an illustration along with relevant facts about this "highest point" in their state.
5. Invite students to log on to Colorado's official Web site at http://www.colorado.gov/. After learning as much as possible about the state, encourage students to assemble some display that features some of the sites, attractions, and highlights of the state.

6. Colorado has 54 mountains that are over 14,000 feet high. Invite students to log on to one of the following Web sites to learn as much as they can about these towering peaks:

   http://www.14ers.com/

   http://www.fourteeners.org

   http://www.14ers.org

   After they have gathered sufficient information, invite them to plot the location of (and one relevant fact about) selected mountain peaks on a blank map of Colorado.

7. Invite students to log on to the Colorado Mountain Club Web site at http://www.cmc.org. Here they will discover lots of information about Colorado's mountains. After they have collected sufficient information, ask them to assemble it into an appropriate display—particularly suited for students and their families who are planning to visit Colorado (in summer or winter).

8. Plan time to talk with students about courage. What is it? When do we need it? Are some people more courageous than others? Are boys more courageous than girls, or the other way around? What are the similarities between courage and bravery? Invite students to discuss times in their lives when they were courageous.

9. If possible, invite members of a local hiking club (check your local phone book) to visit your classroom or library to discuss hiking with students. What equipment do they use? How do they prepare for a hike? What precautions are necessary? After the visit, encourage students to form their own hiking club and plan regular outings in and around the school grounds.

10. After students have gathered information about Colorado, invite them to create a series of imaginary postcards that they would send to friends back home as they were traveling through Colorado (on a summer vacation trip, for example). What would they want to describe for their friends? What Colorado sites are they visiting? What are they learning about Colorado? Students can download photos from the Internet and paste them onto 3-by-5-inch index cards to use for their "postcards."

I Have Heard of a Land

Joyce Carol Thomas

New York: Harper Collins, 1998

SUMMARY

Inspired by the author's own family's westward journey to Oklahoma in the late 1880s, this gentle, yet powerful, story tells of one African American woman's trip into the frontier to start a new life for herself. With well-chosen words and evocative sentences, the author has crafted a book that begs to be shared with children, not just for its language, but also because it reveals a slice of American history not typically covered in textbooks: women on the frontier. This is a story of hope, courage, and determination—one that should be part of every study of the westward movement. Share this with students and be prepared for lots of discussion.

SOCIAL STUDIES DISCIPLINES

History, geography, economics, anthropology

NCSS THEMATIC STRANDS

Time, Continuity, and Change; Individual Development and Identity; Civic Ideals and Practices

CRITICAL THINKING QUESTIONS

1. If you had to move away to a place that was unknown to you and start all over, how do you think you would feel?
2. What kinds of feelings do you think the people who participated in the Oklahoma Territory runs experienced?
3. Why do you think that so many people wanted to travel to the Oklahoma Territory?
4. If you could, what would you like to say to the woman in the story—especially at the end?
5. How do you think the woman will survive in her new home?

RELATED BOOKS

Antle, Nancy. *Beautiful Land: A Story of the Oklahoma Land Rush.* New York: Puffin Books, 1997.

Ladoux, Rita. *Oklahoma.* Minneapolis, MN: Lerner Publications, 2002.

Scillian, Devin. *S Is for Sooner: An Oklahoma Alphabet.* Chelsea, MI: Sleeping Bear Press, 2003.

ACTIVITIES

1. Invite students to create a sequel to the story. What happens to the people who moved to the Oklahoma Territory? Is the woman happier? Do they build anything other than houses? Allow time for students to share their sequels.
2. Encourage students to think of some of the different things that these people may have brought with them on their journey to the new land. Have students then pack a small "suitcase" to fit in a wagon. They could include actual objects or illustrations of objects that they would bring with them if they were to journey to a new land today.
3. Invite students to write five entries in a journal, pretending that they have just traveled to the Oklahoma Territory in the late 1880s. Students should include their feelings, how they obtained their food and what their food was for each day, what they were living in, etc.
4. Invite students to discuss the many hardships that people who were journeying to the Oklahoma Territory must have faced as they traveled.
5. Invite students to access the resources of the school library to locate other literature in which a woman is the prominent character (fiction or nonfiction) in a historical event. Plan time to talk with students about why women have not been featured as central characters throughout American history—particularly as that history has been depicted in textbooks.

6. As an extension of the activity in item 5, invite students to do the same thing with African American individuals or characters. What is the ratio of African American characters or individuals in books about American history to individuals or characters of European descent? Why are there so few history books with African Americans as central figures?

7. Invite students to log on to Oklahoma's official Web site at www.ok.gov. Encourage them to gather as much information as possible about the state and organize it into an informative poster or PowerPoint™ presentation to present to other students in the school.

8. Students may be interested in listening to a firsthand account of the Oklahoma Land Rush of 1889. Log on to the following site—http://www.eyewitnesstohistory.com/landrush.htm—download the article, and spend time reading this to students. Invite students to compare the account of the land rush on this site with that in the book. How are they similar? How are they different?

9. Students may be interested in the settlement of Oklahoma by African Americans. Log on to one or more of the following Web sites and share the information with students:

   http://www.ok-history.mus.ok.us/enc/allblack.htm

   http://www.afrigeneas.com/states/ok/

   http://www.soulofamerica.com/towns/oktowns.html

   After sharing the information with students, invite them to create a book about the settlement of Oklahoma by African Americans. They may wish to use a word processing program to produce the book, which can be featured in the classroom or school library.

10. Invite a student to take on the role of the woman in the story. Encourage other students to "interview" the woman as though the time were 1889 and she was settled on her new land. What questions would they want to ask? What would they like to know?

Quilt of States: Piecing Together America

Adrienne Yorinks

Washington, DC: National Geographic, 2005

SUMMARY

In a wondrously creative book, readers are provided with an imaginative look at all 50 states. Using individual state quilts created by the author and the descriptions of those states by librarians across the country, this book weaves a vision of the United States that will be hard to put down. Teachers and librarians will value this incredible resource above all others. It is exciting, detailed, and dynamic—an engaging book for any classroom or library. Don't miss this one!

SOCIAL STUDIES DISCIPLINES

Geography, history, political science

NCSS THEMATIC STRANDS

Culture; People, Places, and Environment; Power, Authority, and Governance; Civic Ideals and Practices

CRITICAL THINKING QUESTIONS

1. If you could live in any state, what state would it be, and why?
2. Why do you think that the author chose to represent the states on different pieces of a quilt?
3. What fun fact from the back of the book did you find most interesting, and why?
4. If you could ask the author any question, what would it be?
5. How is this book different from other books about the 50 states?

RELATED BOOKS

Gutman, Bill. *The Look-It-Up Book of the 50 States*. New York: Random House Books for Young Readers, 2002.

The Kids' Book of the 50 Great States. New York: Scholastic, 1999.

ACTIVITIES

1. Enlarge a blank map of the United States. Assign each student a state, and invite students to create something that represents their assigned state (state bird, symbol, agricultural crop, manufactured item) in its correct location on the map.
2. Provide students with sheets of construction paper. Ask them to cut out the shapes of all 50 states from the construction paper. Invite students to write relevant facts about each state on its respective shape. Tie a length of string from one end of the classroom or library to the other. Place clothespins on the string and ask students to hang the state outlines on the string, from the first state (Delaware) to the fiftieth state (Hawaii).
3. Encourage students to play the game "Around the States." This game is played by having one student stand behind another student's chair. The teacher will hold a card with a state's name on it, and both students have to quickly think of that particular state's capital. Whoever shouts the correct answer first gets to move to the next person. If the student standing says the answer first, he or she moves to stand behind the next person's chair. If the student sitting in the chair says the answer first, he or she stands up and moves to the next person, while the student who was standing sits in his or her opponent's chair. The first student to make it back around to where he or she started, without having to sit down, is the winner.
4. Invite students to create a large collage about quilting or sewing. Encourage them to cut out pictures and illustrations from old magazines and paste them onto a large sheet of paper. Examples of clothing, sewing materials, dyes, sewing machines, etc., can all be included on the collage. Invite students to prepare an explanatory sheet about the finished product.
5. Students may wish to create a time line that illustrates the events and historical stories as depicted in the book. Encourage students to contribute personal descriptions and original drawings.
6. Each of the state descriptions in this book is like a miniature "time capsule" of the state's history. Invite students to create a time capsule of selected events in their lives. What occurrences, celebrations, or events would each student like to include in her or his time capsule? Invite each student to create a collection of illustrations or photographs that would be "sealed" until opened by another child in the future (in 100 years, for example). What mementos should students include in their time capsules?
7. Invite each student to bring in a piece of fabric from an outgrown item of clothing. Create a classroom quilt by using tacky glue and attaching the fabric squares to card-

board. Students may wish to work in small groups and stitch the squares into strips, and then combine them to form a large quilt-top. They can then sew the quilt-top to a plain blanket and hang it on the wall. (Note: Before engaging in this activity, discuss with students a possible theme for the quilt—States, Nation, Our Community, Our State, etc.)

8. Check with a local woman's club or in the local telephone book to locate a sewing or quilting organization in your area. Invite several members of the group to demonstrate their craft to students. You may wish to provide them with a copy of this book to review beforehand and then ask them to talk about some of the featured quilts. Provide an opportunity for students to interview club members on the intricacies of quilt making.
9. Encourage students to develop a quilt (or quilting square) that tells of an important event in their lives or an important event in the history of your state. Plan opportunities for students to share their quilts with each other.

The Tsunami Quilt: Grandfather's Story

Anthony D. Fredericks

Chelsea, MI: Sleeping Bear Press, 2007

SUMMARY

Each April, young Kimo and his grandfather travel to Laupahoehoe on the Big Island of Hawaii. Grandfather talks about the sea and this special place, but only after his grandfather passes does Kimo learn about the personal and lasting effects of a long-ago and tragic tsunami. It is in the Pacific Tsunami Museum in Hilo that he faces his history and learns the secret his grandfather carried for so long.

SOCIAL STUDIES DISCIPLINES

History, geography, anthropology

NCSS THEMATIC STRANDS

Culture; Time, Continuity, and Change; People, Places, and Environment; Individual Development and Identity; Science, Technology, and Society

CRITICAL THINKING QUESTIONS

1. Why do you think that Grandfather chose to place a lei on top of the marble monument each year?
2. Why do you think that Grandfather wanted to wait until Kimo was older to tell him why Laupahoehoe was a sacred place?

3. What do you think Grandfather meant when he said that "the ocean gives, but it also takes"?
4. If you could say something to Kimo at the end of the story, what would it be?

RELATED BOOKS

Fredericks, Anthony D. *Tsunami Man: Learning About Killer Waves with Walter Dudley.* Honolulu: University of Hawaii Press, 2002.

Souza, D. M. *Powerful Waves.* Minneapolis, MN: Carolrhoda Books, 1992.

Thompson, Luke. *Tsunamis.* New York: Children's Press, 2000.

ACTIVITIES

1. Invite students to conduct research about the monuments located in their own state that represent important people or events. Encourage them to develop an appropriate information guide (geared to other students) for display in the classroom or library.
2. Students may enjoy creating their own tsunami dictionary. Invite them to form small groups, with each group responsible for gathering words and definitions for several letters of the alphabet. For example:

   A—Aleutian Islands
   Alaska
   B—Big waves
   C—Crest Coast Guard
   Caldera
   D—Destruction
   E—Earthquake
   Emergency
   Evacuation

   Students may wish to contribute their class dictionary to the school library.
3. If possible, obtain a copy of the National Geographic Society video *Killer Wave: Power of the Tsunami* (Catalog #51904C). This film is an excellent introduction to the power and force of this natural disaster. Invite students to view the video. Afterward encourage them to compare the information in the book with that presented in the video. What was similar? What was different? Do students have any unanswered questions after reading the book and viewing the video?
4. Here's an activity that will give students an opportunity to create a "homemade" ocean in a bottle:

   Materials: empty 1-liter soda bottle (with a screw-on top), salad oil, water, blue food coloring

   Directions: (1) Fill an empty 1-liter soda bottle one-third of the way up with salad oil. (2) Fill the rest of the bottle (all the way to the brim) with water dyed with a few drops of blue food coloring. (3) Put on the top securely and lay the bottle on its side. Now, slowly and gently tip the bottle back and forth. The oil in the bottle will begin to roll and move just like the waves in the ocean. This is a miniature ocean in a bottle.

5. Here are some great Web sites on tsunamis, including how they are formed, the destruction they cause, where they occur, simulations and animations, and a host of up-to-date information:

   http://www.germantown.k12.il.us/html/tsunami.html

   http://www.geophys.washington.edu/tsunami/welcome.html

   http://www.pmel.noaa.gov/tsunami/

   http://www.usc.edu/dept/tsunamis/

   http://www.thirteen.org/savageseas/neptune-main.html

6. Students can stay up-to-date on the latest events, discoveries, and news about tsunamis by accessing the Web site of the Pacific Tsunami Museum at http://www.tsunami.org. Here they can learn about latest happenings at the museum, contests, and ongoing displays. They may wish to gather selected information together in the form of descriptive brochures or pamphlets for the classroom library.

7. Students may also wish to write to the Pacific Tsunami Museum to inquire about their educational offerings and displays. The address is:

   Pacific Tsunami Museum
   P.O. Box 806
   Hilo, Hawaii 96721

   NOTE: This museum is one of the few tsunami museums in the world. It includes tales of tsunami survivors, information on the dangers of tsunamis, as well as a variety of tsunami artifacts.

8. Students may be interested in a listing of the most frequently asked questions about tsunamis and the work of the International Tsunami Warning System. They can access that information at http://www.geocities.com/CapeCanaveral/Lab/1029/TsunamiFAQ.html. After students have viewed the site, ask them to think of any additional questions they may have about tsunamis. Where might they go to discover the answers?

9. If possible, obtain a copy of the video *Raging Planet: Tidal Wave* (Catalog #51904C) from the Discovery Channel. Invite students to view the video and to focus on the ways in which buildings (particularly those in Hilo, Hawaii) have been constructed so that they can withstand the force of a tsunami. Invite students to check on selected buildings in their town or community. How are those buildings different from those in a tsunami-prone area? What would have to be done to some of the local buildings to make them "tsunami proof"? Encourage students to create diagrams or illustrations of the necessary changes.

10. Invite students to imagine that they are in a tsunami-prone area. What types of precautions should they take in advance of a tsunami? What types of actions should they take if a tsunami alarm were sounded in their area? Invite students to assemble a "tsunami safety book" that could be distributed to local schools through a local chapter of the American Red Cross or other disaster relief agency.

11. Invite small groups of students to each assemble an almanac of various natural disasters that have struck the United States within the last five years. Students may wish to assemble descriptions of the 10 most dangerous and deadly natural disasters to strike the United States, or they may wish to develop a booklet of the worst tsunami, the worst hurricane, the worst tornado, etc. Make these available for sharing in the school library.

CHAPTER 10

Nation and Country

A Is for America: An American Alphabet

Devin Scillian

Chelsea, MI: Sleeping Bear Press, 2001

SUMMARY

This book combines all the sights, sounds, traditions, customs, and history of the United States in one alphabetical arrangement. It's brimming with characters and capitals, destinations and discoveries, and monuments and maps that will provide youngsters with a thorough and engaging look at this country. This book would be a wonderful addition to any study of U.S. history —one kids will dip into time after time.

SOCIAL STUDIES DISCIPLINES

History, geography, political science

NCSS THEMATIC STRANDS

Culture; Time, Continuity, and Change; People, Places, and Environment; Individuals, Groups, and Institutions; Power, Authority, and Governance; Civic Ideals and Practices

CRITICAL THINKING QUESTIONS

1. What do you think makes America unique?
2. What is your favorite letter in the book, and why?
3. What is one thing that you learned from the book that you did not know before?
4. Is there a historical site you would like to visit? Which one?
5. Do you think there was something missing in or left out of the book?

RELATED BOOKS

Peterson, Christine, and David Peterson. *United States of America*. New York: Children's Press, 2002.

Scillian, Devin. *One Nation: America by the Numbers*. Chelsea, MI: Sleeping Bear Press, 2002.

ACTIVITIES

1. Invite students to cut out a shape of the United States using construction paper. Ask students to write various facts that they learned from the book on their papers. Hang these on a classroom or library bulletin board or wall.
2. Encourage students to use the book and to conduct further research about important dates in American history. Invite students to create a time line illustrating and displaying these important events. The time line can be posted along one wall of the classroom or library.
3. Assign each student a letter of the alphabet and ask the students to add to the story. Encourage them to write about and illustrate other important American facts, people, or symbols that go along with each letter that the book did not mention.
4. Encourage students to create their own rhyming story about American customs, facts, historical events, famous people, etc. Students can then create illustrations to go along with their story. These short poems (similar to those in the book) can be developed into a book, which can be placed in either the classroom or school library.
5. Invite students to cut out 50 stars from white paper. Distribute the stars to all the students. Invite students to record significant events, people, sites, or facts about the United States, one on each star. Arrange the stars around an oversized map of the United States.

6. Invite students to create a large scrapbook of pictures and photographs of various locations around the United States. Provide small groups of students with several old magazines or newspapers. Invite each group to select illustrations of important sites and significant places around the country. These can be arranged in the scrapbook according to states or regions in the United States.

7. As a variation of the activity above, invite students to create a giant wall collage of the United States. Encourage students to arrange pictures and photographs cut from a variety of old magazines randomly on an oversized sheet of newsprint. You may wish to call this the "Collage of America." This project can take several weeks as students continuously add new material to the collage on a regular basis.

8. Invite each student to randomly select one letter from the book. Ask each person to develop the information or facts about that letter into a newspaper article. Provide youngsters with sample articles from your local newspaper and take time to analyze them for the five Ws and one H. After students have written a series of articles, combine them into a newspaper (*The USA News*).

9. Invite students to interview their parents or grandparents about the sites, events, or facts they think should be in an alphabet book about America. How do those suggestions compare with the ones in the book? Perhaps students will want to create a new book—one generated by the ideas and suggestions of their parents and grandparents.

10. As a variation of the idea above, ask students to interview other students for their ideas on the events and facts that should be included in a U.S. alphabet book. Write a letter of the alphabet on each of 26 large sheets of newsprint and post them in the library. Encourage students to draw, paint, and write appropriate descriptions of a "kid's-eye view" of America. Encourage students to add to these over a period of several weeks or months.

Coming to America: A Muslim Family's Story

Bernard Wolf

New York: Lee & Low Books, 2003

SUMMARY

This book explores the life of a Muslim family who have immigrated to the United States. Life is very different and filled with all kinds of uncertainties, but the family members learn new customs and make new friends. Their religion is what sustains them and offers them both comfort and a connection with their homeland. This book is a revealing exploration of the Muslim faith and one family's determination to succeed in their adopted country.

SOCIAL STUDIES DISCIPLINES

Geography, economics, anthropology

NCSS THEMATIC STRANDS

Culture; People, Places, and Environment; Individual Development and Identity; Individuals, Groups, and Institutions; Global Connections

CRITICAL THINKING QUESTIONS

1. Why do you think people immigrate to America?

2. What did you admire most about the family in the story?
3. What would you find to be the scariest part of moving to a new country?
4. Do you think that the family was happier once they had been in America for a few years? Why or why not?
5. How was this family's life different from your life? How was it similar?

RELATED BOOKS

Gravois, Michael. *Hands-on History: Immigration*. New York: Scholastic, 2004.

Hoobler, Dorothy, and Thomas Hoobler. *We Are Americans: Voices of the Immigrant Experience*. New York: Scholastic, 2003.

ACTIVITIES

1. Invite students to create a list of five things that they think an immigrant would need to know or have to live in America. Allow time for students to share their lists to see if any items are repeated in the lists.
2. Encourage students to pretend that they just came to America, but without their families. Have students write a letter home to their family members, describing the many new things that they have seen and learned, and what they have been doing.
3. Encourage students to discuss and record some of the hardships and challenges faced, as well as benefits received, by this family when moving to America.
4. Invite students to consult other literature as well as Internet sites about life in Egypt. What are some of the daily practices of children in Egypt? How is school different in Egypt? Students may wish to construct a chart that displays both the similarities and differences of childhood in Egypt and the United States.
5. If possible, invite one or two individuals of the Muslim faith to visit your classroom or library. Invite students to interview these individuals about their faith. What are some of the major features or beliefs? How does the Muslim faith differ from Christianity or Judaism, for example? As appropriate, invite a discussion on why some people find tenets of the Muslim faith difficult to understand.
6. As appropriate, invite students to discuss the role of religion in people's lives. Why is religion so important? Why are there so many different kinds of religions in the world? Most important, plan time to talk about the importance of understanding all religions as well as the importance of religious freedom and religious tolerance.
7. Post a large world map on a wall of the classroom or library. Invite students to put a push pin into each country represented in a group or class of students. If any students are recent immigrants to the United States, invite them to indicate their country of origin. Students may wish to expand this activity and use push pins to represent the

countries of origin for all the students at a particular grade level or, if appropriate, all the students in the school. Invite students to make a chart of the various countries represented by students in a class, a grade level, or the entire school.

8. Students may be interested in learning more about Muslim life in America. The following Web sites were current as of the writing of this book. They offer youngsters some valuable information and insights:

   http://usinfo.state.gov/products/pubs/muslimlife/

   http://www.pbs.org/wgbh/pages/frontline/shows/muslims/

   http://www.muslimheritage.com/

   http://library.thinkquest.org/28505/islam/mecca.htm

   These Web sites have lots of information, but much of it is geared to adult readers. Plan to share this information with students and invite them to create a brochure or newsletter that summarizes it for elementary students.

9. Invite students to write an imaginary letter to a family member in the book. What kinds of questions would they like to ask that individual? What would they like to learn about that individual's life after this book was written?

10. Invite students to assemble a bibliography of books about immigrants from other countries. Students may wish to arrange their bibliographies into geographic regions (for example, people from Europe, people from Africa, people from Asia, etc.). Invite students to read selected books and to share their perception of life in America as seen by people from other countries, other religions, other beliefs, and other cultures.

Martin's Big Words: The Life of Dr. Martin Luther King, Jr.

Doreen Rappaport

New York: Hyperion Books, 2001

© Judy Grupp

SUMMARY

The author interweaves the story of the life of Martin Luther King Jr. with his words and speeches to create a book that is both captivating and compelling. In concert with the incredibly creative illustrations of Bryan Collier, the message rings loud and clear for all readers. This is a story of hope, concern, and determination and how one man's words resonated across the country and beyond the years. This is a book of significance and compassion that will ignite discussions and deliberations for many years to come. It was a 2001 Caldecott Honor Book.

SOCIAL STUDIES DISCIPLINES

History, geography, sociology

NCSS THEMATIC STRANDS

Culture; Time, Continuity and Change; Individuals, Groups, and Institutions; Power, Authority, and Governance; Civic Ideals and Practices

CRITICAL THINKING QUESTIONS

1. What do you think are some of the pros and cons of using nonviolence to bring about change?
2. What did the phrase "big words" really mean?
3. What are some reasons that Martin Luther King Jr. only wanted to use nonviolent actions?
4. Martin Luther King Jr. was considered an American hero. What are the attributes or characteristics of heroes?
5. How did the illustrations contribute to your enjoyment of this book?

RELATED BOOKS

Dekay, James T. *Meet Martin Luther King, Jr.* New York: Random House Books for Young Readers, 2001.

Marzollo, Jean. *Happy Birthday, Martin Luther King*. New York: Scholastic, 2006.

Ringgold, Faith. *My Dream of Martin Luther King*. New York: Dragonfly Books, 1998.

ACTIVITIES

1. Encourage students to cut out pictures from old magazines or newspapers of people of various races, genders, etc. Invite students to create a collage using these pictures and post it on a classroom or library bulletin board stating, "We may have many differences, but we all have equal rights."
2. Invite students to create their own "I have a dream" speech. Encourage students to write about something that they wish to see changed about America today. How do they think America can become a better place? Allow time for students to share their speeches.
3. Encourage students to research various social issues in the United States (e.g., racism, poverty, welfare, etc.). Can any of these issues be addressed through nonviolence? You may wish to organize a debate in which one group of students defends the use of nonviolence while another group advocates violent methods of social change.
4. Invite students to pretend that they need to change something important regarding their school or their community. Ask them to create a list of nonviolent ways that they could go about trying to implement this change.
5. Which African Americans besides Martin Luther King Jr. have achieved greatness or have received honors? Invite students to create a list with a description of each individual and some of her or his significant contributions.
6. Give each student a cloud made out of construction paper. Just as Martin Luther King Jr. had a dream, invite students to write a "dream" on their clouds. These "dreams" can

be personal issues, national issues, or worldly issues. Plan time to share and discuss the various "dreams" students have.

7. Invite students to discuss why this book was placed in the category "Nation and Country." What elements or features of the story or illustrations make this a national book? Does the message of this book apply to every region of the country? Are the words of Martin Luther King Jr. as powerful in the West or Northeast or Southwest as they are in the South?

8. Students may wish to assemble a list of "powerful words." What words, by themselves, are incredibly powerful or particularly strong? Some of those words are in this book, for example, "love," "hate," and "courage." Invite students to interview family members or neighbors for some words they believe to be particularly powerful. Students may wish to create a large wall chart of "Big Words" or "Powerful Words."

9. At the end of the book, the author notes that there are more than 200 Web sites about Martin Luther King Jr. Invite students to log on to several of those sites to obtain information on additional biographical events in his life. What important events did the author leave out of this story? What events helped shape Martin Luther King Jr.'s life or philosophy?

10. Invite students to read the Illustrator's Note at the beginning of the book. Then ask students to look at each of the illustrations and determine the metaphor, symbolism, or imagery depicted in each piece of art. How do the illustrations help tell the story of Martin Luther King Jr.?

11. Invite students to put together a collection of books about Martin Luther King Jr. They may wish to start with the bibliography in the back of this book. How many books are available in the school library? Students may wish to develop an annotated bibliography for use by students at specific grade levels.

Pearl Harbor Warriors: The Bugler, the Pilot, the Friendship

Dorinda Makanaonalani Nicholson

Kansas City, MO: Woodson House Publishing, 2001

© Judy Grupp

SUMMARY

This is an incredible book that weaves a wonderfully rich story about two men—former enemies, now friends—who come to understand the value of forgiveness and reconciliation. With deft strokes the author tells the events of the attack on Pearl Harbor, its aftermath, and the coming together of two old warriors. Through a series of letters between a grandmother and her granddaughter, readers are drawn into a tale that resonates across the years and provides an important lesson for all. This is a moving and beautifully told story that will be read and reread for many years.

SOCIAL STUDIES DISCIPLINES

History, sociology, political science, geography

NCSS THEMATIC STRANDS:

Culture; time, continuity, and change; People, places and environment; Individual development and identity; Global connections; Civic ideals and practices.

CRITICAL THINKING QUESTIONS

1. What did you admire most about these two men?
2. What are some acts of forgiveness that you have done in your life?
3. How would you describe this story to your friends?
4. How did the photographs and illustrations help you appreciate this story?

5. What is the most memorable event in the story?
6. What would you like to say to Mr. Fiske? To Mr. Abe?

RELATED BOOKS

McGowen, Tom. *The Attack on Pearl Harbor*. New York: Children's Press, 2002.

Nicholson, Dorinda M. *Pearl Harbor Child—A Child's View of Pearl Harbor from Attack to Peace*. Kansas City, MO: Woodson House Publishing, 2001.

Tanaka, Shelley. *Attack on Pearl Harbor: The True Story of the Day America Entered World War II*. New York: Hyperion, 2001.

Taylor, Theodore. *Air Raid-Pearl Harbor: The Story of December 7, 1941*. New York: Harcourt Brace, 2001.

ACTIVITIES

1. Since its publication, this book has won awards from various organizations around the country. Invite students to create and develop their own special award for this book. What qualities or features make it so outstanding? Encourage students to create a fictitious organization (e.g., The American Forgiveness Society) and design an appropriate award.
2. Invite students to share and discuss some of the feelings Mr. Fiske and Mr. Abe may have experienced during their first meeting. Encourage youngsters to share incidents from their own lives in which they reconciled with someone they previously didn't like. Ensure a comfortable environment for discussion and provide opportunities for students to share their feelings and to respect those of others.
3. Encourage students to interview their grandparents or other older adults about their recollections of World War II. Students may be interested in obtaining more than one retelling about a specific event (e.g., V-J day) or a series of events (e.g., food rationing, women in the workforce) to determine whether different people remember it the same way. When they have completed the interviews students may wish to combine their data into a series of short chapter books, a classroom time line, or a directory of important World War II events.
4. Invite students to create a time line of the events leading up to the first meeting in Honolulu between Mr. Fiske and Mr. Abe. Students may wish to create an alternate time line of events that occurred after that initial meeting. Be sure these are posted prominently in the classroom.
5. Divide students into two groups. Assign one group the task of writing a prequel to the story and the other group the task of writing a sequel. Encourage students to discuss the various types of events and actions (internationally or for each of the two men) they could include in their prequels or sequels. Individual students may wish to craft a sequel with the title *How Two Men Taught the World Forgiveness*.

6. Set up a special bulletin board titled *My Goals*. Encourage each child to list affective goals he or she has for the coming week or month (e.g., treat others with more respect, be kind to my neighbors, help others without being asked, etc.). Take time to discuss the importance of these affective goals, goal setting in general, and ways students can achieve their self-initiated goals. At the end of each week or month, take time (as a class) to discuss those goals, whether they were reached, and what might be done in the future to achieve those goals. Invite students to compare their goals with those established by Mr. Fiske and Mr. Abe.
7. Invite youngsters to write a letter of appreciation to a relative (real or imaginary) who lived during World War II. What would they like to celebrate or acknowledge about their relatives' lives during that time? What makes a particular relative so special? What lesson(s) or example(s) has that relative provided them that will help them become better human beings?
8. Invite students to create posters on forgiveness and reconciliation. You may wish to work with the school's guidance counselor to share and disseminate these posters throughout the school or district.
9. Plan time to talk with students about hatred between people and between countries. What events or circumstances cause people to dislike each other? What events or circumstances cause countries to dislike each other? Are there any similarities? Any differences? Schedule opportunities for students to share their thoughts and perceptions.
10. As an extension of the activity above, invite students to write a letter to the editor of the local newspaper about the importance of forgiveness and reconciliation. Invite students to express their personal thoughts and reflections on this topic in terms of what they have learned from the book.
11. Invite students to log on to one or more of the following Web sites about Pearl Harbor and the attack on December 7, 1941.

    http://plasma.nationalgeographic.com/pearlharbor

    http://www.ibiscom.com/pearl.htm

    http://www.thinkquest.org/library/lib/site_sum_outside.html?name=J0112601&url=J0112601

    http://members.aol.com/azmemph/phdec7.htm

    http://www.nps.gov/usar

    http://memory.loc.gov/ammem/today/dec07.html

So You Want to Be President? (revised and updated ed.)

Judith St. George

New York: Philomel Books, 2004

© Judy Grupp

SUMMARY

This Caldecott Award–winning book provides young readers with everything they would ever want to know about the presidency, in a light and fun-filled compendium of information. Profiled are fat presidents (William Howard Taft), small presidents (James Madison), and old presidents (Ronald Reagan). Readers get inside information on presidential hobbies, sports, and food preferences. The tone is fun, but the theme is that presidents are an interesting collection of individuals who run the gamut from great to mediocre. There's an addendum at the end with a wealth of vital statistics and one-line bios for all past presidents.

SOCIAL STUDIES DISCIPLINES

History, political science, sociology

NCSS THEMATIC STRANDS

Time, Continuity, and Change; Individuals, Groups, and Institutions; Power, Authority and Governance; Civic Ideals and Practices

CRITICAL THINKING QUESTIONS

1. Who was the most interesting president? Why?
2. Who was the least interesting president? Why?
3. What information surprised you the most?
4. If you could vote for any person in this book, who would it be?
5. After reading this book, would you like to be president? Why?

RELATED BOOKS

Cronin, Doreen. *Duck for President.* New York: Simon & Schuster, 2004.

Piven, Hanoch. *What Presidents Are Made Of.* New York: Atheneum, 2004.

ACTIVITIES

1. Designate each student in a class as president of the United States. Invite students to design their own letterhead (stationery) for this high office. Encourage them to use typography or a word processing font that is "presidential" in nature. They may wish to include an illustration that reflects their interests or lifestyles.
2. Encourage students to each select one president from this book. Invite them to each prepare an informational brochure on the life and events of that person. They may wish to create brochures that can be made part of a classroom or library display, or they may wish to focus on brochures designed for a specific audience (e.g., recent immigrants to this country, children under the age of 12, etc.).
3. Brainstorm with students all the requirements to be president of the United States (e.g., age, place of birth, etc.). Invite students to discuss whether these requirements are appropriate. Are there too many requirements to be president? Should there be other requirements? Students may wish to turn their discussions into a survey or questionnaire. They may wish to poll other students or faculty in the school for their views on this issue.
4. Invite students to each select one president. Ask them to imagine that they are the campaign manager for that individual. Invite students to each create a presidential campaign poster for that individual, using the language and events of that person's time period. How are the posters similar? How are they different? How does each poster reflect the period of American history for which it was created?
5. Invite a member of your local League of Women Voters (check your local phone book) to visit your classroom or library. Ask that person to talk with students about the electoral process, particularly for presidents. After the visit, students may wish to develop a large flow chart that illustrates the various steps in the presidential electoral process.

6. Invite students to discuss the laws, regulations, or bills they would endorse if they were the president of the United States. What would be their "platform" if they were running for office? What current events or legislation would get their immediate attention if they were running for president or had just been elected president? As in a previous activity, students may wish to survey other students and faculty members about their views on selected issues.

7. Obtain some large sheet cake boxes from your local bakery. Invite students to work in small groups to collect artifacts or memorabilia that might be representative of a certain president (for example, jelly beans for Ronald Reagan, a picture of a stovepipe hat for Abraham Lincoln, a model of a horse for Theodore Roosevelt). Invite students to arrange their collection in the bottom of a cake box, label each of the items, and cover the box with a sheet of plastic wrap. This will create a museum display box that can be set up on a table or bookshelf for viewing.

8. Invite students to make a list of all the presidents. Ask them to record the most unusual or strangest fact about each president. What was something each president did that was out of the ordinary or just plain strange? Students may wish to vote for the strangest fact of all.

9. Invite students to write a letter to the current president. They may wish to do this individually or in small groups. They may want to ask about the job, some of the problems being addressed, or simply to request a photograph. They should address their letters to:

   The White House
   1600 Pennsylvania Avenue NW
   Washington, DC 20500

   Be sure students understand that due to the large volume of mail received by the White House each day, they may not receive a reply.

10. Here are some Web sites students may wish to use to obtain current and relevant information about the presidency:

    http://www.pbs.org/wgbh/amex/presidents/

    http://www.npg.si.edu/exh/travpres/index6.htm

    http://www.primarygames.com/holidays/presidents/presidents.htm

    http://www.mce.k12tn.net/us_presidents/hangman.htm

    http://www.pbs.org/wnet/amerpres/

The Star-Spangled Banner

Francis Scott Key

Markham, ONT: Quarry Press, 2003

NOTE: I found it particularly interesting that this book was printed, bound, and published in Canada. Cheers to our northern neighbors!

SUMMARY

This book contains the full text of the "Star-Spangled Banner," a song most Americans can sing only up through the first stanza. Also included is a history of the song—its various names as well as some of the stories surrounding the "Star-Spangled Banner" itself. This is a book for every study of American history—whether in a classroom or school library. Please note that a CD of the "Star-Spangled Banner" (sung by Lee Greenwood) is also included with the book.

SOCIAL STUDIES DISCIPLINES

History, geography

NCSS THEMATIC STRANDS

Time, Continuity, and Change; Individuals, Groups, and Institutions

CRITICAL THINKING QUESTIONS

1. If you could choose a different song to be our national anthem, what song would you choose, and why?

2. If you could add one line to the national anthem, what would it be, and why?
3. What do you feel when you hear the national anthem?
4. What is your favorite part of the song?
5. Do you think all Americans should know the words to this song?

RELATED BOOKS

Bowdish, Lynea. *Francis Scott Key and "The Star-Spangled Banner."* New York: Mondo Publishing, 2002.

Key, Francis Scott. *The Star-Spangled Banner*. New York: Random House, 2002.

Pingry, Patricia A. *The Story of "The Star-Spangled Banner."* Nashville, TN: Candy Cane Press, 2005.

Welch, Catherine A. *The Star-Spangled Banner*. Minneapolis, MN: Carolrhoda Books, 2004.

ACTIVITIES

1. Encourage students to research other countries' flags and national anthems. Have students create each country's flag using construction paper, and underneath each flag, post the country's national anthem on a bulletin board.
2. Invite students to create their own version of what they feel the American flag should look like—a version that represents America today.
3. Give every student a star, and invite students to write one thing that makes America great on the star. Create an American flag out of construction paper, and place these stars in their correct location on the flag.
4. This country's first flag had 13 stars to represent the states. Today, we have 50 stars on the flag. Invite students, in small groups, to research some of the changes that led to the addition of stars to the flag. Encourage students to prepare a time line listing the ratification of states 14 through 50. This time line can be illustrated on a large sheet of butcher paper and displayed in either the classroom or library.
5. Invite students to write a series of newspaper articles about the events surrounding the writing of "The Star Spangled Banner." Encourage students to assemble their articles into a newspaper for publication and distribution throughout the school.
6. Invite selected groups of students to create a bulletin board of some of the symbols that represent the United States. For example, the Statue of Liberty, "The Star Spangled Banner," the flag, the Washington Monument, and the bald eagle. Encourage students to write a short description of each of the symbols posted.
7. Invite students to create a series of history cards (similar to baseball cards) about some of the events surrounding the War of 1812. Using 4-by-6-inch index cards, students

can design illustrations for the upper half of each card. On the bottom half of each card students can record selected facts about the event or person portrayed.

8. Ask students to create a classroom or library stamp collection. Invite each student to create stamps that symbolize what America means to her or him. The stamps can be made larger than life size on construction paper using stamps, markers, or colored pencils. After students have created their stamps, put them into a photo album for permanent display. (Note: For an interesting possibility, students may wish to create actual postage stamps using their own designs. Log on to http://www.photostamps.com for prices and information on how citizens can create their own legal photo stamps.)

9. Challenge students to create a new name for "The Star Spangled Banner." Explain to them that Francis Scott Key had problems coming up with a title for his song (he first called it "Gallant Defense of Fort McHenry") . Tell students that they are Key's musical assistant and have been charged with developing an appropriate title for his new song. After students have generated a few potential titles, invite them to explain the reasoning behind their choices and the appropriateness of each title.

10. Students can obtain information about Fort McHenry from the National Park Service Web site at http://www.nps.gov/fomc/. Invite students to use the data on this site to create an informative brochure for other students who may want some background information about this national monument and historic shrine.

Vote

Eileen Christelow

New York: Clarion Books, 2004

SUMMARY

This book is a complete and thorough review of the American voting process. Through straight text and a series of cartoons, young readers are introduced to all the elements involved in an election, from start to finish. The author has left nothing out (she even devotes attention to recounts in close elections). Here is a book that will be used over and over again for local, regional, and national elections. Informative and inviting, it clarifies voting for young and old alike.

SOCIAL STUDIES DISCIPLINES

History, political science, sociology, economics

NCSS THEMATIC STRANDS

Individuals, Groups, and Institutions; Power, Authority, and Governance; Civic Ideals and Practices

CRITICAL THINKING QUESTIONS

1. Why do you think that it is important to vote?
2. What different positions and things do people vote for?
3. Do you think that voting is an appropriate way for people to decide various things? Why?

4. Should kids be allowed to vote in local elections? Why?
5. Why would some people choose not to vote in an election?

RELATED BOOKS

Granfield, Linda. *America Votes: How Our President Is Elected.* Toronto: Kids Can Press, 2003.

Sobel, Syl. *Presidential Elections: And Other Cool Facts.* Hauppauge, NY: Barron's Educational Series, 2001.

ACTIVITIES

1. If possible, invite a local politician to speak to your class about the various steps it takes to run an election. Encourage students to create questions to ask the politician before he or she visits the class.
2. Invite students to pretend that they are running for class president. Have students create their own campaign ads, including a fun slogan, and display these on a bulletin board.
3. Encourage students to study various presidential elections. Create a scavenger hunt for students to complete while they are conducting their research. Questions that could be included are: Who ran in the first presidential election? Who lost the last presidential election? How many candidates were there in the last election?
4. Invite students to research the two primary political parties. Encourage students to choose a party that they think they would like to join, and have them write why they chose that particular party.
5. If there are forthcoming elections in your area, in your state, or in the country, have students follow the candidates' campaigns. Hold a class election to see which candidate was most liked among the students in the class.
6. Have a day on which students have the opportunity to vote for many things. Various things that students can vote for include a particular book to be read, a game or activity to be played, and an assignment to be completed for a specific subject.
7. Discuss why the author and illustrator chose to include both straight text and cartoons throughout this book. What would be the advantages of this approach? Which of those two elements was most effective for students?

8. The author lists several Web sites in the back of the book. Students may wish to log on to some of the following sites and collect additional information about elections and voting. Afterward encourage them to create a special Web page that summarizes the important information in advance of a forthcoming local, regional, or national election.

   http://www.vote-smart.org

   http://www.kidsvotingusa.org

   http://takeyourkidstovote.org

   http://pbs.org/democracy/votinginamerica

   http://fairvote.org

9. Plan time to talk with students about reasons some people have been denied the right to vote in this country (e.g., women, African Americans). Some of the reasons are presented on pages 44–45 of the book. Help students understand that voting has not been guaranteed for all Americans throughout our history.

10. Contact your local League of Women Voters (check your local phone book). Invite a member of the League to visit your classroom or library to share information about the voting process on both the local and national level. Encourage students to pose questions and record responses. After the visit, the youngsters may wish to gather the data together and create a PowerPoint™ presentation to share with other classes or grades.

CHAPTER 11

World

Antarctic Journal: Four Months at the Bottom of the World

Jennifer Owings Dewey

Honesdale, PA: Boyds Mills Press, 2001

SUMMARY

With sketchbook in hand, the author and illustrator travels to one of the most barren and most desolate places in the world—Antarctica. Here she spends four months observing the wildlife, experiencing the elements, and sailing past building-sized icebergs. In a series of letters to her family she describes this incredible wilderness and the equally incredible adventures she has almost every day. This book is a delightful exploration of a land few will visit but all admire.

SOCIAL STUDIES DISCIPLINES

Geography, sociology, economics

NCSS THEMATIC STRANDS

Time, Continuity, and Change; People, Places, and Environment; Global Connections

CRITICAL THINKING QUESTIONS

1. What did you enjoy most about this book?
2. Based on the author's adventure, would you like to visit Antarctica?
3. Which of the animals was most interesting to you?
4. Why do scientists spend so much time and money studying Antarctica?
5. If you could ask the author one question, what would it be?

RELATED BOOKS

Myers, Walter Dean. *Antarctica: Journeys to the South Pole*. New York: Scholastic, 2004.

Webb, Sophie. *My Season with Penguins: An Antarctic Journal*. Boston: Houghton Mifflin, 2004.

ACTIVITIES

1. If possible, obtain a copy of the DVD *March of the Penguins* (2005). Show this movie (or parts of the movie) to students. Afterward invite students to create an oversized poster of a penguin and post it on one wall of the classroom or library. Ask students to record various facts and information about penguins inside the borders of the penguin illustration.
2. As a variation of the activity above, invite students to create a large illustration of the continent of Antarctica. Post this on a wall of the classroom or library. Encourage students to collect factual information about Antarctica (they may wish to begin with the data on pages 16–17 of the book) and write that information across the illustration. New facts can be added periodically.
3. Encourage students to create a large Venn diagram that compares Antarctica with the United States (or any other country). What are some of the similarities? What are some of the differences? Are there more similarities or more differences?
4. Invite students to talk about how Palmer Station might be similar to or different from the town in which they live. What do they have in their town that they wouldn't find at Palmer Station (e.g., a movie theater, a car wash, a grocery store)? What would Palmer Station have that they wouldn't find in their town (e.g., science labs, permanent ice cover, penguins).

5. Invite selected students to imagine that they are residents of Palmer Station. Ask them to write imaginary letters to their parents and family members about some of their adventures. What do they see? What kind of weather conditions do they experience? What are some of the animals they encounter regularly?

6. Invite small groups of students to imagine that they are travel agents and that they must prepare travel plans for one of the following:

   – A trip to the South Pole
   – A three-day trip across Weddell Sea
   – An all-day trip to Litchfield Island
   – A snowmobile trip across the Ross Ice Shelf
   – A visit to Cormorant Island

   Students may wish to obtain some initial information from the book and then supplement it with information from library books and other resources.

7. Invite students to select favorite scenes or illustrations from the book. Ask them to make dioramas of their selections. They may wish to create original drawings and use clay, construction paper, pipe cleaners, and wire to construct three-dimensional objects to be placed in the diorama. Each diorama can be displayed in the classroom or school library.

8. Provide students with opportunities to act out selected pages or chapters of the book. Divide a large group of students into several smaller groups. Ask each group to select a chapter or an event described in the book. Invite a narrator to read the events as they happen as each group mimes the appropriate actions.

9. Invite students to consult various weather information sources (e.g., http://www.wunderground.com/). Invite them to record the daily weather in Antarctica over a period of two to three weeks. They can record the temperature, wind conditions, thickness of the ice pack, cloud cover, or other factors. Students may wish to create a chart that records daily weather conditions in Antarctica and daily weather conditions in their home town. What differences do they note?

10. Provide students with several library resources on continents. Invite them to make a list of the elements or features of a continent. Based on their listing, does Antarctica constitute a continent? You may wish to invite students to form two debate groups—one arguing that Antarctica is a continent, the other that Antarctica is not a continent. Be sure students are able to substantiate their positions with relevant data.

Beautiful Blackbird

Ashley Bryan

New York: Atheneum Books for Young Readers, 2003

SUMMARY

All the birds think that Blackbird is the most beautiful creature of all. And, they all want to look like him; they all want to have some black on their feathers or their bodies so that they, too, can be beautiful. Well, Blackbird mixes up some black roots in his gourd and paints the other birds with stripes and rings and dots and splashes of black. And they all become beautiful. This book is an adaptation of a folktale from Zambia—a tale of rhythm, rhyme, and universal meaning. The author has woven a story, coupled with stunning cut paper illustrations, that will be shared again and again.

SOCIAL STUDIES DISCIPLINES

Geography, sociology

NCSS THEMATIC STRANDS

Culture; Individual Development and identity

CRITICAL THINKING QUESTIONS

1. What makes each of us a special individual?
2. What message do you think the author was trying to share in this story?
3. Why does the author keep saying, "Black is beautiful"?
4. Why was Blackbird considered the most beautiful bird in the forest?
5. How would you define the word "beautiful"?

RELATED BOOKS

Bryan, Ashley. *Ashley Bryan's ABC of African American Poetry*. New York: Aladdin, 2001.

Nolen, Jerdine. *Thunder Rose*. New York: Silver Whistle, 2003.

ACTIVITIES

1. Encourage students to locate pictures of various individuals who have done great things for the people of the world. Place their names, pictures, and what they did on a bulletin board. Note to students that it was inner beauty, not physical appearance, that placed these individuals on their bulletin board.
2. Invite students to bring in pictures of their heroes. These heroes can be athletes, actors or actresses, family members, etc. Encourage students to discuss who their heroes are and why they chose those particular people.
3. Invite students to talk a walk around the school grounds. Ask them to look for items that are beautiful for their simplicity. For example, a smooth rock may be beautiful simply because of its rounded shape. A leaf may be beautiful simply because of its fragility. Invite students to create a special bulletin board display of some of the beautiful things in nature or in everyday life.
4. Encourage students to write and illustrate their own stories about inner beauty. They may wish to comment on their own inner beauty or the inner beauty of a close family member. As appropriate, invite students to share these stories in a warm and supportive discussion group.
5. Encourage students to create and decorate a bumper sticker expressing the main point of the story. Place these bumper stickers on a bulletin board, around a car made out of construction paper.
6. Invite students to collect from the classroom or school library a sampling of books focusing on African folktales. Invite students to assemble a bibliography or collection of African folktales that would be appropriate for sharing in the classroom or library. How are these folktales similar to or different from the folktales with which they are most familiar (e.g., Grimms')?
7. Invite students to create an alphabet book about places, people, cities, and other features of the country of Zambia. Encourage them to identify at least one important item for each letter of the alphabet (there may not be an item for every letter, however). Be sure these books are appropriately displayed in the classroom or library.
8. Obtain some simple instruments from the school's music teacher. Instruments such as bongo drums, sticks, claves, recorders, or xylophones would all be appropriate. Encourage students to practice with several instruments and develop their own beats or rhythms that could be used as an accompaniment to a retelling of the story.

9. Students may wish to locate some information about the country of Zambia. Here are some Web sites to get them started:

   https://www.cia.gov/cia/publications/factbook/geos/za.html

   http://fotw.fivestarflags.com/zm.html

   http://www.lib.utexas.edu/maps/cia00/zambia_sm00.jpg

   After they have collected information from the Web as well as books in the school library, invite the students to assemble important facts into an informational guide specifically directed at students.

10. Peanut soup is a very popular dish in many African countries, partly because Africa is one of the world's largest suppliers of peanuts. Here is a recipe you may wish to share with students:

    2 each: celery sticks, carrots, onions, potatoes, tomatoes

    4 cups water

    2 bouillon cubes (any flavor)

    2 teaspoons salt

    1 teaspoon pepper

    1 cup chunky peanut butter

    1 cup milk

    2 tablespoons brown sugar

    6 tablespoons rice

    Cut all the vegetables into small pieces and place in a large saucepan. Add the water, bouillon cubes, salt, and pepper and boil gently for about 20 minutes, stirring occasionally. Blend the peanut butter, milk, and brown sugar together in a mixing bowl and add to the saucepan. Stir in the rice and allow all the ingredients to simmer on low heat for about 30 minutes. Ladle into bowls and enjoy.

11. Invite students to read other books by Ashley Bryan. Encourage them to discuss some of the themes that Bryan emphasizes in his books. What messages is he trying to convey? What does he believe? What do you know about this author and illustrator as a result of reading his books? Why have his books won so many awards?

12. Although this book celebrates a folktale from the country of Zambia, the message is universal. Invite students to select other African folktales and to assemble a collection of "messages" that are shared via those stories. Are any of those "messages" universal in nature? Are some of the "messages" specific to their country of origin?

Horse Hooves and Chicken Feet: Mexican Folktales

Neil Philip

New York: Clarion Books, 2003

SUMMARY

This is a delightful and engaging collection of 15 folktales from Mexico. These stories invite readers (and listeners) into an enchanted world populated by cats and kings, priests and tricksters, ordinary people, and, of course, supernatural beings. The collection is both rich and varied and offers a unique sampling of tales and stories that transmit the Mexican culture and preserve its storytelling heritage. This book is a delightful adventure into the wit, spirit, and imagination of Mexico's past.

SOCIAL STUDIES DISCIPLINES

Geography, anthropology, history

NCSS THEMATIC STRANDS

Culture; Time, Continuity, and Change; People, Places, and Environment; Global Connections

CRITICAL THINKING QUESTIONS

1. Which folktale was your favorite, and why?
2. Do any of the folktales remind you of other stories you have heard? If so, what are they?
3. What is one thing that you like about the Mexican folktales?
4. What is one thing that you found strange or unusual about these tales?

5. What did you learn about Mexican history or culture (from these tales) that you didn't know before?

RELATED BOOKS

Ehlert, Lois. *Cuckoo*. New York: Voyager Books, 2000.

ACTIVITIES

1. Read one of the folktales to students, without showing them the illustrations. Invite students to create their own illustrations for the story using bright colors, like the other illustrations in the book.
2. Place students in groups and allow each group to choose a different folktale from the book. Encourage students to create props and puppets out of brown paper bags and construction paper. They may wish to use these props to retell their favorite folktale.
3. Invite small groups of students to each choose a folktale from the book. Invite each group to change the beginning, middle, or end of their selected story. Allow time for students to share their changes and how each change may alter the reading or interpretation of the story.
4. Using appropriate library resources, encourage students to read other Mexican folktales that were not included in the book. Invite students to select stories that they feel would be worthy of being added to the book (in a second edition, for example).
5. Invite students to write their own Mexican folktales and create illustrations to go along with their stories. Collect these stories in one large, class book and place it in the classroom or school library.
6. Students may wish to create large Venn diagrams that compare a story selected from this book with a folktale from another country or culture. For example, the story "The Two Marias" is similar in form and nature to "Cinderella." What are the similarities? Invite students to discuss how and why some stories seem to be universal irrespective of culture, country, or time.
7. If possible, invite a professional storyteller into your classroom or library (these individuals can often be located in the local telephone book or through your local public library). Ask the storyteller to share one or more stories and to talk about the role of storytelling in most cultures and countries. What are some of the elements of a good story? Why do some stories appear in most lands and cultures? Why has storytelling been valued by almost every culture in the world?
8. Post a large map of Mexico on a wall of the classroom or library. Invite students to locate large cities, important sites, and historical locations. These can be identified by inserting push pins into the map. Invite students to post informational cards around the map that provide important details about the location.

9. Students may wish to develop one of the stories into a readers theatre script. Using the examples in part III of this book, invite small groups of students to each select one story from this collection and develop a brief readers theatre presentation to share with students in another class or grade.

10. Invite individuals in your local area who have traveled to Mexico to visit your classroom or library. Ask them to share photographs, slides, or artifacts from their travels that would illustrate sites and customs of Mexico. Encourage students to "match" some of those items to events or details presented in one or more of the stories in this collection. For example, they may wish to "match" a photograph of a Mexican church with the church depicted in the story "The Priest Who Had a Glimpse of Glory."

Jabuti the Tortoise: A Trickster Tale from the Amazon

Gerald McDermott

New York: Harcourt, 2001

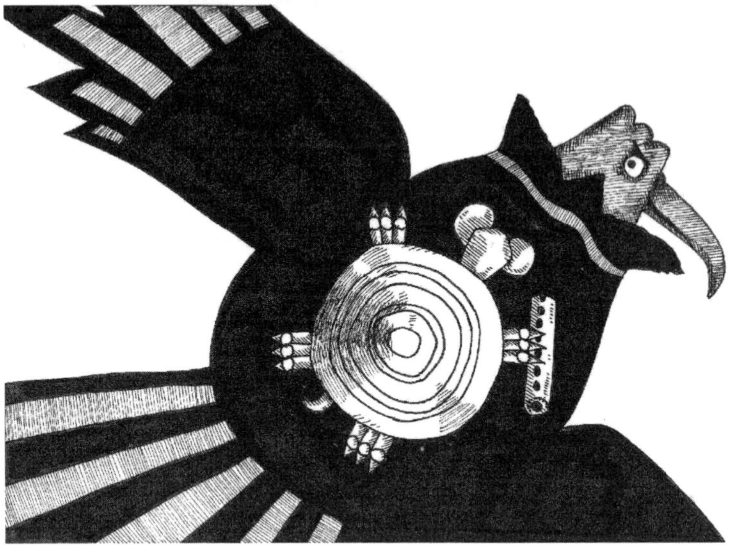

SUMMARY

Jabuti the tortoise played a song on his flute. He created music in the rain forest. One day all the birds were invited to a festival, and Jabuti wanted to go, too. The vulture tricked him, and Jabuti fell from the clouds, shattering his shell. But all was not lost, because he emerged changed and altered . . . and all the more beautiful. This is a delightful tale to share with youngsters—made all the more colorful with lively and vibrant illustrations that capture the eye and the imagination.

SOCIAL STUDIES DISCIPLINES

Geography

NCSS THEMATIC STRANDS

Culture; People, Places, and Environment; Individual Development and Identity

CRITICAL THINKING QUESTIONS

1. Who do you think was/were the hero/heroes in this story?
2. Why do you think the birds who touched Jabuti took on new colors?
3. Why was the vulture still black at the end of the story?
4. Would you say that this story had a happy ending? Why?
5. What would you like to say to the vulture at the end of the story?

RELATED BOOKS

Cherry, Lynne. *The Great Kapok Tree*. New York: Voyager Books, 2000.

Cherry, Lynne, and Mark J. Plotkin. *The Shaman's Apprentice: A Tale of the Amazon Rain Forest*. New York: Gulliver Green, 1998.

Fredericks, Anthony D. *A Is for Anaconda: A Rainforest Alphabet.* Chelsea, MI: Sleeping Bear Press, 2008.

Munduruku, Daniel. *Tales of the Amazon: How the Munduruku Indians Live*. Berkeley, CA: Publishers Group West, 2000.

ACTIVITIES

1. Using construction paper, cut out a tortoise body and shell. Cut the shell into small pieces and give each piece to a student to decorate. Place the pieces of the shell back together and attach the shell to the body. Display the tortoise in the classroom or library.
2. Encourage students to research more about the Amazon and the animals that can be found there. Invite students to use the information that they acquired to create their own story using a single Amazon animal.
3. Invite students to research and locate the Amazon rain forest and other rain forests around the world on a large map. They may wish to use their information to label a large world map (posted on the wall), indicating the various rain forest areas.
4. Invite students to alter the end of the story so that Jabuti dies. What eventually happens to the vulture? What is his fate in life?
5. Have students imagine that they are one of the creatures in the story. Ask them to create posters that say, "Save Our Home." They should include a full-color drawing of their selected creature and write a convincing advertisement for preserving the rain forest.
6. The Rainforest Action Network provides students with an incredible array of activities and information. Invite students to log on to its Web site at http://www.ran.org/ran. Encourage students to share the information learned through a special display in the classroom or library.
7. Students may be interested in obtaining additional information about life in the rain forests of the world. Here are a few Web sites to get them started:

    http://www.zoomschool.com/subjects/rainforest/

    http://www.mbgnet.net/sets/rforest/index.htm

    http://passporttoknowledge.com/rainforest/intro.html

    http://www.livingrainforest.org/for/kids/

    After students have had sufficient opportunities to collect information, invite them to construct a series of informational brochures about selected aspects of the rain forest, such as animals, plants, climate, food products, destruction, or any other topics students may wish to explore.

8. Form an Ecology Club. Interested students can initiate school and community projects aimed at improving the environment. Get a copy of *No Sweat Science: Nature Experiments* by Anthony D. Fredericks (New York: Sterling Publishing, 2005) for possible projects and ideas.

9. Students may wish to grow some rain forest plants in the classroom or library. Invite them to visit a large supermarket, garden shop, or nursery and look for one or more of the following rain forest plants: African violet, begonia, bird's-nest fern, bromeliad, Christmas cactus, corn plant, croton, dumb cane, fiddle-leaf fig, orchid, philodendron, prayer plant, rubber plant, snake plant, umbrella plant, and zebra plant. Inform students that the plants they grow will be somewhat smaller than the plants normally found in the rain forest.

Lord of the Cranes

Kerstin Chen

New York: North-South Books, 2000

SUMMARY

One day a wise old man, Tian, decided to go down to the city to see if people were kind and generous. He met many people, including the owner of a small inn. The owner welcomed him and provided Tian with food and drink. Tian responded by painting beautiful cranes on the wall of the inn, and the inn soon became very popular. The owner became very wealthy but always had food and drink for those in need. This ancient Chinese tale is one of acceptance and generosity. It is both timeless and instructive—for young and old alike. The illustrations are dynamic and delightful in their scope.

SOCIAL STUDIES DISCIPLINES

Sociology

NCSS THEMATIC STRANDS

Culture; People, Places, and Environment; Individual Development and Identity; Civic Ideals and Practices

CRITICAL THINKING QUESTIONS

1. Whom do you think the Lord of the Cranes represents?
2. Would you have offered Tian food if you were Wang? Why or why not?
3. In today's world, do you feel that it is important to help everyone?
4. What is something you have done recently to help others?

5. What is the role of the cranes in this story?
6. What does this book tell you about Chinese culture?

RELATED BOOKS

Tucker, Kathy. *The Seven Chinese Sisters*. Morton Grove, IL: Albert Whitman, 2003.

Wang, Gia-Zhen. *Auntie Tigress and Other Favorite Chinese Folk Tales*. New York: Purple Bear Books, 2006.

ACTIVITIES

1. Students may wish to collect food and clothing items from friends and family and donate them to a local homeless shelter. Plan time beforehand to discuss the reasons the donations might be important. Afterward talk with students about other acts of charity that they might be able to do in their local community.
2. Invite students to write about a time when they helped another person without expecting anything in return. Ask students to create an illustration to go along with their writing. These may be developed into a series of murals (as in the Chinese tradition) for posting on one wall of a classroom or library.
3. Place students in small groups and give each group various scenarios in which individuals need some sort of help (e.g., homeless individuals, people in severe financial difficulty, senior citizens, single parents). Encourage students to write different ways that they would help these individuals, and have each group share their scenarios and solutions.
4. Invite students to pretend that they are Wang and need to convince and teach others to be kind and generous to the poor. Have students create a list of ways they would go about doing this. Take time to talk about items on these lists and how they might be put into practice in your local community.
5. Invite students to retell the story from the perspective of the innkeeper. What were some of the things he dealt with prior to Tian's arrival? How did his life change significantly after Tian left? Students may wish to collect their stories into an "anthology" for display in the classroom or library.
6. Obtain a copy of *Lon Po Po: A Red Riding Hood Story from China* by Ed Young (New York: Philomel, 1989). How does that story compare with *Lord of the Cranes*? Are the themes universal? Are the themes appropriate for all cultures and all countries?
7. Invite students to create a diary ("A Day in the Life of a Chinese Student") based on library investigations and Internet searches. What does a typical Chinese boy or girl (the same age as your students) do during the course of a typical day? Students may wish to construct oversized Venn diagrams of the information on large sheets of newsprint.

8. Encourage your students to form themselves into a theater group and act *Lord of the Cranes* for other classes. Students may wish to visit lower grades and share the story with younger students. Or they may wish to produce a video production, which can be contributed to the classroom or school library.

9. Invite students to assume roles of newspaper reporters and to report on the events in *Lord of the Cranes* as though they were part of the local newspaper. What are some significant events, background information (real or imaginary), or photographs (illustrations) that could be included in a *Lord of the Cranes* newspaper?

10. Students may want to obtain the most current information about China. They can do so at the following Web sites:

    http://library.thinkquest.org/26469/

    http://lcweb2.loc.gov/frd/cs/cntoc.html

    http://www.china-embassy.org/eng/

    http://www.fi.edu/fellows/fellow1/apr99/abc/

    http://www.worldalmanacforkids.com/explore/nations/china.html

11. Discuss the illustrations in this book. How is this style of illustration similar to or different from other styles with which students may be familiar? Invite students to research books in the library with other examples of Chinese art. Is *Lord of the Cranes* a representative example of Chinese illustration? Students may wish to create a PowerPoint™ presentation or slide show of Chinese art, both ancient and modern.

This Place I Know: Poems of Comfort

Georgia Heard, ed.

Cambridge, MA: Candlewick Press, 2002

SUMMARY

This masterful collection of poetry was assembled after the tragic events of 9/11. Poets such as Emily Dickenson, Lillian Morrison, and Walt Whitman offer words of comfort and solace for these troubled times. Eighteen renowned artists have provided special illustrations for each poem that also offer comfort and consolation. This book is beautiful in so many ways, not just for its array of comforting poetry and drawings, but also because it is a book needed by both children and adults for its effervescent hope and optimism.

NOTE: Because of where it falls in the alphabet, this book is listed as the final piece of children's literature for this social studies concept—World. It is also the last piece of children's literature profiled in *Much More Social Studies Through Children's Literature*. That is both prophetic and ironic. As "Much More" was being written (in summer 2006) conflicts, wars, and invasions predominated in the news. Fighting in the Middle East, dictatorial takeovers in Latin America, the subjugation of Tibet by China, civil wars in Africa and the Pacific Rim, territorial conflicts in Asia, incursions, insurrections, and invasions still appear on the evening news regularly. These are troubling times—particularly for children. This book can be a valuable tool in helping youngsters deal with these all too frequent events. It doesn't provide children with all the answers, but it can offer them comfort and solace in both pictures and poems.

SOCIAL STUDIES DISCIPLINES

Sociology, anthropology

NCSS THEMATIC STRANDS

Individual Development and Identity; Individuals, Groups, and Institutions

CRITICAL THINKING QUESTIONS

1. Which of the poems did you enjoy most? Why?
2. Which of the illustrations did you enjoy most? Why?
3. Did you find comfort in this collection of poetry?
4. If you could say anything to the children of the world, what would it be?
5. If you could say anything to the leaders of the world, what would it be?

RELATED BOOKS

Greive, Bradley. *The Blue Day Book for Kids: A Lesson in Cheering Yourself Up*. Kansas City, MO: Andrews McMeel Publishing, 2005.

ACTIVITIES

1. Invite students to a poetry festival. Provide copies of these poems to youngsters and ask that they practice them several times. Afterward ask selected students to each read a poem to the entire group. After each reading, you may wish to spend a little time discussing the implications and meanings in the poem.
2. Invite small groups of students to each select one of the poets. Encourage each group to conduct library research on the other poems written by that individual. Ask the groups to each assemble a collection of poems by that poet. These collections can be bound between sheets of cardboard and displayed in the classroom or library.
3. Invite students to create their own poems of comfort. What are some words, phrases, or sentences they could use? What would they like to say to other students that would help them through a troubling time in their lives or in the world? These collections, too, can be assembled into notebooks and displayed in a classroom or the school library.
4. Invite a small group of students to carefully look at one of the illustrations in the book (before sharing the accompanying poems with them). Ask them to discuss the meaning or implications of that specific illustration. What is the message? What is the artist trying to say? Why is the illustration a comforting one?
5. As appropriate, invite youngsters to discuss special places they go to when they need to be alone or when they just want some peace and quiet. What are the features or fac-

tors that make that particular place so special? Why are some places more special than others? Should everyone have a special place to go?

6. Ask children why the author of *Much More Social Studies Through Children's Literature* included this book in the section entitled "World" rather than the section entitled "Child and Self." What features or characteristics of the book made it more appropriate for "World"? Ask students if this book would be appropriate for children in any country.

7. Invite children to each design an "illustration of comfort." What should the picture have that would make it comforting to others? What artistic medium (oils, acrylics, watercolors, etc.) would work best for a "comforting illustration"? Students may wish to assemble a collection of these illustrations on a special wall entitled "Wall of Comfort."

8. Invite students to audio record each of these poems. Place an audiotape of the poems and a tape player in a special location in the classroom or library. As appropriate, invite students who may need some "time out" or a quiet place to be to put on a set of headphones and listen to the poems on their own. There's no special project they have to complete. They are simply being offered a chance to ponder, think, and contemplate as they listen to comforting poetry read by their peers.

9. Provide a large sheet of newsprint for students. In very large letters, write the word "HOPE" in the center of the sheet. Provide each student with a marker and ask her or him to write what "hope" means. Students can put words, phrases, personal definitions, sentences, sayings, or quotes all over the sheet. When completed the sheet may be posted on the classroom or library wall.

10. Ask the school counselor to visit your classroom or library to talk with students about things that make us sad. Ask the individual to recommend ways that both children and adults can deal with some of the inevitable sad events in their lives. You may wish to provide the individual with a copy of this book and ask her or him to talk about the comfort that words, particularly poetry, often provide people.

11. Invite a child to lie on a sheet of butcher paper or newsprint. Ask another child to trace an outline of the child on the paper. Invite each child to cut out her or his outline and post it on a wall of the classroom or library. During the next several weeks, invite students to write in each of their classmates' outlines; encourage them to write positive phrases or observations about the specific individual. Encourage children to add comments in the outlines of their classmates continuously throughout the month or year. You may wish to put up an outline of yourself and invite students to record appropriate observations (positive, of course).

Part III
Readers Theatre

Readers theatre is a storytelling device that stimulates the imagination and promotes *all* of the language arts. Simply stated, it is an oral interpretation of a piece of literature read in a dramatic style. Readers theatre is an act of involvement, an opportunity to share, and a time to creatively interact with others. It provides numerous opportunities for youngsters to make stories and literature come alive and pulsate with their own unique brand of perception and vision. Literature becomes personal and reflective—children have a breadth of opportunities to be authentic users of language.

Of no less importance is the significance of readers theatre as a method to enhance an appreciation of social studies. Too many youngsters envision social studies as a collection of facts and figures to be committed to memory and regurgitated on standardized tests or workbook pages. As you have probably gathered from the intent and focus of this book, social studies is an active engagement with the dynamics of children's literature. That focus can also be promoted with readers theatre. In fact, when teachers and librarians incorporate readers theatre into their respective programs, youngsters are offered multiple opportunities to, as one third-grade teacher put it, "become actively and personally involved in all that literature has to offer."

When children are provided with regular opportunities to use readers theatre, they develop a personal stake in the literature shared. They also begin to cultivate personal interpretations of that literature—interpretations that lead to higher levels of appreciation and comprehension. Practicing and performing stories is an involvement endeavor—one that demonstrates and utilizes numerous languaging activities. So, too, do youngsters learn to listen to their classmates and appreciate a variety of presentations.

WHAT IS THE VALUE OF READERS THEATRE?

I like to think of readers theatre as a way to interpret social studies without the constraints of skills, rote memorization, or assignments. Readers theatre allows children to breathe life and substance into social studies concepts—an interpretation that is colored by kids' unique perspectives, experiences, and vision. It is, in fact, the readers' interpretation of an event that is intrinsically more valuable than some predetermined and/or preordained "translation" (something that might be found in a teacher's manual or curriculum guide, for example).

With that in mind, I'd like to share with you some of the many values I see in readers theatre—particularly as it applies to elementary social studies:

- Readers theatre is a participatory event. The characters as well as the audience are all intimately involved in the design, structure, and delivery of the story. Children begin to realize that learning social studies is not a solitary activity, but one that can be shared and discussed with others.
- Readers theatre stimulates curiosity and enthusiasm for learning. It allows children to experience learning in a supportive and nonthreatening format that underscores their active involvement.
- Since it is the performance that drives readers theatre, children are given more opportunities to invest themselves and their personalities in the production of a readers theatre. The same story may be subject to several different presentations depending on the group or the individual youngsters involved. Children learn that readers theatre can be explored in a host of ways.
- Children are given numerous opportunities to learn about the major features of selected social studies concepts.
- Readers theatre is informal and relaxed. It does not require elaborate props, scenery, or costumes. It can be set up in any classroom or library. It does not require large sums of money to "make it happen." And, it can be "put on" in any kind of environment—formal or informal.
- Readers theatre enhances the development of cooperative learning strategies. It requires youngsters to work together toward a common goal and supports their efforts in doing so. Readers theatre is not a competitive activity, but rather a cooperative one in which children share, discuss, and band together for the good of the production.
- Teachers and librarians have also discovered that readers theatre is an excellent way to enhance the development of communication skills. Voice projection, intonation, inflection, and pronunciation skills are all promoted within and throughout any readers theatre production.
- The development and enhancement of self-concept is facilitated through readers theatre. Since children are working in concert with other children in a supportive atmosphere, their self-esteem mushrooms accordingly. Again, the emphasis is on the presentation, not necessarily the performers. Youngsters have opportunities to develop levels of self-confidence and self-assurance that would not normally be available in more traditional class productions.

- Creative and critical thinking are enhanced through the utilization of readers theatre. Children are active participants in the interpretation and delivery of a story; they develop thinking skills that are divergent rather than convergent and interpretive skills that are supported rather than directed.
- Readers theatre provides wonderful opportunities for classroom teachers and school librarians to work together in a shared activity. Language arts and literature can be shared beyond the usual constraints of walls, textbooks, and curriculum guides. Teachers and librarians can plan cooperative ventures that expand the social studies program in a host of new dimensions.
- Readers theatre is fun! Children of all ages have delighted in using readers theatre for many years. It is delightful and stimulating, encouraging and fascinating, relevant and personal. Indeed, try as I might, I have not been able to locate a single instance (or group of children) in which (or for whom) readers theatre would not be an appropriate learning activity. It is a strategy filled with a cornucopia of possibilities and promises.

USING READERS THEATRE

Consider some of the following ideas for your classroom or library:

- Use a readers theatre script in conjunction with a specific book or group of books.
- Use a readers theatre script as a "stand-alone"—that is, as a complete, total event.
- Use a readers theatre script as part of a larger unit. The unit may focus on a discipline of social studies (e.g., sociology, history) or as part of a thematic unit (e.g., The Westward Migration, Making Rules and Laws).
- Use a readers theatre script to lead off a unit, in the middle of a unit, or as a final activity for a unit.
- Use a readers theatre script as a classroom activity with follow-up in the library studying related children's literature.
- Use a readers theatre script in the library with follow-up in the classroom via a thematic unit or relevant materials in the social studies textbook.
- After completing a unit, invite students to create their own original readers theatre script for presentation to another class or group.

As you can see, the possibilities for using readers theatre in the classroom or the library are limitless. A coordinated effort between teachers and librarians can result in a plethora of learning opportunities throughout the social studies program.

PRESENTATION SUGGESTIONS

Here are some ideas for readers theatre that you and the students with whom you work may wish to keep in mind—whether in a classroom setting or the school library:

- After a script has been selected for presentation, make sufficient copies. A copy of the script should be provided for each actor. In addition, making two or three extra copies (one for you and "replacement" copies for scripts that are accidentally damaged or lost) is also a good idea. Copies for the audience are unnecessary and are not suggested.
- Emphasize that a readers theatre performance does not require any memorization of the script. It's the interpretation and performance that count.
- Readers should have an opportunity to practice their script before presenting it to an audience. Take some time to discuss voice intonation, facial gestures, body movements, and other features that could be used to enhance the presentation.
- For most presentations readers will stand and/or sit on stools or chairs. The physical location of each reader has been indicated for each of the scripts in this book. Usually all of the characters will be on stage throughout the duration of the presentation. For most presentations it is not necessary to have characters enter and exit. If you place the characters on stools, they can face the audience when they are involved in a particular scene and then turn around whenever they are not involved in a scene.
- You may wish to make simple hand-lettered signs with the name of each character. Loop a piece of string or yarn through each sign and hang it around the neck of each respective character. That way, the audience will know the identity of each character throughout the presentation.
- Each reader will have her or his own copy of the script in a paper cover (see above). If possible, use a music stand for each reader's script (this allows readers to use their hands for dramatic interpretations as necessary).
- Several presentations have a narrator to set up the story. The narrator serves to establish the place and time of the story for the audience so that the characters can "jump into" their parts from the beginning of the story. Typically, the narrator is separated from the other "actors" and can be identified by a simple sign.
- Much of the setting for a story should take place in the audience's mind. Elaborate scenery is not necessary—simple props are often the best. For example:

    A branch or potted plant can serve as a tree.

    A drawing on the chalkboard can illustrate a building.

    A hand-lettered sign can designate one part of the staging area as a particular scene (e.g., swamp, castle, field, forest).

    Children's toys can be used for uncomplicated props (e.g., telephone, vehicles).

    A sheet of aluminum foil or a remnant of blue cloth can be used to simulate a lake or pond.

- Costumes for the actors are unnecessary. A few simple items may be suggested by students. For example:

    Hats, scarves, or aprons can be used by major characters.

    A paper cutout can serve as a tie, button, or badge.

    Old clothing (borrowed from parents) can be used as warranted.

Readers theatre holds the promise of "energizing" your classroom social studies curriculum, stimulating your library program, and fostering an active and deeper engagement of students in all the dynamics of books and literature. For both classroom teachers and librarians its benefits are enormous and its implications endless.

REFERENCES

Fredericks, Anthony D. *Frantic Frogs and Other Frankly Fractured Folktales for Readers Theatre*. Westport, CT: Teacher Ideas Press, 1993.

———. *Mother Goose Readers Theatre for Beginning Readers*. Westport, CT: Teacher Ideas Press, 2007.

———. *Nonfiction Readers Theatre for Beginning Readers*. Westport, CT: Teacher Ideas Press, 2007.

———. *Readers Theatre for American History*. Westport, CT: Teacher Ideas Press, 2001.

———. *Science Fiction Readers Theatre*. Westport, CT: Teacher Ideas Press, 2002.

———. *Silly Salamanders and Other Slightly Stupid Stories for Readers Theatre*. Westport, CT: Teacher Ideas Press, 2000.

———. *Tadpole Tales and Other Totally Terrific Treats for Readers Theatre*. Westport, CT: Teacher Ideas Press, 1997.

The First Thanksgiving

SOCIAL STUDIES CONCEPT

Nation

SUMMARY

This script offers students an opportunity to discover the roots of a favorite American holiday—Thanksgiving. This is done through a description made to a student (Assad) from another country in which Thanksgiving is not practiced. As a result students have an opportunity to view this traditional American holiday through the eyes of a child from another country.

SOCIAL STUDIES DISCIPLINES

Sociology, economics, history

NCSS THEMATIC STRANDS

Culture; Time, Continuity, and Change; Production, Distribution, and Consumption

CRITICAL THINKING QUESTIONS

1. If you could ask Assad one question, what would it be?
2. What do you think he found most unusual about Thanksgiving?
3. What other traditional holidays might immigrants not understand?
4. How could you help someone from another country understand a holiday such as the Fourth of July, President's Day, or Labor Day?
5. What American holidays do you have difficulty understanding?

The First Thanksgiving

STAGING: There is no narrator for this script. All of the characters may stand at individual music stands or be seated on stools. They may wish to move around or stay in one place. Make clear to students that "Assad" is a student from another country—a country that has holidays that are different from those celebrated in the United States. In "Assad's" native country there is no Thanksgiving holiday.

		Assad X		
	Michael X		Sarah X	
Cindy X				Tyrone X

TYRONE: Hey, Assad, welcome to the United States. And. welcome to our class. I think you are going to like it here.

ASSAD: Thank you very much. The United States is a special place. It is very different from the country I grew up in.

CINDY: How is it different?

ASSAD: Your buildings all look different. The people who live here wear different kinds of clothes. And, your school is different from the one I used to go to.

SARAH: How was your school different?

ASSAD: I went to a school that had only three rooms. We did not have a blackboard. And, we did not have all the books that you have here.

MICHAEL: It sure sounds like it was really different.

ASSAD: Yes. I also know that in the United States there are different holidays. There are lots of holidays here.

TYRONE: You're right. Holidays help us remember special people. They also help us remember special times in our history.

CINDY: That's right. Holidays are times that everyone celebrates together. When we celebrate we do special things. We do them with our family or with our friends.

ASSAD: Tell me about the holiday you call Thanksgiving.

MICHAEL: O.K. You see, many years ago . . . .

SARAH: . . . It was more than 400 years ago.

MICHAEL: That's right. 400 years ago a group of people left England. They sailed across the Atlantic Ocean to come to this land. They were called Pilgrims.

ASSAD: Why did they leave England?

TYRONE: They left because the king didn't like their religion. They wanted to practice their religion in a different way. But, the king wouldn't let them. So, they left and came here.

ASSAD: That happens in my country, too. Some people think their religion is best. Other people think their religion is best. Sometimes they fight about it.

CINDY: Well, the pilgrims didn't want to fight. So, they came here.

SARAH: When they got here they discovered Indians living nearby. The Indians were friendly. They taught the Pilgrims how to grow food. They learned how to grow corn and other vegetables.

TYRONE: Then, in the fall they gathered all those vegetables. They were very thankful for all the food they had.

MICHAEL: They were so thankful that they all decided to celebrate.

CINDY: Yeah. The women cooked cornbread and fish stew. It took about three days to cook all the food. The men hunted some turkeys. And the kids gathered berries and nuts.

SARAH: And, don't forget the Indians. The Indians came, too. They brought some deer meat. They also brought some wild turkeys.

MICHAEL: So, everyone sat around and ate all that food. The Pilgrims and Indians ate together. It was a big celebration.

ASSAD: We have celebrations in my country with lots of food, too.

TYRONE: Well, this celebration was a special one. It was the first Thanksgiving. People were very thankful for the food they had.

SARAH: And, we have been celebrating Thanksgiving ever since. It is always the last Thursday in November.

CINDY: Yeah, the whole country gives thanks for what we have.

ASSAD: That is very interesting. I like your holiday called Thanksgiving. But, you know what?

ALL: What?

ASSAD: I am just like the Pilgrims. Because I am thankful to be in the United States. This is my new country.

Adapted from Anthony D. Fredericks, *Nonfiction Readers Theatre for Beginning Readers* (Westport, CT: Teacher Ideas Press, 2007).

Three Ways of Living

SOCIAL STUDIES CONCEPT

City and country

SUMMARY

Communities come in all shapes and sizes—from very large to very small. Most communities are designated as urban, suburban, or rural. While those categories are broadly defined, they help students understand that this country is a tapestry of different living environments, each with its own distinctive personality.

SOCIAL STUDIES DISCIPLINES

Sociology, political science, geography

NCSS THEMATIC STRANDS

People, Places, and Environment; Civic Ideals and Practices

CRITICAL THINKING QUESTIONS

1. What type of community do you live in?
2. If you could live in any community you wanted, which one would you choose?
3. What did you like most about each of the three communities?
4. What did you like least?

Three Ways of Living

STAGING: The narrator should be standing off to the side and in back of the other players. The three actors can be seated on stools or chairs throughout this script.

Narrator X			
	Urban X	Suburban X	Rural X

NARRATOR: Ladies and gentlemen, welcome to our panel discussion today. We've invited three very special guests to be with us today. We've asked each one of them to talk about themselves. As you can see by their signs they each represent a different way to live. First, we have Urban. Next we have Suburban. And, finally, we have Rural. Let's get started with Urban. Excuse me, sir, can you tell us a little about yourself?

URBAN: Yes, thank you. I'm actually the biggest of the three of us here. I'm what is known as a large, large community. Often thousands and thousands of people will live in me. Sometimes it may be millions and millions of people.

NARRATOR: Wow, that's a lot of people. Can you give our audience some examples?

URBAN: Sure. The largest of me is New York City with more than 8 million people. Then there's Los Angeles, with millions and millions of people. And, of course, there's Chicago up on Lake Michigan. They have a couple of million people. And down in Texas there's the city of Dallas, which has a whole bunch of people, too.

NARRATOR: So, it seems as though one of the things you're most known for is all the people that you have.

URBAN: You got that right!

NARRATOR: What else can you tell us about yourself?

URBAN: I also have lots of tall buildings—what you folks would call skyscrapers. There are lots and lots of businesses in these tall buildings. Lots and lots of people go to work in these buildings, too.

NARRATOR: Doesn't it get noisy there?

URBAN: Yeah, that's one of the things I really don't like. There's always a lot of traffic, a lot of cars, buses, and trucks all over the place. Of course, I have lots and lots of roads, streets, and freeways for all the transportation to travel on. And all that traffic sure does make a lot of noise.

NARRATOR: It sure sounds like a busy place.

URBAN: Yes, it is. There's always something going on. It's always busy. Busy, busy, busy.

NARRATOR: Well, thank you. Now, I'm wondering if we could ask Suburban to share a little information.

SUBURBAN: I'd love to. You see, I'm sorta like my friend Urban, but I'm a little different. You see I'm usually smaller than an urban area. I'm like the area that surrounds an urban area. Sure, I have lots of shopping malls, movie theaters, stores, and other things, but I'm not as noisy as my friend there [points].

NARRATOR: How else are you different?

SUBURBAN: There are lots of commuters inside me. Commuters are people who live in one place and drive to another place to work. Because there are lots of commuters, there are also lots of streets for the commuters to travel on. I also have lots of houses and housing developments.

NARRATOR: So, you are a special place.

SUBURBAN: Yes, lots of people like to live in me because I have lots of places in which they can live. There are lots of neighborhoods and lots of different kinds of communities. And, of course, there are lots of shopping malls!

NARRATOR: Well, thank you. Let's turn now to our third and final guest, Rural. Please tell us about yourself.

RURAL: Thank you very much. I'm not at all like my two friends here. There are no large buildings, big housing developments, or busy streets where I am. I'm usually pretty quiet. I'm really spread out. My roads may be far apart and my houses may be far apart, too.

NARRATOR: It sounds like you are quieter than these other two.

RURAL: Usually I am. The houses are apart from each other and there are also farms and ranches where I am. Yeah, there are usually lots of farms. The farms may grow cotton, corn, vegetables, apples, and a thousand other kinds of food. In fact, most of the food that those people in Urban and Suburban eat comes from me.

NARRATOR: What else can you tell us?

RURAL: Well, I have stores and banks and restaurants and hardware stores just like you'd find in Urban and Suburban. It's just that there aren't as many of them. They're sorta far apart from each other. But that's the way we like it. Lots and lots of wide open spaces. Lots and lots of wide open land. We've got a lot of room out here.

NARRATOR: Well, thank you all three. We've learned something new about all of you. Hopefully we'll be able to use that new knowledge in some way. Maybe that new knowledge will help us make some decisions about where we might want to live during our lives. Thank you again for sharing your time and your information.

ALL: You're welcome!

A Conversation with Thomas Jefferson

SOCIAL STUDIES CONCEPT

Nation

SUMMARY

This readers theatre script provides youngsters with insight into the drafting of the Declaration of Independence. They have an opportunity to "look into" the mind of one of the primary architects of that document and the reasons for its existence. Here, students take on the roles of the actual participants.

SOCIAL STUDIES DISCIPLINES

Sociology, political science, history

NCSS THEMATIC STRANDS

Time, Continuity, and Change; Individuals, Groups, and Institutions; Power, Authority, and Government; Civic Ideals and Practices

CRITICAL THINKING QUESTIONS

1. If you were a reporter, what question would you like to ask Thomas Jefferson?
2. Why is the Declaration of Independence so important?
3. What was the most challenging question Mr. Jefferson had to answer in this interview?
4. Have you ever wanted to declare your independence from anything?
5. What would you have found most interesting about living during these times?

A Conversation with Thomas Jefferson

STAGING: The narrator can be placed at a podium or lectern near the front of the staging area. The 3 reporters should be standing. Thomas Jefferson can be seated on a stool.

	Reporter 1 X	
Thomas Jefferson X		Reporter 2 X
Reporter 3 X		
	Narrator X	

NARRATOR: The time is 1775. The Revolutionary War has begun. The colonists are angry at the laws being imposed on them by England. They feel they are being unfairly treated and unfairly ruled. The colonists feel they should be able to pass their own laws. King George of England thinks otherwise.

The congress decides to tell the king in a public letter that the colonies now consider themselves independent. The job of writing this Declaration of Independence was given to a young lawyer from Virginia, Thomas Jefferson.

As we look in on this scene, Mr. Jefferson has just completed drafting the Declaration of Independence. In this fictionalized scene, he is being interviewed by 3 newspaper reporters.

REPORTER 1: Mr. Jefferson, I'm Benjamin Bonnely from the *Patriot News*. Can you tell us, please, what you and Benjamin Franklin, Robert Livingston, John Adams, and Roger Sherman hope to accomplish by writing this so-called Declaration of Independence?

JEFFERSON: Certainly, Mr. Bonnely. One purpose in writing this document was to tell the world the reasons why the colonists were rebelling.

REPORTER 2: Mr. Jefferson, Patrick Engalls from the *Colonist's Gazette*. Tell me, sir, why exactly are the colonists rebelling against the king of England? Hasn't England provided the colonists with materials and supplies enough to sustain them?

JEFFERSON: Well, you see, it's not as easy as all that. You remember back in 1754 when England and France were fighting over the lands in the Ohio River Valley?

REPORTER 2: Yes.

JEFFERSON: Well, that war, what you reporters called the French and Indian War, lasted for nearly 9 years. It was an expensive war for both sides. The English ran up large debts as a result of the war. The king of England thought that the colonists should help pay for the war and so he levied taxes on the colonists. Up until that point the colonists had paid taxes to their colonial governments, but now they were being asked to pay taxes to an overseas government.

REPORTER 3: Sir, I'm Cecil Randolph from the Freedom Press. Sir, wasn't there another reason why the colonists began to have problems with the English?

JEFFERSON: Well, yes. After the war, the English wanted the colonists to stay out of Indian lands. By keeping the colonists away from those lands, the English would not need to protect settlements with their soldiers.

That did not stop the colonists. They went into Indian lands and began to settle there. Unfortunately, there were many battles between the settlers and the Indians. The settlers called for help from the English, but help never came. Instead the English passed laws forbidding any settlement west of the Proclamation Line of 1763.

REPORTER 1: I suppose that law angered the colonists.

JEFFERSON: Indeed it did. And there were other laws passed by the British that angered colonists. One was the Stamp Act, which made colonists pay a tax on every letter they wrote or every newspaper they bought.

REPORTER 2: I imagine that that was not a very popular tax.

JEFFERSON: Correct. In fact, between 1765 and this year England imposed many taxes on the colonies and then sent soldiers here to make sure that everyone paid their taxes to the mother country.

REPORTER 3: What was done about those taxes, sir?

JEFFERSON: There were many boycotts. People refused to buy goods that were made in England. They refused to buy English cloth and English tea and English paper.

REPORTER 1: But didn't the colonists know that a government needs to raise taxes in order to pay for the services it provides to its citizens?

JEFFERSON: Yes, that's right. The colonists did not have a problem with the question of taxation—they knew that taxes were necessary. The problem was that the taxes were being imposed by a foreign government who had no interest in the colonies other than the raising of money. The colonists believed that taxes should only be imposed by elected representatives of the people—representatives who had the best interests of the people at heart.

REPORTER 2: Isn't that what is meant by "taxation without representation?"

JEFFERSON: Yes. The colonists didn't want their money going overseas to finance another government. They believed that their money should stay here, in the colonies, and should be used for the betterment of the colonies.

REPORTER 3: Wasn't it shortly after that that the Revolutionary War began?

JEFFERSON: Yes, since the battles at Concord, Lexington, and Bunker Hill the English and Americans have been in a full scale war. This Revolutionary War is an action by Americans that they do not like the way they are being governed. It is also a reaction by the English that they have the authority to govern a colony or group of colonies anyway they see fit.

REPORTER 1: During the early part of this Revolutionary War you and Benjamin Franklin, Robert Livingston, John Adams, and Roger Sherman met in Philadelphia, didn't you?

JEFFERSON: Yes, we were there for a meeting of the Second Continental Congress. During that meeting we wrote a letter to King George asking him to repeal the laws that we felt were unjust. As you may recall, he refused to do so.

REPORTER 2: So that was what precipitated this Declaration of Independence?

JEFFERSON: Yes, as Mr. Bonnely had stated earlier, we wish to tell the king that we don't like what he is doing and that we want our independence from England. We want to tell him and the rest of the world why we are rebelling and the liberties that we felt we should be granted.

REPORTER 3: So, tell us Mr. Jefferson, what's in the Declaration of Independence?

JEFFERSON: There are three main parts to the document. The first part lists all the wrongs that have been done to the colonies by England.

REPORTER 1: What were some of the wrongs you put in the Declaration?

JEFFERSON: I stated that England had cut off our trade with the rest of the world. I stated that England had taxed us unfairly and without our approval. And, I wrote that England did not allow us to elect our own representatives.

REPORTER 2: I imagine that you knew that those kinds of statements would anger the king.

JEFFERSON: Yes, I was well aware of that. But, more important, it was necessary to let the king and the world know that we had been unfairly treated and unfairly ruled.

REPORTER 3: What was the second major part of the Declaration of Independence?

JEFFERSON: This part may have been the most important part of all. Basically it says that we did not wish to be ruled by a king. It said that, as a people, we had certain rights that could not be controlled or governed by any king.

REPORTER 1: What were some of the rights you talked about?

JEFFERSON: Here is what I wrote in the Declaration: "We hold these truths to be self-evident: That all men are created equal; that they are endowed by their Creator with certain unalienable rights; that among these are life, liberty, and the pursuit of happiness."

REPORTER 2: Those are very powerful words, Mr. Jefferson.

JEFFERSON: Yes, they are meant to be. I believe that every human being has rights that cannot be controlled or taken away by any other human being. And people can and should oppose anyone who takes away those rights—even if that person is a king.

REPORTER 3: What else did you put in the Declaration of Independence?

JEFFERSON: The last part of the document was a declaration of war against England. We believed that the time for compromise with England had passed. If England would not grant us our rights, then it was time for us to take our rights.

REPORTER 1: This seems to be a most important document . . . a most unusual document.

JEFFERSON: Indeed it is! It is a document that guarantees certain rights and makes provisions for obtaining those rights.

REPORTER 2: What happens now?

JEFFERSON: The Declaration of Independence will be presented to the Second Continental Congress for a vote.

NARRATOR: The Declaration of Independence was presented to Congress on June 28, 1776. However, before it was approved the delegates decided to cut out the part that blamed George III for the slave trade. Delegates from slave states did not want to threaten slave owners who were both rich and powerful. After that, events moved quickly and Congress adopted the Declaration of Independence on July 4, 1776. Since then, the Declaration of Independence has been a model of government for people all over the world. Today, more than 200 years after its signing, it is still a powerful and effective document.

Adapted from Anthony D. Fredericks, *Readers Theatre for American History* (Westport, CT: Teacher Ideas Press, 2001).

All Together Now

SOCIAL STUDIES CONCEPT

Communities and neighborhoods

SUMMARY

This script provides students with a basic introduction to communities—what they are and how they function. Students need to understand that communities have several elements and several functions. While they may take their own community for granted, children must comprehend the values of their respective communities to their daily lives.

SOCIAL STUDIES DISCIPLINES

Sociology, political science, economics

NCSS THEMATIC STRANDS

Individuals, Groups, and Institutions; Production, Distribution, and Consumption; Civic Ideals and Practices

CRITICAL THINKING QUESTIONS

1. What are some things you like about the community in which you live?
2. What are some things you would like to change?
3. What are three different services offered in your local community?
4. Why do people enjoy living in communities?
5. If you could live in any community in the United States, where would it be?

All Together Now

STAGING: Each of the individuals should be standing or seated in a permanent position. The narrator moves from person to person with a fake or imaginary microphone. You may wish to designate the narrator as a reporter for one of your local TV stations.

Person 1 X		Person 2 X
	Narrator X	
Person 3 X		Person 4 X

NARRATOR: We are standing on the street looking at all the people. There seems to be many different people in this town. I'm hoping some of them can help me. Excuse me, can you answer a question for me?

PERSON 1: I'd be happy to.

NARRATOR: Well, can you tell me what a community is?

PERSON 1: It's been a long time since I was in school, but here goes. A community is a place where people live, work, and play.

PERSON 2: And, don't forget one of the most important things about a community.

NARRATOR: What's that?

PERSON 2: People who live in a community depend on one another in many ways.

NARRATOR: What do you mean?

PERSON 3: Maybe I can help. You see I may need some lumber to build a house. I can go to a store that sells lumber.

The person working in that store is helping me by providing me with something that I need. In this case, it's lumber.

PERSON 4: You're right. Let's say that I need some chocolate chip ice cream. I mean, I really, really need some chocolate chip ice cream. Since I don't have any at home, I can go to the grocery store. Somebody there will sell me some chocolate chip ice cream. Yum, yum, yum. That person is helping me. Or, I depend on that person to sell me something I want.

NARRATOR: So, a community is where people sell things?

PERSON 3: It's actually more than that. It's also where people provide services.

NARRATOR: What do you mean by that?

PERSON 1: Well, let's say you had a washing machine that didn't work. You don't know how to fix washing machines. So, you call somebody to come to your house. That person then fixes the broken washing machine.

PERSON 2: Or, let's say that your car is really dirty. You can take it to a car wash. Somebody there will wash the car for you.

NARRATOR: Oh, I get it. People in a community provide services for other people in the same community.

PERSON 4: That's right! A community is made up of people who sell things. And, a community is made up of people who provide services.

NARRATOR: What are some of the other services in a community?

PERSON 3: A school is a service that every community has. A library is a service in many communities. Stores, gas stations, banks, hardware stores, hospitals, police and firefighters are all community services.

PERSON 1: There's one more thing that every community has.

NARRATOR: What's that?

PERSON 1: Most communities have people who make the rules. They have people who make the laws for the community.

PERSON 2: The rules or laws are important. They make sure everyone does the right thing. They make sure everyone is safe and protected.

PERSON 3: Yeah, there are rules for traffic in the community. There are rules about littering and pollution. There are rules for noise. There are rules for . . . .

NARRATOR: . . . It seems like there are lots of rules in a community.

PERSON 4: It may seem that way. Actually, the rules are there so everyone is treated the same. Everyone is protected.

PERSON 1: But, the best thing is that people are always around to help. If someone is sick, there are people to help. If a terrible storm damages property, there's someone to help. If someone is handicapped or needs a special service, there is always someone around to help.

NARRATOR: O.K., now I get it. A community is people helping people.

PERSON 1: Right. And, it's a place where people live . . . .

PERSON 2: . . . and work . . . .

PERSON 3: . . . and play . . . .

PERSON 4: . . . and share.

Adapted from Anthony D. Fredericks, *Nonfiction Readers Theatre for Beginning Readers* (Westport, CT: Teacher Ideas Press, 2007).

The Shapiros' New Adventure

SOCIAL STUDIES CONCEPT

World

SUMMARY

Many people have come to the United States as immigrants. They have come for many reasons—political, religious, and social. In fact, that immigration process is alive and well, as may be indicated by the number of recent immigrants in any elementary classroom. This script allows students to experience the joys and fears of this process firsthand.

SOCIAL STUDIES DISCIPLINES

Sociology, political science, geography, history

NCSS THEMATIC STRANDS

Time, Continuity, and Change; Individual Development and Identity; Civic Ideals and Practices

CRITICAL THINKING QUESTIONS

1. What fears would you have about moving to a new country?
2. Which person in this script is most like you? Why?
3. How would this story have been different if the children had not had their parents with them?
4. What question would you like to ask the Shapiros?
5. What did you learn about immigration that you didn't know before?

The Shapiros' New Adventure

STAGING: The narrator can sit on a stool or stand at the rear of the staging area. The four main characters can be standing or may be seated on stools. If possible, hang an old sheet in the background with waves painted on it to make it seem as though all the action is taking place on a large ship.

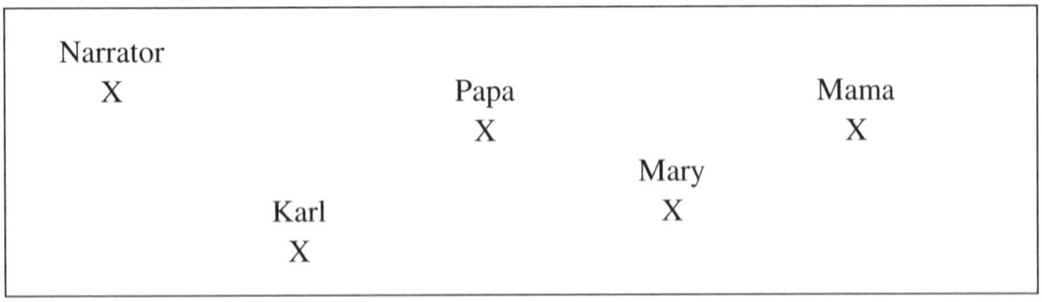

Narrator X		Papa X		Mama X
	Karl X		Mary X	

NARRATOR: The year is 1892. Thousands of people in eastern and southern Europe are flocking to the shores of America to seek new land, religious freedom, and political independence.

Most of these immigrants are from southern and eastern Europe, primarily from Italy, Poland, Russia, and Hungary. People in these regions of the world are facing economic disaster. Lots of unemployment, overpopulated cities, and unproductive agricultural techniques are spurring many people to travel to "The Land of Plenty"—the United States. Many people suffer religious persecution as well. Jews, for example, are forbidden to own land, engage in certain trades, or move out of areas that have been set aside for them. As a result, there is widespread poverty and widespread discrimination. Many immigrants see the United States as a place of personal safety, religious freedom, and economic opportunity

One such family is the Shapiros (a fictitious family). The Shapiros are from Russia and because they are Jewish they have suffered a great deal of persecution. Their beliefs have not been tolerated and they find their life more and more difficult each day. They have heard of a new land—a land where there is plenty of space and plenty of freedom. This new land is America. It is a land of both promise and opportunity. After many weeks of thinking, the Shapiros decide to set sail for this new land—leaving behind everything they have known.

As we look in on the Shapiros, they are on a large steamship bound for America. They are hopeful, yet still worried.

MARY: Papa, tell me again about this new land. What is it like?

PAPA: It is a land of opportunity, daughter. It is a land where people can find work, where they can find good housing, and where families can be together.

MARY: But, I am still frightened, father. I am leaving all my friends behind. We are leaving our village behind. We are leaving our home for a place we know little about.

MAMA: Rest easy, child. We are all frightened. We are all a little unsure of what lies before us. Just look around. Over there [points] are the Krinsky's. An old grandmother and seven children in the family and they, too, have decided to sail to America. Do you not think they are as frightened as we are?

KARL: And look over there [points]—the Paduks who have left a profitable dress making business to go live in

America. We are all leaving what we know. We are all leaving that with which we are familiar. We are all travelers on an unknown sea . . . not knowing what we will find or where we will live.

PAPA: You are right, son. We have all—every one of us on this ship—given up our heritage, our memories, our friends and relatives to go and live a better life. Yes, we do not know what that life holds for us. But, we do know that it must be a life much better than the one we leave. There must be a carpenter's job for me so I may put bread on our table. There must be a seamstress's job for your mother to help us pay the rent. And there must be good schools for both of you [points to the two children] to learn English and to do math.

MARY: Oh, Papa, you are always thinking the best. But, I am still scared. We do not know the people in this new land, we do not know their ways, and we do not know their language. What will they think of us? What will they say about us?

MAMA: Your papa and I are scared, too, my child. It is a big adventure for everyone. There are many things we do not know. There are many things we will need to learn. There are many things that await us.

NARRATOR: The trip from Europe to the United States is not easy. Besides the cost of the trip, the difficulties of travel make the journey even more difficult. Many immigrants have to book passage in *steerage*. This is a section of the ship set aside for people who pay the lowest fares. Generally, the accommodations are crowded, dirty, and uncomfortable.

The Shapiros are about halfway through the trip. The conditions on board ship are barely tolerable. Word filters through the immigrants that there have been some deaths due to the crowded and unsanitary conditions.

KARL: Papa, I have just heard about another family in steerage. The word is that two of their children have died from high fever.

PAPA: I have heard that, too. It is very crowded in here and I am sure that it is not as sanitary as we would like it to be.

MAMA: I'm afraid that there might be others who will not be able to see the new land. There will be other deaths and other burials at sea. This is not an easy journey for anyone.

KARL: Why do so many have to die? Why is this journey so long and so dangerous? I do not like the bad food we have to eat or the dirty beds we have to sleep in. I am afraid that one or more of us will get very sick. This is not what I thought the journey would be like.

MARY: I, too, am frightened. I do not like this ship or the people who run it. I do not trust them and they seem not to notice the passengers. We are like baggage to them.

MAMA: Do not worry so, child. In a short time we shall be docking in our new country—our new land—and then everything will be all right. Just be patient, my child. Just be patient.

NARRATOR: Upon their arrival in the United States all immigrants had to be checked for any criminal records or communicable diseases. This processing took place at Ellis Island in New York Harbor. Ellis Island is next to the Statue of Liberty, which was a symbol of hope for a better life for many immigrants.

It is now nearing the end of the voyage and the Shapiros, like most of the immigrants on board the ship are eager to see their new land. Excitement is high and conversation is lively as the ship nears New York Harbor.

MAMA: You Uncle Lucas wrote to us of New York City and told us that we would sail into the harbor and pass by the great statue of the famous lady.

MARY: Famous Lady?

MAMA: Yes, she is the lady they call Lady Liberty. I believe that Uncle Lucas called her the Statue of Liberty. [reflects] Liberty . . . ah, what a sweet word!

MARY: Then what, Mama, then what?

MAMA: Then we will get off the ship at a place called Ellis Island. It is a place where all new people to America arrive. There will be many of us there—many new adventurers, many new travelers, and many new explorers from all over the world.

PAPA: We will be with many freedom-loving people the world over—people seeking a new life like us.

KARL: I have heard that we will be given new names . . . American names . . . a new family name.

PAPA: Perhaps. But we will become Americans. And most important, we will become free. We will be free of the tyrants of our old land. We will be free of the persecution we faced every day. We will be free of the poor land of our ancestors. We will be free! We will be Americans . . . free Americans!

MARY: I am still anxious, Papa.

PAPA: So am I, dear Mary. And so is your Mama. And so is your brother.

MAMA: Yes, my child, we are all anxious. But we are also filled with hope. And that hope and our faith will help us make good in our new land.

PAPA: We will survive and we will succeed. It will not be easy and there may be difficult times ahead, but we will live a better life.

MARY: I hope you are right, Papa, I hope you are right.

KARL: So do I, so do I.

NARRATOR: A few days later, on a misty chilly morning, the ship sails into New York Harbor. They pass by the Statue of Liberty—their first view of their new country. A short time later the ship docks at Ellis Island. There, along with 1200 other passengers, the Shapiros set foot on a new land—a new homeland. There are no promises here—only possibilities. Just like the other adventurers with whom they have traveled the past two weeks, there are lots of questions and lots of unknowns. But there is also lots of hope. It is with that hope that the Shapiros begin the first day of their new life in a new country.

Most immigrants, just like the Shapiros, have to adjust to life in their new land. Most immigrants settle in the cities because that's where most of the jobs are. Others settle on farms and take up a lifestyle that they were accustomed to in their old country. Many immigrants settle in communities made up of people from the same area of origin. This provides them with opportunities to practice familiar celebrations and customs. It is a new land, but one filled with old traditions.

Adapted from Anthony D. Fredericks, *Readers Theatre for American History* (Westport, CT: Teacher Ideas Press, 2001).

Day of the Wave

NOTE: This script is based on the book *The Tsunami Quilt: Grandfather's Story* by Anthony D. Fredericks, which is profiled on pages 127–130 of this resource book. It illustrates how a single book can be used to develop an accompanying readers theatre script. Both teachers and librarians will find numerous opportunities to develop readers theatre scripts from other examples of children's literature profiled throughout *Much More Social Studies Through Children's Literature*.

SOCIAL STUDIES CONCEPT

States and regions

SUMMARY

On April 1, 1946, shortly after sunrise, a series of giant waves devastated the northern coast of the island of Hawai'i. Traveling 2,300 miles from the Aleutian Islands in less than five hours, the waves struck without warning and claimed 159 lives. Of all the states in the United States, Hawai'i is most prone to natural disasters—hurricanes, tsunamis, volcanic eruptions, earthquakes, and oceanic storms have long been a part of Hawaiian history. There is also a human impact as well.

SOCIAL STUDIES DISCIPLINES

Geography, history

NCSS THEMATIC STRANDS

Time, Continuity, and Change; People, Places, and Environment; Science, Technology, and Society

CRITICAL THINKING QUESTIONS

1. What did you enjoy most about this story?
2. Have you ever been in a situation in which you were really scared?
3. What else would you like to learn about tsunamis?
4. What question would you like to ask Kimo?
5. Is this story similar to any other story you have heard?

Day of the Wave

STAGING: The narrator should be placed off to the side and in front of the other actors. The actors should be seated on stools or chairs.

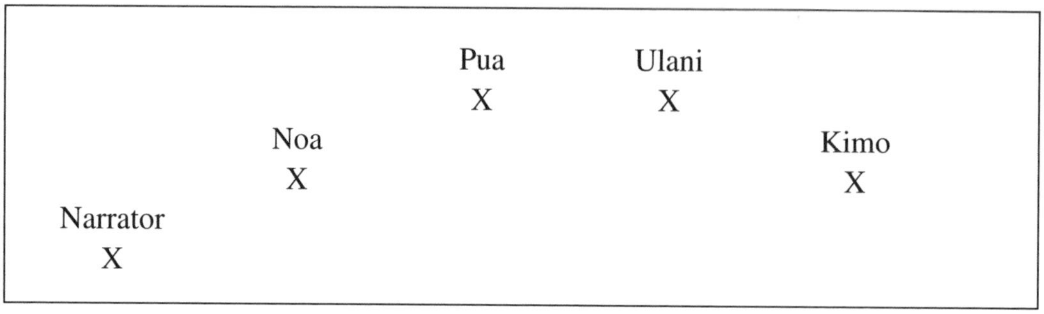

		Pua	Ulani	
		X	X	
	Noa			Kimo
	X			X
Narrator				
X				

NARRATOR: One of the ancient traditions of native Hawaiians is "Talking Story." It is one way Hawaiians preserve and share their history. More than just a factual history, it is often personal recollections of the members of a specific family; the funny anecdotes, humorous stories, and fond reminiscences about relatives that are shared during family gatherings. Because Hawaii is such a cultural melting pot, "talking story" is also a way of preserving qualities from each culture while blending them into a composite story. "Talking story" is similar to the conversations friends might have at a party.

NOA: So, Kimo, I understand that your grandfather was a very special person. You say that he was a big influence in your life.

KIMO: Yes, my grandfather was my all-time best friend. He always took me fishing down at the ocean. We would sometimes take long walks along the shore. But, maybe the best times we had were when he told me stories.

PUA: What kind of stories did he tell you?

KIMO: He liked telling fishing stories the best. He had been a fisherman all his life and he used to tell fish tales whenever he could. Of course, as a fisherman, he was known to stretch the truth now and again. But, that was O.K., I still liked to hear him tell stories—especially the stories of long ago.

ULANI: Your grandfather sounds like a real neat guy. He must have had a lot of stories.

KIMO: Yes, but I think it was when he and I went down to Laupa-hoehoe every spring that I remember the most.

NARRATOR: Laupa-hoehoe (LAH-pah-hoy-hoy) is a small peninsula the juts out from the northern coast of the big island of Hawaii. It was formed by an eruption of Mauna Loa many thousands of years ago.

KIMO: Each spring my grandfather and I would walk along the shore. We never said much on those special visits. But, each time my grandfather would walk over to a marble monument, lay his hands on the top, and look out over the sea.

NOA: Did he say anything to you?

KIMO: No, this was the only time in his life that I ever saw him so quiet.

PUA: Then, what?

KIMO: He said that one day he would tell me a story about this special place. He said the place was one of remembrance and also one of tragedy.

ULANI: What did he mean by that?

KIMO: I didn't know at the time. It wasn't until after my grandfather died that I learned what he meant.

NOA: What did he mean? What did he mean by a place of remembrance?

KIMO: Well, it was actually my father who told me the story. He said that many many years ago there was a school at Laupahoehoe. One day, all the kids were getting off the bus when they saw something happening to the ocean water.

PUA: What was happening?

KIMO: The water was moving away from the shore. There were lots of fish flapping on the sand.

ULANI: I think I know what's going to happen.

KIMO: Yes, there was a tsunami coming. Before anyone knew what happened, the waves of the tsunami rolled onto the land. They were big. They were fierce. They swept everything around like in a giant washing machine.

NARRATOR: A tsunami can race across an open ocean at 500 mph. When a tsunami nears shore it slows down very quickly and the water beneath the wave piles up. In a brief moment, a 2-foot-high wave at sea may be transformed into a 30-foot-high wave on the shore. Typically, there are several waves in a row—a tsunami wave train.

NOA: Was your grandfather there?

KIMO: Yes, he was. And so was his little brother. But he didn't know where his little brother was. My grandfather was on some high ground and as soon as he saw the tsunami hit he ran uphill as fast as he could go. But he didn't know where his brother was.

PUA: And then what happened, Kimo?

KIMO: My grandfather kept running and running uphill. All he could hear were people crying. Children and adults were screaming and crying. It was awful, he said.

ULANI: Did a lot of people die?

KIMO: Yes, when it was over 24 people had died. Students and teachers had all been caught in the power of the tsunami. It was terrible.

NOA: Don't tell me! Don't tell me!

KIMO: Yes, one of the people who was killed that day was my grandfather's little brother. He felt helpless, because there was nothing he could do to save him. He was gone forever.

PUA: So, is that why he went to Laupa-hoehoe every year?

KIMO: Yes, he wanted to honor the memory of his little brother. He wanted to remember his little brother in a special way.

ULANI: That is a sad story . . . a very sad story.

KIMO: Yes, and it is a story we should never forget. Because as my grandfather used to say, "The ocean gives, but it also takes."

NOA: What else, Kimo?

KIMO: Well, there is something else. But I cannot tell you. It is something you must see for yourself.

PUA: What is it?

KIMO: You must go to The Pacific Tsunami Museum in Hilo to see it for yourself. When you see it you will never be the same. It is something very special. It is something you will always remember. It will touch you in a very magical way.

ULANI: What is it?

NARRATOR: It is "The Tsunami Quilt." But, that is something for another story and another time. In the meantime, perhaps you will read the children's book about that story and about that time. The book is called *The Tsunami Quilt: Grandfather's Story*. It, too, is a story to remember.

Part IV
Activity Sheets

This section of the book includes a collection of activity sheets that can be used with a wide range of children's literature. Duplicate and distribute these to individuals, small groups, or an entire class. The sheets are not requirements for any single piece of children's literature, but rather are learning options that will help you extend and expand the learning experiences for the students with whom you work. They are generic in nature and can be used as extensions of the hands-on, minds-on activities for almost any trade book.

The sheets also provide extended opportunities for classroom teachers and school librarians to work in concert within a theme or a specific social studies topic. For example, a sheet may be duplicated and distributed by a classroom teacher for completion by students while visiting the library. By the same token, another sheet may be assigned by the school librarian for students to work on in the classroom as an extension of the week's library activities. Their intrinsic value for students will be determined by the collaborative spirit shared by teachers and librarians within and throughout the social studies curriculum.

1. **Literature Log I**—This sheet provides students with opportunities to think about a nonfiction book and to organize their thoughts into a systematic piece of writing. There are no right or wrong answers to any literature log. The logs can be used by individuals or small groups of students as a way to record information and thoughts about a particular book.

2. **Literature Log II**—This sheet can be used by students as a way to summarize information in a narrative or fiction book. Again, there are no right or wrong responses—but plenty of opportunities for additional research. You may find either literature log appropriate as a summary sheet for inclusion in each student's portfolio.

3. **Story Map**—This "organizer" helps students determine the essential elements of a well-crafted story. Not only can students focus on important details (such as setting, characters, and problem), but more important, students begin to see how these "parts"

of a story are woven together into a coherent whole. Students can complete and discuss a sheet after reading a selected trade book.

4. **Story Pyramid**—A story pyramid helps students focus on main characters, important settings, and the problem/solution of a selected piece of literature. It can be used with individual readers or may be presented as a group activity or guided reading lesson.

5. **Character Analysis Frame**—This sheet provides students with an opportunity to focus on the specific features, traits, or personality dynamics of a particular character within a story. You may wish to assign individual sheets for individual characters within a book.

6. **I Wonder . . .**—This sheet can be used with a wide range of social studies literature. It provides students with opportunities to think about the plot, characters, theme, setting, and point of view of both fiction and nonfiction works. After students complete a sheet, invite them to discuss their various reactions to a designated book.

7. **A Reader's Menu**—This sheet can be used with any of the books profiled in this resource or with any books you choose to share with students. You can duplicate the sheet and check off those activities you want a whole class, small group, or single individuals to pursue. This sheet provides you with a quick and easy way to individualize assigned activities for any one book. Students should also be afforded the opportunity to self-select activities that interest them.

8. **Author Study**—This sheet allows students to investigate a favorite author. Students have the option of working independently or with one or two partners. Depending on available time, you may wish to assign options or have students self-select an appropriate number of choices.

9. **Word by Word**—This sheet provides students with key words that can be used to describe a book or the impression the book made on the reader. Students get to select any five words and use those words in a written report about the book and its impact.

10. **Book by Book**—After completing a unit or study, you may wish to invite students to fill in this activity sheet. Students can think about the various books they have read over several days or weeks and match those titles with appropriate descriptions. Undoubtedly, students will think of more than one book for each description. That's O.K. They are welcome to write multiple titles in each blank. You may wish to post selected sheets on a classroom or library bulletin board.

Literature Log I

Name: ____ **Date:** ___________

Book Title: ____

Author: ____

Publisher: ____

Date of Publication: _________________________

Before Reading

I want to read this book because ____________________________________

____

Here's what I know about the topic: __________________________________

____

These are some questions I would like to ask before I read __________________

____

____

I think I will learn ____

____

During Reading

Here's what I'm learning as I read this book: ___________________________

____

This is what I do when I don't understand something in the book: _____________

____

I want to finish this book because ____________________________________

____

This is how I find answers to some of my questions: ______________________

____

After Reading

I think the author wrote this book because ______________________

____

I am satisfied with this book because ______________________

____

I can write a brief summary of the book: ______________________

____

____

____

____

____

There are questions I still need answers to: ______________________

____

____

I will find that information here: ______________________

____

Here's what I would like to say to the author: ______________________

____

____

Literature Log II

Name: ______________________________ **Date:** ____________________

Book Title: ____

Author: ____

My favorite part was ____

____

My least favorite part was ____

____

The central problem was ____

____

____

Some important words were ____

____

Words I need to learn are ____

____

My favorite character was ____

My least favorite character was _____________________________________

I didn't understand ____

I will never forget ____

I would recommend this book to _______________ because _______________

____

____

Story Map

Title: ____

Setting:

Characters: ____________________ ____________________

____________________ ____________________

____________________ ____________________

Problem:

Event 1: ____

Event 2: ____

Event 3: ____

Event 4: ____

Solution:

Theme: ____

Story Pyramid

Name: ____ **Date:** ________________

Line 1:	Name of a character
Line 2:	Two words describing the character
Line 3:	Three words describing the setting
Line 4:	Four words stating a problem
Line 5:	Five words describing the main event
Line 6:	Six words describing a second main event
Line 7:	Seven words describing a third main event
Line 8:	Eight words stating the solution to the problem

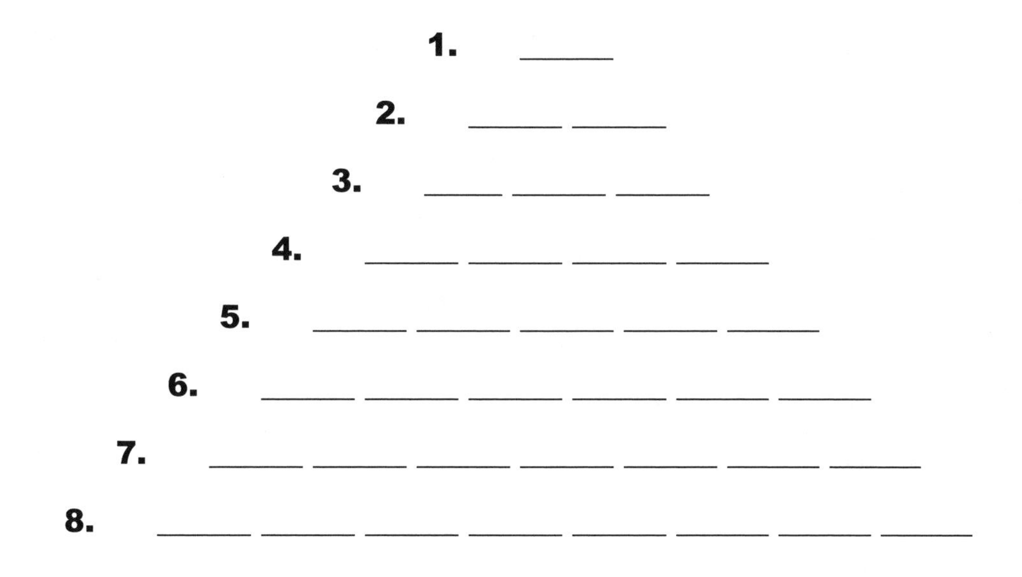

Character Analysis Frame

Name: ________________________________ **Date:** ________________

Book Title: ____

Author: ____

________________________________ is an important character in this story.

______________________________ is important because ____________

____

____

____

____.

Once, she/he ____

____

____

____.

Another time, ____

____

____

____.

I think that _______________________ is _________________________

because ____

____.

She/he is also ____

______________________________________ because ____________

____

____.

I Wonder . . .

Name: ______________________________________ **Date:** ____________

1. I wonder why . . .

2. Why did . . .

3. I really liked . . .

4. I didn't understand . . .

5. I don't believe . . .

6. I was surprised . . .

7. I was upset when . . .

8. I found myself thinking about . . .

9. When I finished the book, I thought . . .

10. I wish the author would . . .

A Reader's Menu

Name: ______________________________

Date: ______________

Book Title: ______________________________

Author: ______________________________

☐ Create a poster that "advertises" the book. What will encourage others to read that book?	☐ Create a 3-dimensional artistic display (diorama, mobile, etc.) of the characters, plot, and/or setting.	☐ Develop the story into a readers theatre presentation. Work with others to present the script.
☐ Create a Web page based on the book. Include information about the characters, plot, and author.	☐ Create a PowerPoint™ presentation that introduces the book to other students.	☐ Create a series of puppets that can be used to retell the story. Construct the puppets from classroom materials.
☐ Collect a series of artifacts that could be used as part of a storytelling experience.	☐ Develop the plot of the story into a newspaper article. Print it in a newspaper format.	☐ Create a list of thinking questions for other students to answer after reading the book.

Other Presentation Options:

☐ model
☐ storytelling
☐ book
☐ play
☐ DVD
☐ newspaper
☐ letter
☐ dictionary
☐ scale model
☐ salt map
☐ tabletop museum
☐ diorama
☐ video
☐ portfolio
☐ drama
☐ trivia quiz
☐ 3-sided display
☐ diary
☐ rebus story
☐ poll
☐ chart
☐ magazine
☐ time line
☐ CD
☐ guidebook
☐ scrapbook
☐ centers
☐ panel discussion
☐ poem
☐ puzzle
☐ pictograph
☐ advertisement
☐ slide show
☐ card file
☐ calendar
☐ music
☐ audiotape
☐ journal
☐ article
☐ story map
☐ graph
☐ map
☐ cartoon
☐ papier-mâché

Author Study

Name: ____________________

Date: ____________________

Author: ____________________

☐ Investigate (if available) the Web site of the author. What information did you find especially appealing?	☐ Prepare an annotated bibliography of the author's books.	☐ Prepare a biography of the author to share with other students. Present your information in a creative display.
☐ Create a poster or trifold display of the author and her/his books.	☐ Review an article about the author. Summarize the article and share it with other students.	☐ Read a review of one of the author's books and summarize it. What did you learn that you didn't know before?
☐ Write a newspaper article about the author and her/his books.	☐ Assemble a chronological listing of the author's books and describe how the author's work has changed over time.	☐ Read one or more of the author's books to other students. Solicit their reactions, comments, or evaluations.

Word by Word

Name: ______________________________ **Date:** ______________

Directions: There are certain words that can be used to describe a book or the impression that book has on a reader. Some of those words are listed in the squares below. Go through this chart and place a check mark in five individual boxes. Select those words you think would apply to your book. Then, use those five words in a report about the book. Be sure to use complete sentences.

Book Title: ____

☐ **question**	☐ **puzzle**	☐ **enjoyed**	☐ **favorite**	☐ **dislike**
☐ **detail**	☐ **ending**	☐ **author**	☐ **character**	☐ **setting**
☐ **wonder**	☐ **situation**	☐ **unknown**	☐ **fact**	☐ **purpose**
☐ **sense**	☐ **beginning**	☐ **location**	☐ **title**	☐ **satisfied**
☐ **wished**	☐ **time**	☐ **place**	☐ **simple**	☐ **great**

Book by Book

Name: ______________________________ **Date:** ______________

Directions: Read the first description in the left-hand column. Think of a book that matches that description and write its title in the space in the right-hand column. Complete the remainder of the chart in the same way.

Description	Book Title
I had a lot of unanswered questions when I finished reading this book.	
After reading this book I definitely want to read more books by this author.	
After reading this book I definitely want to read more about this topic/subject.	
I thought that the illustrations in this book were exceptional.	
This book really got me thinking about things I'd never thought of before.	
This book had lots and lots of details.	
I'm not sure I liked the ending to this book. If I were the author, I would have done something else.	
This book really made me use my imagination.	
This book had one of the strongest characters I've ever met.	
I don't think I would recommend this book to any of my friends.	
I would love to travel to the time or place of this book.	
This book is one of the best social studies books I've ever read.	

APPENDIX A

An Annotated Bibliography of Children's Literature

The number of books available in social studies is limitless. My own investigations led me to thousands of literature possibilities—many of which could be easily integrated into all aspects of the social studies curriculum. Obviously, no resource book this size could do justice to the scores of literature selections you can choose for your classroom or library program. I have therefore tried to provide you with a variety of possibilities—with an emphasis on the new and fascinating books available for every aspect of a social studies curriculum.

This appendix contains two annotated bibliographies. The first is a collection of trade books organized according to the seven basic concepts of all social studies curricula: self, family, communities and neighborhoods, city and country, states and regions, nation, and world. The second is a selection of trade books arranged according to the six major topics of social studies: geography, anthropology, sociology, political science, economics, and history. Any one book may, of course, encompass more than one concept as well as more than one topic. There are also many more books in your local bookstore or community library. In other words, the organization of books within each of the two bibliographies may be arbitrary and certainly arguable. Nevertheless, I hope these selections offer a plethora of potential literature selections for all areas of your social studies curriculum—no matter what its scope, sequence, or instructional emphasis. Both classroom teachers and school librarians will find much to savor here—and much to explore!

THE CONCEPTS OF SOCIAL STUDIES

Self

Beaumont, Karen. *I Like Myself!* New York: Harcourt, 2004.

A delightful story about a young girl who accepts herself for who she is no matter what the circumstances.

Bowen, Anne. *How Did You Grow So Big, So Soon?* Minneapolis, MN: Carolrhoda, 2003.

A curious boy learns how he grew into the child that he is today and anticipates his first day of school.

Cote, Nancy. *It's All About Me!* New York: G. P. Putnam's Sons, 2005.

A young boy grows up and learns how to adapt to his increasing family size.

Curtis, Jamie Lee. *It's Hard to Be Five: Learning How to Work My Control Panel*. New York: Joanna Cotler Books, 2004.

An amusing story about the challenges and benefits of being five years old as seen through the eyes of a young boy.

Drachman, Eric. *It's Me!* Los Angeles: Kidwick Books, 2004.

An imaginative young girl enjoys playing dress up, but also loves to be herself.

Falconer, Ian. *Olivia*. New York: Anne Schwartz Books, 2000.

Young Olivia keeps herself busy from the time she gets up until her mother makes her go to bed.

Medearis, Angela Shelf, and Michael Medearis. *Daisy and the Doll*. Middlebury: Vermont Folklore Center, 2000.

Based on a true story, this inspiring book discusses the strength and courage of a young African American girl.

Recorvits, Helen. *My Name Is Yoon*. New York: Frances Foster Books, 2003.

Yoon, a Korean girl, has just moved to America and learns to overcome some of her insecurities about her new country.

Richmond, Marianne. *Hooray for You!* Minneapolis, MN: Marianne Richmond Studios, 2001.

This book truly illustrates the uniqueness of every child.

Vaughan, Marcia. *Up the Learning Tree*. New York: Lee & Low Books, 2003.

A young slave is extremely determined to learn, even if that means taking great risks.

Family

Adoff, Arnold. *Black Is Brown Is Tan*. New York: HarperCollins, 2001.

A beautiful picture book about the many colors that make up an interracial family.

Browne, Anthony. *My Mom*. New York: Farrar, Straus & Giroux, 2005.

A story about the love that one child has for his mother.

Browne, Michael Dennis. *Give Her the River: A Father's Wish for His Daughter*. New York: Atheneum Books for Young Readers, 2004.

A father discusses the many things that he wishes his daughter to have.

Carlson, Nancy. *My Family Is Forever*. New York: Viking, 2004.

An adopted child shares her story and discusses the love that her family members have for one another.

Cox, Judy. *My Family Plays Music*. New York: Holiday House, 2003.

Talented family members differ in the various types of music that they play. However, they do share the love they have for one another.

Crystal, Billy. *I Already Know I Love You.* New York: HarperCollins, 2004.
A patient grandfather discusses the various things he is excited to experience and teach his future grandchild.

Desimini, Lisa. *My Beautiful Child.* New York: Blue Sky Press, 2004.
A touching story about the many things that parents want to show their children.

Downey, Roma. *Love Is a Family.* New York: HarperCollins, 2001.
A young girl is nervous about being the only one at Family Fun Night with a single parent.

Ericsson, Jennifer A. *Home to Me, Home to You.* New York: Little, Brown, 2005.
A daughter and father patiently await the return of their mother and wife, after she has been away for several days.

Karim, Roberta. *Faraway Grandpa.* New York: Henry Holt, 2004.
A moving story about the closeness of a granddaughter and her grandfather.

Communities and Neighborhoods

Brumbeau, Jeff. *The Quilt Makers Journey.* New York: Orchard Books, 2004.
An inspiring story about a girl who decides to leave the only village she ever knew.

Bunting, Eve. *Market Day.* New York: Joanna Cotler Books, 1996.
A story about a special day, called Market Day, which takes place in an Irish community on the first Thursday of every month.

Bunting, Eve. *Pop's Bridge.* New York: Harcourt, 2006.
A young boy watches his father work as he helps to build the Golden Gate Bridge.

Cummins, Julie. *Country Kid, City Kid.* New York: Henry Holt, 2002.
A wonderful look into two children's daily lives, one who lives in the city and the other who lives in the country.

Cunnane, Kelly. *For You Are a Kenyan Child.* New York: Anne Schwartz Book, 2006.
This book allows readers the opportunity to follow a young boy around Kenyan villages in Africa.

Gay, Libba Moore. *Miss Tizzy.* New York: Aladdin Paperbacks, 1998.
When Miss Tizzy falls ill, the children in her neighborhood come together to help her feel loved.

Grifalconi, Ann. *The Village of Round and Square Houses.* New York: Little, Brown, 1986.
In the unique village of Tos in the Cameroons, the women and children live in round houses and the men live in square houses.

San Souci, Robert D. *The Birds of Killingworth.* New York: Dial Books for Young Readers, 2002.

When the farmers in the town of Killingworth decide to rid the town of its birds, a young girl, a schoolmaster, and many neighborhood children devise a plan to save the birds and their town.

Taylor, Debbie A. *Sweet Music in Harlem.* New York: Lee & Low Books, 2004.

News spreads fast around the neighborhood of Harlem.

City and Country

Climo, Shirley. *City! San Francisco.* New York: Macmillan, 1990.

This book is a wonderful introduction to a city many adults feel is the most intriguing of any in the United States.

Gerstein, Mordicai. *The Man Who Walked Between the Towers.* Brookfield, CT: Roaring Brook Press, 2003.

An account of Philippe Petit, the man who walked on a tightrope between the twin towers.

Melmed, Laura Krauss. *New York, New York! The Big Apple from A to Z.* New York: HarperCollins, 2005.

Examines the many wonderful things that can be found throughout New York.

Neubecker, Robert. *Wow! City!* New York: Hyperion Books for Children, 2004.

A young girl takes a trip to a busy city with her father and observes her surroundings.

Ransom, Candice. *Liberty Street.* New York: Walker, 2003.

An intriguing story of a young slave in the city of Fredericksburg and her chance at freedom.

Soentpiet, Chris K. *Around Town.* New York: Lothrop, Lee & Shepard Books, 1994.

Toy shops on the sidewalks, underground railroads, and face painting are just a few of the things that can be found in a large city.

Steele, Philip. *A City Through Time: The Story of a City—From Ancient Colony to Vast Metropolis.* New York: DK, 2004.

This delightful picture book takes readers through the history and growth of a city.

Wellington, Monica. *Crepes by Suzette.* New York: Dutton Children's Books, 2004.

Readers have an opportunity to visit various places in the city of Paris with Suzette, a woman who makes crepes for people in the town.

States and Regions

Altman, Linda Jacobs. *The Legend of Freedom Hill*. New York: Lee & Low Books, 2000.
A young California girl has to find a way to dig enough gold to free her mother after she is captured.

Antle, Nancy. *Beautiful Land: A Story of the Oklahoma Land Rush*. New York: Puffin Books, 1997.
A family eagerly participates in the first Oklahoma land rush.

Bockenhauer, Mark H. *Our Fifty States*. Washington, DC: National Geographic, 2004.
A stunning book of pictures, maps, and information about the many states and regions of the United States.

Burgan, Michael. *The Trail of Tears*. Mankato, MN: Compass Point Books, 2001.
An informative book about the Cherokee Indians' removal from their homes, and their journey to Oklahoma.

Harrington, Janice N. *Going North*. New York: Melanie Kroupa Books, 2004.
An African American family travels from Alabama to Nebraska in hope of a better life.

Hopkinson, Deborah. *Apples to Oregon*. New York: Atheneum Books for Young Readers, 2004.
This book portrays the many challenges a family faces as they journey from Iowa to Oregon.

Kay, Verla. *Orphan Train*. New York: G. P. Putnam's Sons, 2003.
An excellent introduction to what life was like for the many orphans who experienced riding on the orphan trains.

MacLachlan, Patricia. *Sarah, Plain and Tall*. New York: HarperTrophy, 2004.
A Midwestern farmer places an ad in the paper requesting a bride, and Sarah from Maine responds.

Mortensen, Denise Dowling. *Ohio Thunder*. New York: Clarion Books, 2006.
Wonderfully depicted, a thunderstorm moves across an Ohio farm, disrupting a family's daily chores.

Nation

Bunting, Eve. *Dreaming of America: An Ellis Island Story*. Mahwah, NJ: BridgeWater Books, 2000.
An account of the journey of Annie Moore, the first immigrant to enter America through Ellis Island.

Cheney, Lynne. *A Is for Abigail: An Almanac of Amazing American Women*. New York: Simon & Schuster, 2003.

Many of the various women who had a positive impact on American history are portrayed throughout this book.

Cheney, Lynne. *America: A Patriotic Primer*. New York: Simon & Schuster, 2002.

Revisit U.S. history and what makes our nation one to be appreciated, through each letter of the alphabet.

Curlee, Lynn. *Liberty*. New York: Aladdin Paperbacks, 2000.

The Statue of Liberty from 1865 to the present as it becomes an important symbol to America.

DiPucchio, Kelly. *Liberty's Journey*. New York: Hyperion Books for Children, 2004.

An enjoyable story of the Statue of Liberty and the many things she sees on her journey across America.

Hopkinson, Deborah. *Under the Quilt of the Night*. New York: Atheneum Books for Young Readers, 2001.

Follow along on the journey of a group of runaways from slavery to freedom.

Jarrie, Martin. *ABC USA*. New York: Sterling Publishing, 2005.

Delightful illustrations highlighting many unique aspects of America.

Johnson, Angela. *A Sweet Smell of Roses*. New York: Simon & Schuster Books for Young Readers, 2005.

During the civil rights movement, African American adults and children played an important part in helping to establish equal rights.

Minor, Wendell. *Yankee Doodle America*. New York: G. P. Putnam's Sons, 2006.

A story about a journey along a colonial road from 1765 to 1783.

Ryan, Pam Munoz. *The Flag We Love*. Watertown, MA: Charlesbridge Publishing, 1996.

An inspiring text about the history surrounding the American flag.

World

Elvgren, Jennifer Riesmeyer. *Josias, Hold the Book*. Honesdale, PA: Boyds Mills Press, 2006.

A young boy, living in Haiti, is determined to find a way to make his bean crops grow.

Hoffelt, Jane E. *We Share One World*. Bellevue, WA: Illumination Arts, 2004.

This story illustrates the many things that we all share on this Earth.

Hoffman, Mary. *The Color of Home*. New York: Phyllis Fogelman Books, 2002.

A young boy tells a story of the attack that occurred in his native country—Somalia—and how he adjusted to his new home in America.

Jackson, Ellen. *It's Back to School We Go*. Brookfield, CT: Millbrook Press, 2003.
Describes the school experiences of children from 11 countries.

Lauber, Patricia. *How We Learned the Earth Is Round*. New York: HarperCollins, 1990.
This book examines all the great explorers of the world and their fabulous adventures.

Lewis, Patrick J. *Blackbeard the Pirate King*. Washington, DC: National Geographic, 2006.
The story of a mysterious pirate's journey across the seas.

Montanari, Donata. *Children Around the World*. Toronto: Kids Can Press, 2001.
Introduces 12 children from varying parts of the world, describing the many aspects and characteristics of the places they live.

Myers, Tim. *Basho and the River Stones*. Tarrytown, NY: Marshall Cavendish, 2004.
The intriguing tale of how Matsuo Basho became one of Japan's most inspired poets, and a great friend to the foxes of Fukagawa.

Nelson, Kadir. *He's Got the Whole World in His Hands*. New York: Dial Books for Young Readers, 2005.
The beautiful illustrations truly bring the words to life in this well-known song.

Shulevitz, Uri. *The Travels of Benjamin of Tudela: Through Three Continents in the Twelfth Century*. New York: Farrar, Straus & Giroux, 2005.
The story about the dangerous yet courageous journey of a Jewish traveler during the twelfth century.

Spier, Peter. *People*. New York: Doubleday Books for Young Readers, 1980.
A quick look into what makes our world so diverse.

THE DISCIPLINES OF SOCIAL STUDIES

Geography

Aardema, Verna. *Bringing the Rain to Kapiti Plain*. New York: Dial Press, 1981.
The story of the effects of a terrible drought on a region of Africa that lives and dies according to the amount of rainfall it receives.

Fritz, Jean. *Around the World in a Hundred Years: From Henry the Navigator to Magellan*. New York: PaperStar Group, 1998.
A fascinating account of many explorers who helped to discover and uncover parts of what was considered the unknown world.

Hurwitz, Laura, and Amanda Lumry. *Adventures of Riley: Safari in South Africa*. Bellevue, WA: Eaglemont Press, 2003.
Young Riley goes on an exhilarating African safari, where he has the opportunity to meet much magnificent native wildlife.

Jakobsen, Kathy. *My New York*. New York: Little, Brown, 2003.
Bright, colorful illustrations and a descriptive text take readers on a tour around the busy city of New York.

Leeuwen, Jean Van. *Bound for Oregon*. New York: Penguin Young Readers Group, 2003.
The journey of a family from Arkansas to Oregon in 1852.

Montanari, Donata. *Children Around the World*. Toronto: Kids Can Press, 2001.
Readers learn various aspects of how children live in other locations around the world.

Siebert, Diane. *Mojave*. New York: Thomas Y. Crowell, 1988.
The beauty and vastness of the Mojave Desert are wonderfully illustrated in this book about the best-known desert in the United States.

Siebert, Diane. *Rhyolite: The True Story of a Ghost Town*. New York: Clarion, 2003.
When two men discover gold in a town in Nevada, the population skyrockets, but only for a short period of time.

Yorinks, Arthur. *The Alphabet Atlas*. New York: Winslow Press, 1999.
Readers are provided with a few facts about each country.

Anthropology

Beeler, Selby B. *Throw Your Tooth on the Roof: Tooth Traditions from Around the World*. Boston: Houghton Mifflin, 2001.
A collection of traditions that children all around the world do with their teeth when they fall out.

Crandell, Rachel. *Hands of the Maya: Villagers at Work and Play*. New York: Henry Holt, 2002.
Experience a day in the life of a Mayan and how they worked to create and obtain their food, clothing, and a lot of the other things they needed in life.

Fox, Mem. *Whoever You Are*. New York: Harcourt, 2001.
This book discusses the differences among people around the world, as well as some of their similarities.

Harris, Nicholas. *Leap Through Time: The First Humans*. New York: Backpack Books, 2002.
Travel through a million years of history, following the evolution of human beings from cave people to modern people.

Hynes, Margaret. *The Best Book of Early People*. Boston: Kingfisher, 2003.
A fascinating look into our prehistoric ancestors and what they did to survive.

Martin, Rafe. *The Rough-Face Girl*. New York: G. P. Putnam's Sons, 1992.
A young girl does not allow her appearance to prevent her from seeing the beauty of her surroundings.

McGovern, Ann. *If You Lived in the Days of the Knights*. New York: Scholastic, 2001.
A wonderful introduction to the life and times of the knights in the Middle Ages.

Rice, Chris, and Melanie Rice. *How Children Lived*. New York: DK Publishing, 2005.
A delightful look into the lives of 16 children throughout different time periods in history.

Ryan, Pam Muñoz. *Esperanza Rising*. New York: Scholastic, 2002.
When she is forced to leave her life and home in Mexico and work on a farm in California, a young girl has to learn to adapt to her new life and environment.

Steele, Philip. *Long Ago*. New York: Kingfisher, 2002.
A collection of questions and answers about various aspects of cultures and things in the world.

Sociology

Ado, Alma. *Gathering the Sun: An Alphabet in Spanish and English*. New York: HarperCollins, 2001.
Bright, colorful paintings highlight this delightful collection of 28 poems.

Fogelin, Adrian. *Crossing Jordan*. Atlanta, GA: Peachtree Publishers, 2002.
An African American girl moves in next door to a Caucasian girl's house, and the two become friends despite prejudices and the opposition of others.

Garza, Carmen Lomas. *Family Pictures*. Chicago: Children's Press, 2005.
A look into the culture of Mexican Americans through a family's everyday experiences.

Heynen, Jim. *Fishing for Chickens: Short Stories about Rural Youth*. New York: Persea Books, 2001.
A collection of short stories that share experiences of living in rural America.

Joseph, Lynn. *The Color of My Words*. New York: HarperCollins, 2002.
A wonderful story about a young girl and her struggles to write and express herself in a place where this is frowned upon.

Polacco, Patricia. *The Keeping Quilt*. New York: Simon & Schuster, 2001.
A Russian Jewish immigrant family creates a quilt of family memories and love to be passed on to many generations.

Rampersad, Arnold, and David Roessel. *Poetry for Young People: Langston Hughes*. New York: Sterling Publishing, 2006.
A delightful collection of poems depicting African Americans in many different locations.

Sheth, Kashmira. *Blue Jasmine*. New York: Hyperion Books for Children, 2006.

A story about a young girl and her family who move from India to Iowa City and the challenges she faces in feeling at home in her new country and city.

Whelan, Gloria. *Homeless Bird*. New York: HarperCollins, 2001.

An excellent story about a young Indian girl and her arranged marriage.

Political Science

Bausum, Ann. *Our Country's Presidents*. Washington, DC: National Geographic, 2005.

Offers a variety of information on the electoral college, political parties, and much more.

Freedman, Russell. *In Defense of Liberty: The Story of America's Bill of Rights*. New York: Holiday House, 2003.

A wonderful explanation of the decisions that were made to create the Bill of Rights.

Gilley, Jeremy. *Peace One Day: The Making of World Peace Day*. New York: G. P. Putnam's Sons, 2005.

The story of how one person met with many political and religious leaders to create a day on which everyone in the world observes peace.

Granfield, Linda. *America Votes: How Our President Is Elected*. Toronto: Kids Can Press, 2005.

This book offers a descriptive and informative look into the presidential election process.

Hale, Sarah Elder. *Abraham Lincoln: Defender of the Union*. Peterborough, NH: Cobblestone, 2005.

A remarkable story of an influential president in American history.

Heilbroner, Joan. *Meet George Washington*. New York: Random House, 2001.

A thorough story on the life, decisions, and presidency of George Washington.

Nobleman, Marc Tyler. *Election Day*. Mankato, MN: Capstone Press, 2004.

A wonderful explanation of what Election Day is, methods of voting, how Election Day was started, and much more.

Economics

Cooney, Doug. *The Beloved Dearly*. New York: Aladdin, 2003.

A 12-year-old boy decides to start a pet funeral business to earn some cash fast.

Cooper, Elisha. *Ice Cream*. New York: HarperCollins, 2002.

A wonderful explanation of where stores get their ice cream, starting with the resources that are needed and obtained to make the ice cream.

Firestone, Mary. *Earning Money*. Mankato, MN: Capstone Press, 2004.

A young boy does whatever he can think of to make money so he can buy himself something special.

Gill, Shelley, and Deborah Tobola. *The Big Buck Adventure*. Watertown, MA: Charlesbridge Publishing, 2000.

When a young girl receives her allowance, she has to decide what she wants to do with it.

Honig, Debbie, and Gail Karlitz. *Growing Money: A Complete Investing Guide for Kids*. New York: Price Stern Sloan, 2001.

This book examines the different ways to invest and save money, and provides children with the knowledge to help them make investment decisions.

Krull, Kathleen. *Supermarket*. New York: Holiday House, 2001.

This book explains how a grocery store receives, organizes, displays, and cares for its food.

Leedy, Loreen. *Follow the Money!* New York: Holiday House, 2003.

Follow a quarter around to its many stops in stores and in a piggy bank. This book introduces readers to a simplistic view of money.

McGillian, Jamie Kyle. *The Kids' Money Book: Earning, Saving, Spending, Investing, Donating*. New York: Sterling, 2003.

A great book to introduce the topics of creating budgets, investing money, and how to spend money most efficiently.

Roberson, Erin. *All About Money*. Chicago: Children's Press, 2005.

An excellent book discussing the concept of money and how people work for, save, and spend money.

Wells, Donald. *Silk Road*. New York: Weigl Publishers, 2004.

An interesting story about trade and trade routes in Asia.

History

Adler, David A. *Heroes of the Revolution*. New York: Holiday House, 2003.

An excellent introduction to some of the many brave heroes of the Revolutionary War.

Ambrose, Stephen E. *The Good Fight: How World War II Was Won*. New York: Atheneum Books for Young Readers, 2001.

An insightful account of the major events of World War II.

Armstrong, Jennifer. *The American Story: 100 True Tales from American History*. New York: Knopf Books for Young Readers, 2006.

A wonderful collection of true tales of America's past.

Ayer, Eleanor. *Parallel Journeys*. New York: Simon & Schuster, 2000.

An outstanding biography of the lives of two people, a Jewish woman and a German man, who lived during World War II.

Cheney, Lynne. *When Washington Crossed the Delaware: A Wintertime Story for Young Patriots*. New York: Simon & Schuster Books for Young Readers, 2004.

An intriguing story of George Washington and his decision to lead his army across the Delaware River.

Koestler-Grack, Rachel A. *The Pilgrims*. Edina, MN: ABDO Publishing, 2005.

A thorough description of life for the first European settlers in America.

Maestro, Betsy. *The New Americans: Colonial Times 1620–1689*. New York: HarperCollins, 2004.

This informative book discusses the various reasons Europeans settled in North America and what took place during colonial times.

Ringgold, Faith. *If A Bus Could Talk: The Story of Rosa Parks*. New York: Aladdin Paperbacks, 1999.

A creative story of the life of Rosa Parks and her influence on others.

Santella, Andrew. *Pearl Harbor*. Mankato, MN: Capstone Press, 2004.

A wonderful introduction to the events that led to the attack on Pearl Harbor, the attack itself, and the aftermath.

Waters, Kate. *Sarah Morton's Day: A Day in the Life of a Pilgrim Girl*. New York: Scholastic, 1989.

Taken from the diary of a child who lived in Plimoth Plantation in 1627, this book illustrates the similarities and differences between children then and those of today.

Weatherford, Carole Boston. *Moses: When Harriet Tubman Led Her People to Freedom*. New York: Hyperion Books for Children, 2006.

An influential woman, Tubman not only led herself to freedom, but helped free hundreds of other slaves as well.

Winters, Kay. *Abe Lincoln: The Boy Who Loved Books*. New York: Aladdin Paperbacks, 2003.

An informative and interesting account of Abraham Lincoln's life growing up and his many contributions to America.

APPENDIX B

Teacher Resources

by

Anthony D. Fredericks

The following books are available from Teacher Ideas Press (88 Post Road West, Westport, CT 06881); 1-800-225-5800; http://www.teacherideaspress.com.

Frantic Frogs and Other Frankly Fractured Folktales for Readers Theatre. ISBN 1-56308-174-1. (123pp.; $19.50)

Have you heard "Don't Kiss Sleeping Beauty, She's Got Really Bad Breath" or "The Brussels Sprouts Man (The Gingerbread Man's Unbelievably Strange Cousin)"? This resource (grades 4–8) offers 30 reproducible satirical scripts for rip-roaring dramatics in any classroom or library.

The Integrated Curriculum: Books for Reluctant Readers, Grades 2–5. 2nd ed. ISBN 0-87287-994-1. (220pp.; $22.50).

This book presents guidelines for motivating and using literature with reluctant readers. The book contains more than 40 book units on titles carefully selected to motivate the most reluctant readers.

Investigating Natural Disasters Through Children's Literature: An Integrated Approach. ISBN 1-56308-861-4. (193pp.; $28.00).

Tap into students' inherent awe of storms, volcanic eruptions, hurricanes, earthquakes, tornadoes, floods, avalanches, landslides, and tsunamis to open their minds to the wonders and power of the natural world. .

Involving Parents Through Children's Literature: P–K. ISBN 1-56308-022-2. (86pp.; $15.00).

Involving Parents Through Children's Literature: Grades 1–2. ISBN 1-56308-012-5. (95pp.; $14.50).

Involving Parents Through Children's Literature: Grades 3–4. ISBN 1-56308-013-3. (96pp.; $15.50).

Involving Parents Through Children's Literature: Grades 5–6. ISBN 1-56308-014-1. (107pp.; $16.00)

This series of four books offers engaging activities for adults and children that stimulate comprehension and promote reading enjoyment. Reproducible activity sheets based on high-quality children's books are designed in a convenient format so that children can take them home.

The Librarian's Complete Guide to Involving Parents Through Children's Literature: Grades K–6. ISBN 1-56308-538-0. (137pp.; $24.50).

Activities for 101 children's books are presented in a reproducible format, so librarians can distribute them to students to take home and share with parents.

More Social Studies Through Children's Literature: An Integrated Approach. ISBN 1-56308-761-8. (225pp.; $27.50).

Energize your social studies curriculum with dynamic, "hands-on, minds-on" projects based on such great children's books as *Amazing Grace*, *Fly Away Home*, and *Lon Po Po*. This books is filled with an array of activities and projects sure to "energize" any social studies curriculum.

Mother Goose Readers Theatre for Beginning Readers. ISBN 978-1-59158-500-8. (168pp.; $25.00).

Designed especially for educators in the primary grades, this resource provides engaging opportunities that capitalize on children's enjoyment of Mother Goose rhymes. There lots to share and lots to enjoy in the pages of this resource.

Nonfiction Readers Theatre for Beginning Readers. ISBN 978-1-59158-499-5. (220pp.; $25.00).

This collection of science and social studies nonfiction scripts for beginning readers is sure to "jazz up" any language arts program in grades 1–3. Teachers and librarians will discover a wealth of creative opportunities to enhance fluency, comprehension, and appreciation of nonfiction literature.

Readers Theatre for American History. ISBN 1-56308-860-6. (173pp.; $30.00).

This book offers a participatory approach to American history in which students become active participants in several historical events. These 24 scripts give students a "you are there" perspective on critical milestones and colorful moments that have shaped the American experience.

Science Adventures with Children's Literature: A Thematic Approach. ISBN 1-56308-417-1. (190pp.; $24.50).

Focusing on the National Science Education Standards, this activity-centered resource uses a wide variety of children's literature to integrate science across the elementary curriculum. With a thematic approach, it features the best in science trade books along with stimulating hands-on, minds on activities in all the sciences.

Science Discoveries on the Net: An Integrated Approach. ISBN 1-56308-823-1. (315pp.; $27.50).

This book is designed to help teachers integrate the Internet into their science programs and enhance the scientific discoveries of students. The 88 units emphasize key concepts—based on national and state standards—throughout the science curriculum.

Silly Salamanders and Other Slightly Stupid Stuff for Readers Theatre. ISBN 1-56308-825-8. (161pp.; $23.50).

The third entry in the "wild and wacky" readers theatre trilogy is just as crazy and just as weird as the first two. This unbelievable resource offers students in grades 3–6 dozens of silly send-ups of well-known fairy tales, legends, and original stories.

Social Studies Discoveries on the Net: An Integrated Approach. ISBN 1-56308-824-X. (276pp.; $26.00).

This book is designed to help teachers integrate the Internet into their social studies programs and enhance the classroom discoveries of students. The 75 units emphasize key concepts—based on national and state standards—throughout the social studies curriculum.

Social Studies Through Children's Literature: An Integrated Approach. ISBN 1-87287-970-4. (192pp.; $24.00).

Each of the 32 instructional units contained in this resource utilizes an activity-centered approach to elementary social studies, featuring children's picture books such as *Ox-Cart Man, In Coal Country,* and *Jambo Means Hello.*

Tadpole Tales and Other Totally Terrific Titles for Readers Theatre. ISBN 1-56308-547-X. (115pp.; $18.50).

A follow-up volume to the best-selling *Frantic Frogs and Other Frankly Fractured Folktales for Readers Theatre*, this book provides primary level readers (grades 1–4) with a humorous assortment of wacky tales based on well-known Mother Goose rhymes. More than 30 scripts and dozens of extensions will keep students rolling in the aisles.

Index

A Is for America: An American Alphabet, 131
Acting activities, 45, 50, 54, 59, 92, 97, 107, 155, 161, 167. *See also* Readers theatre; Role-playing activities
Active learning, 13
Activities
acting, 45, 50, 54, 59, 92, 97, 107, 155, 161, 167
"adoption"
of animal, 108
of senior citizen, 84
advertisement, 33, 39, 42, 56, 79, 101, 150, 163
almanac, 130
alphabet book, 39, 56, 113, 133, 157
anagram, 113
anthology, 166
artifacts, collection of, 145
audiorecording, 33, 85, 104, 116, 170
award creation, 141
baking, 63, 70, 95. *See also* Cooking activities; Eating activities; Recipe activities; Tasting activities
bibliography, 60, 66, 81, 95, 136, 139, 157
birth announcement, 39
book development/creation, 85, 89, 98, 114, 123, 130, 132, 160, 169
booklet creation, 111, 130
brainstorming, 47, 144
brochures, 51, 62, 67, 70, 72, 79, 81, 94, 104, 110, 111, 113, 116, 119, 129, 136, 144, 148, 163
bulletin board display, 32, 35, 38, 51, 59, 63, 76, 78, 94, 105, 113, 132, 138, 142, 147, 150, 157
bumper sticker, 157
campaign ad, 150
campaign poster, 144
charitable donation, 108, 166
chart, 73, 78, 94, 108, 135, 139, 144, 155
clothing collection/donation, 166
club formation, 120, 164
collage, 32, 33, 42, 50, 54, 57, 100, 107, 111, 125, 133, 138
collections
of artifacts, 145
of food/clothing, 166
of poems, 169
of stamps, 148
color, 32–33, 53, 67, 160
coloring, 101. *See also* Drawing activities; Illustration activities; Painting activities
commercial, 42
comparison/contrast, 91, 95, 97, 98, 101, 105, 107, 119, 128, 129, 133, 135, 142, 154, 157, 160, 166
construction paper "models," 35, 66, 70, 88, 94, 125, 132, 138–139, 147, 148, 160, 163
contest
quiz game, 113
tasting, 94
cooking, 63, 95. *See also* Baking activities; Eating activities; Recipe activities; Tasting activities
debate, 54, 107, 138, 155
diagram, 129
diary, 41, 47, 75, 100, 166
dictionary, 78, 128
dioramas, 69, 73, 107, 155
directory, 38, 98, 141
discussion, 41, 47, 53, 59, 56–57, 62, 69, 73, 76, 78, 85, 101, 122, 126, 135, 139, 141, 142, 145, 150, 157, 158, 166, 169
display box, 145
dramatic presentation, 45, 50, 54, 59, 92, 97, 107, 155, 161, 167
drawing, 35, 36, 56, 62, 69, 91, 92, 97, 104, 125, 133, 163
eating, 62, 63, 70, 94, 95, 158. *See also* Baking activities; Cooking activities; Recipe activities; Tasting activities
election, 150
environmental protection plan, 91
experiment, 44–45, 128–129
field guide, 91

Activities (*Cont.*)
- field trip, 72, 84, 94, 104, 116
  - imaginary trip, 76, 97, 104, 116, 155
  - virtual tour, 116
- fill-in-the-blank, 57, 76, 82
- flow chart, 144
- food collection/donation, 166
- fund drive, 108
- game, 133, 125
  - quiz game, 113
- goal setting, 142
- graph, 73, 78
- graphic organizer, 57, 78
- greeting card, 51
- guest speaker, 50, 53, 67, 72, 79, 81, 95, 120, 126, 135, 144, 150, 151, 160, 170
- guest storyteller, 67, 160
- guide, 51, 117, 128, 158
- history cards, 148
- illustration, 35, 41, 44, 45, 53, 59, 62, 67, 69, 78, 84, 89, 91, 105, 113, 119, 122, 125, 129, 132, 139, 144, 154, 157, 160, 166, 169, 170
- imagination, 39, 42, 50, 59, 75, 76, 78, 85, 89, 92, 94, 97, 98, 108, 111, 113, 135, 136, 155
- information request, 91, 100, 103, 117, 129
- informational display, 73, 103, 107, 120, 163, 166
- informational guide, 158
- interview, 36, 38, 41, 44, 51, 53, 60, 62, 70, 75, 78, 79, 82, 85, 97, 111, 113, 119, 123, 133, 139, 141
- journal, 41, 76, 85, 104, 111, 116, 122
- leaflets, 67
- letter writing, 33, 48, 50, 73, 75, 84, 85, 88, 89, 94, 100, 103, 108, 111, 129, 135, 136, 142, 145, 155
  - thank-you letters, 33, 48, 89, 111, 142
- letterhead design, 144
- list making, 35, 38, 47, 50, 51, 54, 72, 84, 94, 97, 104, 110, 113, 116, 117, 119, 129, 135, 138, 139, 145, 150, 155, 166
  - "Top Ten" list, 110, 117
- map, 45, 56, 89, 91, 101, 104, 114, 116, 120, 125, 132, 135–136, 160, 163. *See also* Salt map activities
- masks, 66
- memorial, 53, 89
- memory, 84
- mime presentation, 54, 155
- mobile, 59, 69, 111, 113
- model, 67, 73, 88, 94, 97, 107, 128–129, 163
- mosaic, 104
- mural, 78, 89
- museum display, 111, 145
  - tabletop museum activity, 145
- musical instruments, 157
- nature walk, 33, 47, 72, 91, 92, 157
- newscast, 92
- newsletter, 70, 75, 136
- newspaper, 72, 95, 97, 101, 133, 147, 167
  - advertisements, 39, 101
  - article collection, 84
  - article writing, 133, 147
  - reporting, 60, 95, 97, 167
- observation, 48, 116. *See also* Nature walk activities; Stargazing activities
- outdoor walk, 33, 47, 72, 91, 157
- outline of body, 35, 44, 170
- oversized book, 114
- painting, 66, 104, 114, 133
- pamphlets, 104, 116, 129
- panoramic display, 117
- photo display, 38, 51, 56, 62, 76
- physical activity, 45. *See also* Field trip activities; Walking activities
- picture finding, 157
- plant growing, 164
- play. *See* Dramatic presentation activities; Readers theatre
- plot development, 88
- poem writing, 35, 72, 132, 169
- poetry collection, 169
- poetry festival, 169
- poetry reading, 73
- poll, 144
- portrait, 36
- postcard, 62, 113, 120

poster, 41, 47, 48, 51, 63, 69, 72, 73, 78, 82, 94, 95, 107, 111, 113, 117, 119, 123, 142, 144, 154, 163, 170
pourquoi story, 66
PowerPoint presentation, 54, 67, 72, 81, 95, 117, 123, 151, 167
prequel writing, 141
props, 45, 160
puppets, 35, 160
questionnaire, 78, 144
questions
  thinking, 41
  true-false, 36
quilting, 125–126
quiz game, 113
readers theatre presentation, 50, 69, 92, 110, 161. *See also* Readers theatre
reading, 45, 50, 53, 70, 81, 100, 104, 123, 136, 155, 158, 160, 166, 169
recipe, 62, 63, 70, 76, 95, 104, 114, 158. *See also* Baking activities; Cooking activities; Eating activities; Tasting activities
record book, 89
requests for information, 91, 100, 103, 117, 129
research, 54, 62, 63, 66, 67, 69, 70, 73, 75, 78, 81, 88, 89, 91, 95, 100, 101, 104, 107, 108, 111, 113, 117, 128, 132, 135, 138, 147, 150, 163, 166, 167, 169. *See also* Web research activities
revision to book/story, 44, 98, 160, 163
rhyming story, 62
rhythm, 157
role playing, 75, 82, 85, 97, 111, 119, 123, 167. *See also* Acting activities; Readers theatre
safety book, 130
salt map, 104, 114
sand drawing, 104
scale model. *See* Model-making activities; Three-sided display activities
scavenger hunt, 150
scrapbook, 38, 56, 63, 79, 91, 92, 111, 133
semantic web, 57
sentence stems, 57, 82
sequel writing, 32, 36, 41, 50, 67, 75, 81, 122, 141
shape book, 107
skit, 59, 97, 107. *See also* Acting activities; Mining presentation activities; Readers theatre
slide show, 67, 117, 167
small group discussion, 51, 54, 85, 107, 166
small group exercise, 54, 56, 57, 62, 76, 104, 107, 111, 116, 147, 155, 166, 169
song writing, 35, 42, 97
sound effects, 104, 116
speech, 138
stamp collection, 148
stargazing, 48, 59
stationery design, 144
story map, 57
story writing, 59, 62, 66–67, 88, 108, 132. *See also* Story-revision activities
storytelling, 45, 50, 67, 107, 166. *See also* Guest storyteller activities
survey, 57, 73, 111, 144, 145
tabletop museum, 145
tasting, 45, 94. *See also* Baking activities; Cooking activities; Eating activities; Recipe activities
telephone directory, 84–85, 98
television broadcast, 60, 92. *See also* Newspaper activities
terrarium, 103, 116–117
thank-you letter, 33, 48, 89, 111, 142
three-sided display, 67, 73, 97
time capsule, 84, 125
time line, 38, 44, 62, 89, 107, 111, 125, 132, 141, 147
"Top Ten" list, 110, 117
tours, 94, 116
travel brochure, 62
true-false questions, 36
two-sided display, 67
Venn diagram, 69, 97, 101, 154, 160, 166
video production, 79, 92, 167
video viewing, 101, 128, 129, 154
videotape, 79, 92
virtual tour, 116. *See also* Tour activities

Activities (*Cont.*)
visual display, 41, 48, 59, 60, 67, 72, 89, 97, 103, 107, 113, 117, 120, 126, 145, 147
voting, 150
walking, 33, 47, 72, 91, 92, 157
wall chart, 139
weather investigation/report, 91, 97, 155
Web page, 36, 95, 114, 119, 151
Web research, 38, 54, 59, 63, 66, 67, 72, 73, 75, 78, 81, 89, 91, 98, 100, 101, 104, 107, 108, 110, 111, 114, 116, 117, 119, 120, 123, 129, 135, 136, 139, 142, 145, 148, 151, 155, 158, 163, 166, 167
Webquest, 110, 114
wood-cut illustrations, 105
word meaning, 170
word wall, 33
writing, 35, 36, 39, 41, 42, 44, 48, 50, 53, 56, 59, 62, 67, 69, 75, 78, 81, 84, 88, 91, 95, 98, 133, 138, 139, 147, 150, 157, 166, 170. *See also* Letter-writing activities; Newspaper activities; Poetry activities; Prequel-writing activity; Sequel-writing activities; Song-writing activities; Story-writing activities
yellow pages, 79, 84, 98
Activity sheets, 209–221. *See also* Forms
suggestions for using, 28
Adams, John, 186
"Adoption" activities
animal, adoption of, 108
senior citizen, adoption of, 84
Advertisement activities, 33, 39, 42, 56, 79, 101, 150, 163
campaign ad activity, 150
Africa, 4, 158. *See also* Zambia
African Americans, 121, 123, 138, 151
African folktales, 156, 157
All the Colors of the Earth, 31
"All Together Now" (script), 193–195. *See also* Communities
Almanac activity, 130
Alphabet book activities, 39, 56, 113, 133, 157
Amazon, 163
American West, 106
settlement of, 102
wild horses, 106
Anagram activity, 113
Ancient civilizations, 4
Andreae, Giles, 34
Antarctic Journal: Four Months at the Bottom of the World, 153
Antarctica, 153–155
Anthem, national, 146–148
Anthology activity, 166
Anthropology, 37, 40, 43, 52, 58, 61, 65, 77, 80, 87, 90, 93, 96, 115, 121, 127, 134, 159, 168
Apple harvesting, 93
Arizona, 115–117
Arnold, Tedd, 43
Artifact collection activity, 145
Asia, 4
Audiorecording activities, 33, 85, 104, 116, 170
Author study form, 210, 219
Authority. *See* Power, authority, and governance
Award creation activity, 141

Baking activities, 63, 70, 95. *See also* Cooking activities; Eating activities; Recipe activities; Tasting activities
Barrier islands, life on, 90–92
Barron, T. A., 118
Beaches, 109
Beautiful Blackbird, 156
Bibliography activities, 60, 66, 81, 95, 136, 139, 157
Birth, 37–39
announcement activity, 39
Blackbirds, 156
"Blending" of disciplines, 5, 13
Body parts, 43
"Book by book" form, 210, 221
Book creation activities, 85, 89, 98, 114, 123, 130, 132, 160, 169
Booklet activities, 111, 130
Brainstorming activities, 47, 144
Brisson, Pat, 49, 55
Brochure activities, 51, 62, 67, 70, 72, 79, 81, 94, 104, 110, 111, 113, 116, 119, 129, 136, 144, 148, 163
Bryan, Ashley, 156

Bulletin board display activities, 32, 35, 38, 51, 59, 63, 76, 78, 94, 105, 113, 132, 138, 142, 147, 150, 157
Bumper sticker activity, 157
Bunker Hill, Battle at, 189
Bunting, Eve, 52
Butterflies, 73

California, 112–114
Campaign ad activity, 150
Campaign poster activity, 144
Canada, 4
Cards
  greeting, 51
  history, 148
  postcards, 62, 113, 120
Change. *See* Time, continuity, and change
Character analysis frame form, 210, 216
Charitable donation activity, 166
Chart activities, 73, 78, 94, 108, 135, 139, 144, 155
Chen, Kerstin, 165
Child and self, 31–48
  birth, 37–39
  body parts, 43–45
  difference, embracing, 34–36
  diversity, 31–33
  elementary school social studies program design
    hierarchy, 3
    typical topics, 3
  self-esteem, 40–42
  self-worth, 34–36
  thankfulness, 46–48
China, 165–167
Chinese tale, 165
Christelow, Eileen, 149
Cities, 87–108
  attacks on, 88
  barrier island, life on, 90–92
  city life, 96
  desert life, 103–105
  disasters, dealing with, 87–89
  ecosystems and, 90
  elementary school social studies program design
    hierarchy, 4
    typical topics, 4
  farm life compared, 93–95
  ghost town, 102
  mining town, 102
  mountain town, life in, 96–98
  New York City, 87, 88, 89
  open plains, life on, 106–108
  settlement of American West, 102, 106
  social studies concept, 180
  wetlands environment, life in, 99–101
Civic ideals and practices
  NCSS thematic strand, 5, 7, 49, 52, 61, 74, 77, 80, 88, 96, 102, 112, 121, 124, 132, 137, 140, 143, 149, 165, 180, 185, 192, 196
  relevant courses and disciplines, 7
Clothing collection activity, 166
Club formation activities, 120, 164
Collaboration factor, 19
Collaborative partnership, teacher and librarian, 19–23, 173
  benefits of, 19–20
  forging the partnership, 20–23
  strategies to use, 19–20
  suggestions for librarians/media specialists, 20–21
  suggestions for teachers, 21–22
Collage activities, 32, 33, 42, 50, 54, 57, 100, 107, 111, 125, 133, 138
Color activities, 32–33, 53, 67, 160
Colorado, 118–120
Coloring activity, 101
Comfort, 58
  in troubled times, 168–170
Coming to America: A Muslim Family's Story, 134
Commercial creation activity, 42
Communication skills, 172
Communities, 65–85. *See also* Living environments
  barrier island community, 90–92
  critical thinking questions, 192
  disciplines, 192
  elementary school social studies program design
    hierarchy, 4
    typical topics, 4

Communities (Cont.)
functions of, 192–195
how communities work, 71–73, 192–195
insects, world of, 71–73
Hispanic, 77–79
laws and rules in, 195
makeup of, 77
migrant workers, 80, 81
Native Americans, 65–67
NCSS thematic strand, 192
racial segregation, 74–76
readers theatre, 193–195
rural, 180, 183–184
script for play, 193–195
segregation, 74–76
senior citizens, 83–85
sizes and types of, 180–184
social studies concept, 192
staging of play, 193
suburban, 180, 182–183
urban, 180, 181–182
teachers and teaching, celebration of, 68–70
Compare/contrast activities, 91, 95, 97, 98, 101, 105, 107, 119, 128, 129, 133, 135, 142, 154, 157, 160, 166
Construction paper "model" activities, 35, 66, 70, 88, 94, 125, 132, 139, 147, 148, 160, 163
Constructivism, 9–10
Constructivist philosophy of teaching, 9–10, 15, 19
Consumption. *See* Production, distribution, and consumption
Contests
quiz game, 113
tasting contest, 94
Continuity. *See* Time, continuity, and change
Cooking activities, 63, 95. *See also* Eating activities; Recipe activities; Tasting activities
Cooperative learning strategies, 172
Cornell, Laura, 40
Costumes
for readers theatre, 172, 175
Country
city and, 87–108, 180
nation and, 131–151
social studies concept, 180
Courage, 120
Cowley, Joy, 106
Crab Moon, 109
Crabs
horseshoe crabs, 109
Creative thinking, 173
Criteria for inclusion in *Much More Social Studies,* 25–26
Critical thinking, 173
emphasis on, 20
Critical thinking questions
for *A Is for America,* 132
for *All the Colors of the Earth,* 32
for *Antarctic Journal,* 154
for *Beautiful Blackbird,* 156
for *Coming to America,* 134–135
for *Crab Moon,* 110
for *Fireboat,* 88
for *G Is for Golden,* 112
for *G Is for Grand Canyon,* 115
for *Giraffes Can't Dance,* 34–35
for *Happy Birth Day!,* 37
for *High as a Hawk,* 118–119
for *Horse Hooves and Chicken Feet,* 159
for *How Raven Stole the Sun,* 66
for *I Have Heard of a Land,* 122
for *I'm Gonna Like Me,* 40
for *Island Scrapland,* 90–91
for *Jabuti the Tortoise,* 162
for *Life on an Apple Orchard,* 94
for *Lord of the Cranes,* 165–166
for *Mama Loves Me from Away,* 50
for *Martin's Big Words,* 138
for *Mountain Town,* 96–97
for *My Great-Aunt Arizona,* 68–69
for *Near One Cattail,* 99–100
for *On One Flower,* 71
for *Other Side, The,* 74–75
for *Parts,* 43
for *Pearl Harbor Warriors,* 140
for *Quilt of States,* 124
for *Quinito's Neighborhood,* 77–78
for *Rhyolite,* 102–103
for *Secret of Saying Thanks, The,* 46–47

for *So Far from the Sea,* 53
for *So You Want to Be President?,* 144
for *Star Blanket,* 55
for *Star People,* 58
for *Star Spangled Banner, The,* 146–147
for *Tattered Sails,* 61–62
for *This Place I Know,* 169
for *Tomás and the Library Lady,* 80–81
for *Tsunami Quilt,* 127–128
for *Vote,* 149–150
for *Where Horses Run Free,* 106
for *Wilfrid Gordon McDonald Partridge,* 83–84
Culture
NCSS thematic strand, 5, 6, 46, 52, 58, 65, 68, 74, 77, 80, 102, 115, 124, 127, 132, 134, 137, 140, 156, 159, 162, 165, 176
relevant courses and disciplines, 6
Cumpiano, Ina, 77
Curriculum
expanding environments curriculum, 4, 5
systematic progression in, 4 (fig.)
widening horizons curriculum, 4
Curtis, Jamie Lee, 40

"Day of the Wave" (script), 204–208. *See also* Tsunamis
Debate activities, 54, 107, 138, 155
Declaration of Independence
critical thinking questions, 185
disciplines, 185
drafting of, 185–191
NCSS thematic strands, 185
parts of, 190–191
readers theatre, 185–191
script for play, 186–191
social studies concept, 185
staging of play, 186
Delaware, 110
Delaware Bay, 109, 111
Desert regions, 103–105, 116
Dewey, Jennifer Owings, 153
Diagram activity, 129
Diary activities, 41, 47, 75, 100, 166
Dictionary creation activities, 78, 128
Difference, embracing, 34–36
Diorama activities, 69, 73, 107, 155
Directory activities, 38, 84–85, 98, 141
Disaster relief, 130
Discussion activities, 41, 47, 53, 56–57, 59, 62, 69, 73, 76, 78, 85, 101, 122, 126, 135, 139, 141, 142, 145, 150, 157, 158, 166, 169
small group discussion, 51, 54, 85, 107, 166
Displays
bulletin board displays. *See* Bulletin board display activities
display box activity, 145
panoramic display activity, 117
photo display activities, 38, 51, 56, 62, 76
poster displays. *See* Poster activities
three-sided display activities, 67, 73, 97
two-sided display activity, 67
visual display activities, 41, 48, 59, 60, 72, 89, 103, 107, 113, 117, 120, 126, 147
Distribution. *See* Production, distribution, and consumption
Diversity of people, 31–33
Domeniconi, David, 112
Dramatic presentation activities, 45, 50, 54, 59, 92, 97, 107, 155, 161, 167. *See also* Readers theatre
Drawing activities, 35, 36, 56, 62, 69, 91, 92, 97, 104, 125, 133, 163

Eastern Hemisphere, 4
Eating activities, 62, 63, 70, 94, 95, 158. *See also* Baking activities; Cooking activities; Recipe activities; Tasting activities
Ecological Research and Development Group, 110
Economics, 46, 49, 61, 77, 80, 87, 93, 96, 102, 106, 112, 115, 121, 134, 149, 154, 176, 192
Ecosystems, 90
Election activity, 150
Electoral process, 144
Elementary school social studies curriculum
child/self, typical topics, 3. *See also* Child and self
cities, typical topics, 4. *See also* Cities
communities, typical topics, 4. *See also* Communities
country, typical topics, 4. *See also* Country

Elementary school social studies curriculum (*Cont.*)
families, typical topics, 3. *See also* Families
hierarchy, 3–4
nation, typical topics, 4. *See also* Nation
neighborhoods, typical topics, 4. *See also* Neighborhoods
regions, typical topics, 4. *See also* Regions
states, typical topics, 4. *See also* States
United States, typical topics, 4. *See also* Nation
world, typical topics, 4. *See also* World
Elevation, 119, 120
Ellis Island, 200, 202
Environment. *See also* People, places, and environment
environmental protection plan activity, 91
wetlands, 99, 100, 101
Europe, 4
Expanding environments curriculum, 4, 5
Experiment activities, 44–45, 128–129
tasting experiment, 45

Families, 49–63
elementary school social studies program design
hierarchy, 3
typical topics, 3
getting lost, 58
in internment camps, 52–54
missing family, 58
parents, relationship with, 49–51
Pilgrims, 61–63
prison, parent in, 49, 50
rituals, 55
survival of, 52–54
traditions, 55–57
Farm life, 93–95
Field guide activity, 91
Field trip activities, 72, 84, 94, 104, 116
imaginary trip, 76, 97, 104, 116, 155
virtual tour, 116
Fill-in-the-blank activities, 57, 76, 82
Fireboat: The Heroic Adventures of the John J. Harvey, 87
"First Thanksgiving, The" (script), 177–179. *See also* Thanksgiving
Flow chart activity, 144
Food collection activity, 166
Forgiveness, 140, 141, 142
Forms
author study, 210, 219
book by book, 210, 221
character analysis frame, 210, 216
I wonder . . . , 210, 217
literature logs, 209, 211–212, 213
reader's menu, 210, 218
story map, 209–210, 214
story pyramid, 210, 215
word by word, 210, 220
Fort McHenry, 148
Fox, Mem, 83
Franklin, Benjamin, 186
Fredericks, Anthony D., 71, 99, 127
French and Indian War, 187
Frontier, women on, 121
Fund drive activity, 108

G Is for Golden: A California Alphabet, 112
G Is for Grand Canyon: An Arizona Alphabet, 115
Game activities, 133, 125
quiz game, 113
Garden State, 111
Gardner, Howard, 10, 11
Geisert, Arthur, 96
Geisert, Bonnie, 96
Geography, 52, 61, 68, 80, 87, 90, 93, 96, 99, 102, 106, 109, 112, 115, 118, 121, 124, 127, 131, 134, 137, 140, 146, 154, 156, 159, 162, 180, 196
Ghost town, 102
Giraffes Can't Dance, 34
Global connections. *See also* World
NCSS thematic strand, 5, 7, 134, 140, 154, 159
relevant courses and disciplines, 7
Goal-setting activity, 142
Gold, Melissa, 13
Golden State, 112
Governance. *See* Power, authority, and governance

Gowan, Barbara, 115
Grand Canyon, 115, 117
Graph activities, 73, 78
Graphic organizer activities, 57, 78
Greeting card activity, 51
Groups. *See* Individuals, groups, and institutions
Guest speaker activities, 50, 53, 72, 79, 81, 95, 120, 126, 135, 144, 150, 151, 160, 170
Guest storyteller activities, 67, 160
Guide creation activities, 51, 117, 128, 158

Hamanaka, Sheila, 31
Hands-on, minds-on learning, 9, 14, 17, 25
  hands-on, minds-on activities, discussion of, 26–27, 209
Happy Birth Day!, 37
Harris, Robie H., 37
Harvesting, 93
Hawaii, 127
  Laupahoehoe, 205
  Mauna Loa, 205
  natural disasters in, 203–208. *See also* Tsunamis
  "talking story," 204
  tsunamis. *See* Tsunamis
Heard, Georgia, 168
High as a Hawk: A Brave Girl's Historic Climb, 118
Hiking, 120
Hispanic communities, 77–79
History, 52, 55, 58, 61, 65, 68, 74, 87, 96, 102, 106, 112, 115, 118, 121, 124, 127, 131, 137, 140, 143, 146, 149, 159, 176, 185, 196
History cards activity, 148
Holidays, 176–179
Horowitz, Ruth, 109
Horse Hooves and Chicken Feet: Mexican Folktales, 159
Horses, 107
  wild mustangs, 106
Houston, Gloria, 68
How Raven Stole the Sun, 65
Human intelligences, 11–12

I Have Heard of a Land, 121
"I wonder . . . " form, 210, 217
Illustration activities, 35, 41, 44, 45, 53, 59, 62, 67, 69, 78, 84, 89, 91, 105, 113, 119, 122, 125, 129, 132, 139, 144, 154, 157, 160, 166, 169, 170
I'm Gonna Like Me: Letting Off a Little Self-Esteem, 40
Imagination activities, 39, 42, 50, 59, 75, 76, 78, 85, 89, 92, 94, 97, 98, 108, 111, 113, 135, 136, 155
Immigration, 60, 62, 134, 135, 196–202
  critical thinking questions, 196
  disciplines, 196
  NCSS thematic strands, 196
  readers theatre, 196–202
  script for play, 197–202
  social studies concept, 196
  staging of play, 197
  steerage, 199
Indigenous peoples, 65
Individual development and identity
  NCSS thematic strand, 5, 6, 32, 34, 37, 40, 43, 46, 49, 52, 55, 58, 68, 74, 83, 109, 118, 121, 127, 134, 140, 156, 162, 165, 169, 196
  relevant courses and disciplines, 6
Individuals, groups, and institutions
  NCSS thematic strand, 5, 6, 37, 61, 68, 74, 77, 80, 88, 132, 134, 137, 143, 146, 149, 169, 185, 192
  relevant courses and disciplines, 6
Inflection
  in readers theatre, 172
Information request activities, 91, 100, 103, 117, 129
Informational display activities, 73, 103, 107, 120, 163, 166
Inquiry-based learning, 8
Insects, 71–73
Institutions. *See* Individuals, groups, and institutions
Intelligence, defined, 10
Intelligences
  human, 11–12
  multiple, 10–12
Internment camps, 52–54

Interview activities, 36, 38, 41, 44, 51, 53, 60, 62, 70, 75, 78, 79, 82, 85, 97, 111, 113, 119, 123, 133, 139, 141
Intonation, in readers theatre, 172, 174
Island Scrapland: Dawn to Dusk on a Barrier Island, An, 90
Islands
  barrier island, 90
  ecosystems on, 90

Jabuti the Tortoise: A Trickster Tale from the Amazon, 162
Japanese Americans, 54
Japanese internment camps, 54
Jefferson, Thomas, conversation with, 185–191
  critical thinking questions, 185
  Declaration of Independence, drafting of, 185–191. *See also* Declaration of Independence
  disciplines, 185
  NCSS thematic strands, 185
  readers theatre, 185–191
  script for play, 186–191
  social studies concept, 185
  staging of play, 186
Journal activities, 41, 76, 85, 104, 111, 116, 122

Kalman, Maira, 87
Kay, Verla, 61
Key, Francis Scott, 146
King, Martin Luther, Jr., 137, 138, 139

Lakota Indians, 58, 59
Latin America, 4
Leaflet activities, 67
League of Women Voters, 144, 151
Learning
  active learning, 13
Letter-writing activities, 33, 48, 50, 73, 75, 84, 85, 88, 89, 94, 100, 103, 108, 111, 129, 135, 136, 142, 145, 155
  thank-you letters, 33, 48, 89, 111, 142
Letterhead design activity, 144
Life on an Apple Orchard, 93
List-making activities, 35, 38, 47, 50, 51, 54, 72, 84, 94, 97, 104, 110, 113, 116, 117, 119, 129, 135, 138, 139, 145, 150, 155, 166
  "Top Ten" list, 110, 117
Literature logs
  I, 209, 211–212
  II, 209, 213
Literature-based approach to instruction, 14–17
  benefits of, 14, 15, 16 (fig.), 17
Living environments. *See also* Communities; Neighborhoods
  critical thinking questions, 180
  disciplines, 180
  NCSS thematic strands, 180
  readers theatre, 180–184
  rural, 180, 183–184
  script for play, 181–184
  sizes and types of, 180–184
  social studies concept, 180
  staging of play, 181
  suburban, 180, 182–183
  urban, 180, 181–182
Livingston, Robert, 186
Longs Peak, 118
Lord of the Cranes, 165

Mama Loves Me from Away, 49
Map activities, 45, 56, 89, 91, 101, 104, 114, 116, 120, 125, 132, 135–136, 160, 163. *See also* Salt map activities
Martin's Big Words: The Life of Dr. Martin Luther King, Jr., 137
Mask activity, 66
McDermott, Gerald, 162
Memorial activities, 53, 89
Memorization, 8, 12, 17, 20, 171, 174
Memory, 83
  activity, 84
Menu
  reader's menu form, 210, 218
Mexico, 159–161
Middle East, 4
Migrant workers, 80, 81
Miming activities, 54, 155
Mining town, life in, 102
Mobile creation activities, 59, 69, 111, 113

Model-making activities, 67, 73, 88, 94, 97, 107, 128–129, 163
Montana, 98
Monuments, 128
Mora, Pat, 80
Mosaic activity, 104
Mountain Town, 96
Mountains, 118, 120
  life in mountain town, 96–98
Multiple intelligences, 10–12
Mural activities, 78, 89
Museum display activities, 111, 145
  tabletop museum activity, 145
Musical instrument activity, 157
Muslims, 134, 135, 136
My Great-Aunt Arizona, 68

Nation, 131–151. *See also* United States
  anthem, national, 146–148
  elementary school social studies program design
    hierarchy, 4
    typical topics, 4
  history of United States, 131–133
  holiday celebration, 176. *See also* Thanksgiving
  immigration to United States, 134–136
  Martin Luther King Jr., life of, 137–139
  Pearl Harbor, attack on, 140–142
  presidency, 143–145
  social studies concept, 176, 185
  "Star-Spangled Banner," 146
  voting process, 149–151
National anthem, 146–148
National Council for the Social Studies (NCSS), 3
  standards, 5–7
    relevant courses under, 6–7
    themes of, 5–7. *See also* NCSS thematic strands
National Museum of the American Indian, 67
National Park Service, 148
Native Americans, 65–67
Natural disasters. *See* Tsunamis
Nature walk activities, 33, 47, 72, 91, 92, 157
NCSS thematic strands
  civic ideals and practices, 5, 7, 49, 52, 61, 74, 77, 80, 88, 96, 102, 112, 121, 124, 132, 137, 140, 143, 149, 165, 180, 185, 192, 196
  culture, 5, 6, 46, 52, 58, 65, 68, 74, 77, 80, 102, 115, 124, 127, 132, 134, 137, 140, 156, 159, 162, 165, 176
  global connections, 5, 7, 134, 140, 154, 159
  individual development and identity, 5, 6, 32, 34, 37, 40, 43, 46, 49, 52, 55, 58, 68, 74, 83, 109, 118, 121, 127, 134, 140, 156, 162, 165, 169, 196
  individuals, groups, and institutions, 5, 6, 37, 61, 68, 74, 77, 80, 88, 132, 134, 137, 143, 146, 149, 169, 185, 192
  people, places, and environment, 5, 6, 37, 40, 46, 52, 55, 58, 65, 68, 71, 77, 80, 83, 88, 90, 96, 99, 102, 106, 109, 112, 115, 118, 124, 127, 132, 134, 140, 154, 159, 162, 165, 180
  power, authority, and governance, 5, 7, 52, 88, 96, 115, 124, 132, 137, 143, 149, 185
  production, distribution, and consumption, 5, 7, 93, 102, 115, 176, 192
  science, technology, and society, 5, 7, 90, 93, 109, 127
  time, continuity, and change, 5, 6, 37, 52, 55, 58, 61, 65, 68, 74, 80, 83, 90, 96, 102, 106, 109, 112, 115, 118, 121, 127, 132, 137, 140, 143, 146, 154, 159, 176, 185, 196
NCSS. *See* National Council for the Social Studies (NCSS)
Near One Cattail: Turtles, Logs and Leaping Frogs, 99
Neighborhoods, 65–85, 192. *See also* Communities; Living environments
  elementary school social studies program design
    hierarchy, 4
    typical topics, 4
Nelson, S. D., 58
New Jersey, 111
New York City, 87, 88, 89, 201
New York Harbor, 200, 201, 202

Newscast activity, 92
Newsletter activities, 70, 75, 136
Newspaper activities, 72, 95, 97, 101, 133, 147, 167
advertisement activities, 39, 101
article collection activity, 84
article-writing activities, 133, 147
reporter activities, 60, 95, 97, 167
Nicholson, Dorinda Makanaonalani, 140
9/11, 88, 89, 168
Nonviolence, 138

Observation activities, 48, 116. *See also* Nature walk activities; Stargazing activities
Oklahoma, 121–123
On One Flower: Butterflies, Ticks and a Few More Icks, 71
Open plains, 106
Other Side, The, 74
Outdoor walking activities, 33, 47, 72, 91, 157
Outline-tracing activities, 35, 44, 170
Oversized-book activity, 114

Pacific Tsunami Museum, 127, 129, 207
Painting activities, 66, 104, 114, 133
Palmer Station, 154–155
Pamphlet activities, 104, 116, 129
Panoramic display activity, 117
Parent, in prison, 49. *See also* Families
Partnership between teacher and librarian
benefits of, 19–20
forging the partnership, 20–23
strategies to use, 19–20
suggestions for librarians/media specialists, 20–22
suggestions for teachers, 21–22
Parts, 43
Pearl Harbor, 140, 142
Pearl Harbor Warriors: The Bugler, the Pilot, the Friendship, 140
Penguins, 154, 155
People, places, and environment
NCSS thematic strand, 5, 6, 37, 40, 46, 52, 55, 58, 65, 68, 71, 77, 80, 83, 88, 90, 96, 99, 102, 106, 109, 112, 115, 118, 124, 127, 132, 134, 140, 154, 159, 162, 165, 180
relevant courses and disciplines, 6
Philip, Neil, 159
Photo display activities, 38, 51, 56, 62, 76
Physical activity, 45. *See also* Walking activities
Picture-finding activity, 157
Pilgrims, 61–63, 178, 179
Places. *See* People, places, and environment
Plains
open plains, life on, 106–108
Plant-growing activity, 164
Plot development activity, 88
Poetry activities
collection activity, 169
poem-writing activities, 35, 73, 132, 169
poetry festival activity, 169
poetry-reading activity, 73
Political science, 52, 74, 112, 115, 124, 131, 140, 143, 149, 180, 185, 192, 196
Polling activity, 144
Portrait activity, 36
Postcard activities, 62, 113, 120
Poster activities, 41, 47, 48, 51, 63, 69, 72, 73, 78, 82, 94, 95, 107, 111, 113, 117, 119, 123, 142, 144, 154, 163, 170
Pourquoi story activity, 66
Power, authority, and governance
NCSS thematic strand, 5, 7, 52, 88, 96, 115, 124, 132, 137, 143, 149, 185
relevant courses and disciplines, 7
PowerPoint presentation activities, 54, 67, 72, 81, 95, 117, 123, 151, 167
Prequel-writing activity, 141
Presidency, 143–145
Presidents, 143
Prison, parent in, 49
Problem solving, emphasis on, 20
Process approach to learning, 14
Proclamation Line of 1763, 188
Production, distribution, and consumption
NCSS thematic strand, 5, 7, 93, 102, 115, 176, 192
relevant courses and disciplines, 7
Pronunciation skills
readers theatre, 172
Props
making and using props, 45, 160
in readers theatre, 172, 174

Puppet activities, 35, 160

Questionnaire activities, 78, 144
Questions
  thinking-questions activity, 41
  true-false questions activity, 36
Quilt of States: Piecing Together America, 124
Quilting activity, 125–126
Quinito's Neighborhood, 77
Quiz game activity, 113

Racial segregation, 74–76
Rain forests, 163–164
Rainforest Action Network, 163
Rappaport, Doreen, 137
Reader's menu form, 210, 218
Readers theatre
  activities, 50, 69, 92, 110, 161
  body movements in, 174
  communities, script about. *See* Communities
  copies of script, 174
  costumes, 172, 175
  Declaration of Independence, script about. *See* Declaration of Independence: drafting of
  defined, 171
  facial gestures in, 174
  identification of characters, 174
  immigration, script about. *See* Immigration
  inflection in, 172
  informality of, 172
  intonation in, 172, 174
  Jefferson, Thomas, script about conversation with. *See* Jefferson, Thomas, conversation with
  living environments, script about. *See* Living environments
  narrator, 174
  natural disasters, script about. *See* Tsunamis
  physical location of reader, 174
  practicing of script, 174
  presentation suggestions, 174–175
  pronunciation skills, 172
  props, 172, 174
    examples of simple props, 174
  scenery, 172, 174
  scripts, how to use, 27–28
  self-concept, development of, 172
  self-esteem, development of, 172
  suggestions for use of, 173
  Thanksgiving, script about. *See* Thanksgiving
  tsunamis, script about. *See* Tsunamis
  value of, 171–173
  voice intonation in, 172, 174
  voice projection in, 172
Reading activities, 45, 50, 53, 70, 81, 100, 104, 123, 136, 155, 158, 160, 166, 169
Recipe activities, 62, 63, 70, 76, 95, 104, 114, 158. *See also* Baking activities; Cooking activities; Eating activities; Tasting activities
Reconciliation, 140, 142
Record book activity, 89
Regions, 109–130. *See also* States
  elementary school social studies program design
    hierarchy, 4
    typical topics, 4
  social studies concept, 203
Related books
  for *A Is for America,* 132
  for *All the Colors of the Earth,* 32
  for *Antarctic Journal,* 154
  for *Beautiful Blackbird,* 156
  for *Coming to America,* 135
  for *Crab Moon,* 110
  for *Fireboat,* 88
  for *G Is for Golden,* 113
  for *G Is for Grand Canyon,* 116
  for *Giraffes Can't Dance,* 35
  for *Happy Birth Day!,* 38
  for *High as a Hawk,* 119
  for *Horse Hooves and Chicken Feet,* 160
  for *How Raven Stole the Sun,* 66
  for *I Have Heard of a Land,* 122
  for *I'm Gonna Like Me,* 41
  for *Island Scrapland,* 91
  for *Jabuti the Tortoise,* 163
  for *Life on an Apple Orchard,* 94
  for *Lord of the Cranes,* 166
  for *Mama Loves Me from Away,* 50
  for *Martin's Big Words,* 138

Related books (*Cont.*)
for *Mountain Town,* 97
for *My Great-Aunt Arizona,* 68–69
for *Near One Cattail,* 100
for *On One Flower,* 72
for *Other Side, The,* 75
for *Parts,* 44
for *Pearl Harbor Warriors,* 141
for *Quilt of States,* 125
for *Quinito's Neighborhood,* 78
for *Rhyolite,* 103
for *Secret of Saying Thanks, The,* 47
for *So Far from the Sea,* 53
for *So You Want to Be President?,* 144
for *Star Blanket,* 56
for *Star People,* 59
for *Star Spangled Banner, The,* 147
for *Tattered Sails,* 62
for *This Place I Know,* 169
for *Tomás and the Library Lady,* 81
for *Tsunami Quilt,* 128
for *Vote,* 150
for *Where Horses Run Free,* 107
for *Wilfrid Gordon McDonald Partridge,* 84
Religion, 135
Representation, taxation without, 188–189
Requests for information
activities for students, 91, 100, 103, 117, 129
Research activities, 54, 62, 63, 66, 67, 69, 70, 73, 75, 78, 81, 88, 89, 91, 95, 100, 101, 104, 107, 108, 111, 113, 117, 128, 132, 135, 138, 147, 150, 163, 166, 167, 169
on Web sites, 38, 54, 59, 63, 66, 67, 72, 73, 75, 78, 81, 89, 91, 98, 100, 101, 104, 107, 108, 110, 111, 114, 116, 117, 119, 120, 123, 129, 135, 136, 139, 142, 145, 148, 151, 155, 158, 163, 166, 167
Rethinking the curriculum, 8–9
Revising stories. *See* Story-revision activities
Revolutionary War, 186, 189
Rhyming-story activity, 62
Rhyolite: The True Story of a Ghost Town, 102
Rhythm activity, 157
Rituals, family, 55–57
Rocky Mountain National Park, 119
Rocky Mountains, 118
Role-playing activities, 75, 82, 85, 97, 111, 119, 123, 167. *See also* Dramatic presentation activities; Readers theatre
Rural communities, 180, 183–184. *See also* Communities; Living environments

Safety book activity, 130
Salt map activities, 104, 114
Sand-drawing activity, 104
Scale model. *See* Model-making activities; Three-sided display activities
Scavenger hunt activity, 150
Scenery
for readers theatre, 172
Science, technology, and society
NCSS thematic strands, 5, 7, 90, 93, 109, 127
relevant courses and disciplines, 7
Scillian, Devin, 131
Scope and sequence of social studies programs, 3–4
Scrapbook activities, 38, 56, 63, 79, 91, 92, 111, 133
Seashores, 91
Second Continental Congress, 189, 191
Secret of Saying Thanks, The, 46
Segregation, racial, 74–76
Self. *See* Child and self
Self-concept, development of, 172
Self-esteem, development of, 40–42, 172
Semantic web activity, 57
Senior citizens, 83–85
"adoption" of, 84
Sentence stem activities, 57, 82
Sequel-writing activities, 32, 36, 41, 50, 67, 75, 81, 122, 141
Settlement of American West, 102, 106
Shape book activity, 107
"Shapiros' New Adventure, The" (script), 197–202. *See also* Immigration
Sherman, Roger, 186
Siebert, Diane, 102
Skit activities, 59, 97, 107. *See also* Dramatic presentation activities; Readers theatre
Slide show activities, 67, 117, 167
Small group discussion activities, 51, 54, 85, 107, 166

Small group exercises, 54, 56, 57, 62, 76, 104, 107, 111, 116, 147, 155, 166, 169
So Far from the Sea, 52
So You Want to Be President?, 143
Social studies concepts
  city and country, 180. *See also* Cities; Country
  communities and neighborhoods, 192. *See also* Communities; Neighborhoods
  nation, 176, 185. *See also* Nation
  states and regions, 203. *See also* Regions; States
  world, 196. *See also* World
Social studies, defined, 3
Social studies disciplines
  anthropology, 37, 40, 43, 52, 58, 61, 65, 77, 80, 87, 90, 93, 96, 115, 121, 127, 134, 159, 169
  economics, 46, 49, 61, 77, 80, 87, 93, 96, 102, 106, 112, 115, 121, 134, 149, 154, 176, 192
  geography, 52, 61, 68, 80, 87, 90, 93, 96, 99, 102, 106, 109, 112, 115, 118, 121, 124, 127, 131, 134, 137, 140, 146, 154, 156, 159, 162, 180, 196
  history, 52, 55, 58, 61, 65, 68, 74, 87, 96, 102, 106, 112, 115, 118, 121, 124, 127, 131, 137, 140, 143, 146, 149, 159, 176, 185, 196
  political science, 52, 74, 112, 115, 124, 131, 140, 143, 149, 180, 185, 192, 196
  sociology. *See* Sociology
Social studies programs, scope and sequence of, 3–4
Social studies standards. See NCSS thematic strands
Society. *See* Science, technology, and society
Sociology, 32, 34, 37, 40, 43, 46, 49, 52, 55, 58, 61, 65, 68, 71, 74, 77, 80, 83, 87, 90, 93, 102, 109, 112, 115, 118, 137, 140, 143, 149, 154, 156, 159, 165, 169, 176, 180, 185, 192, 196
Solace, during troubled times, 168–170
Song-writing activities, 35, 42, 97
Sound effects activities, 104, 116
South Pole, 155
Speech activity, 138
St. George, Judith, 143
Stamp Act, 188
Stamp collection activity, 148
Standards, themes of. *See* NCSS thematic strands
Star Blanket, 55
Star People: A Lakota Story, The, 58
Star Spangled Banner, The, 146
Stargazing activities, 48, 59
States, 109–130. *See also* Regions
  Arizona, 115–117
    Grand Canyon, 115
  California, 112–114
  Colorado, 118–120
    Longs Peak, 118
    Rocky Mountains, 118–120
  Delaware, 109–111
    Delaware Bay, horseshoe crabs in, 109–111
  elementary school social studies program design
    hierarchy, 4
    typical topics, 4
  Hawaii, 127, 203. *See also* Hawaii
    tsunamis, 127–130
  natural disasters, 127–130
  New Jersey, 111
  New York, 87, 88, 89, 200, 201, 202
  Oklahoma, 121–123
  quilt of states, 124
  social studies concept, 203
Stationery design activity, 144
Statue of Liberty, 200, 201, 202
Steerage, 199
Story map activity, 57
Story map form, 209–210, 214
Story pyramid form, 210, 215
Story-revision activities, 44, 98, 160, 163
Story-writing activities, 59, 62, 66–67, 88, 108, 132. *See also* Prequel-writing activity; Sequel-writing activities
Storytelling activities, 45, 50, 67, 107, 166. *See also* Guest storyteller activities
Suburban communities, 180, 182–183. *See also* Communities; Living environments
Survey activities, 57, 73, 111, 144, 145

"Talking story," 204
Tasting activities, 45, 94. *See also* Baking activities; Cooking activities; Eating activities; Recipe activities,
Tattered Sails, 61
"Taxation without representation," 188–189
Teachers/teaching, celebration of, 68–70
Technology. *See* Science, technology, and society
Telephone directory activities, 84–85, 98
Television broadcast activities, 60, 92
Terrarium activities, 103, 116–117
Thank-you letter activities, 33, 48, 89, 111, 142
Thankfulness, 46–48
Thanksgiving
  critical thinking questions, 176
  disciplines, 176
  NCSS thematic strands, 176
  readers theatre, 172–179
  script for play, 177–179
  social studies concept, 176
  staging of play, 177
Themes of NCSS standards. *See* NCSS thematic strands
This Place I Know: Poems of Comfort, 168
Thomas, Joyce Carol, 121
Three-sided display activities, 67, 73, 97
"Three Ways of Living" (script), 181–184. *See also* Living environments
Time capsule activities, 84, 125
Time, continuity, and change
  NCSS thematic strand, 5, 6, 37, 52, 55, 58, 61, 65, 68, 74, 80, 83, 90, 96, 102, 106, 109, 112, 115, 118, 121, 127, 132, 137, 140, 143, 146, 154, 159, 176, 185, 196
  relevant courses and disciplines, 6
Time line activities, 38, 44, 62, 89, 107, 111, 125, 132, 141, 147
Tlingit people, 66
Tomás and the Library Lady, 80
Tour activities, 94, 116. *See also* Field trip activities; Nature walk activities
virtual tour activity, 116
Trade books, benefit of, 13–14
Traditions, family, 55–57
Travel brochure activity, 62
Troubled times, comfort during, 168–170
True-false questions activity, 36
Tsunami Quilt: Grandfather's Story, The, 127
Tsunamis, 127–129
  critical thinking questions, 203
  disciplines, 203
  NCSS thematic strands, 203
  readers theatre, 203–208
  script for play, 204–208
  social studies concept, 203
  staging of play, 204
Two-sided display activity, 67

United States. *See also* Nation
  elementary school social studies program design
    hierarchy, 4
    typical topics, 4
  history of, 131
  states. *See* States
Urban communities, 180, 181–182. *See also* Communities; Living environments

Venn diagram activities, 69, 97, 101, 154, 160, 166
Video production activities, 79, 92, 167
Video-viewing activities, 101, 128, 129, 154
Videotape activities, 79, 92
Virtual tour activity, 116. *See also* Tour activities
Visual display activities, 41, 48, 59, 60, 67, 72, 73, 89, 97, 103, 107, 113, 117, 120, 126, 145, 147
Voice projection
  in readers theatre, 172
Vote, 149
Voting activity, 150
Voting process, 149, 151

Walking activities, 33, 47, 72, 91, 92, 157
Wall chart activity, 139
War
  comfort during, 168–170
  internment camps, 52–54
Weather investigation/report activities, 91, 97, 155

Web page creation activities, 36, 95, 114, 119, 151
Web research activities, 38, 54, 59, 63, 66, 67, 72, 73, 75, 78, 81, 89, 91, 98, 100, 101, 104, 107, 108, 110, 111, 114, 116, 117, 119, 120, 123, 129, 135, 136, 139, 142, 145, 148, 151, 155, 158, 163, 166, 167
Webquest activities, 110, 114
Western Hemisphere, 4, 65
Wetlands environment, 99–101
Where Horses Run Free: A Dream for the American Mustang, 106
Widening horizons curriculum, 4
Wilfrid Gordon McDonald Partridge, 83
Williams, Maria, 65
Wolf, Bernard, 134
Wolfman, Judy, 93
Women, historical, 121, 122
Wood-cut illustrations activity, 105
Wood, Douglas, 46
Woodson, Jacqueline, 74
Word by word
  key words form, 210, 220
Word wall activity, 33
Word-meaning activity, 170
World, 153–170
  Amazon, 162–163
  Antarctica, 153–155
  China, 165–167
  conflict, comfort during, 168–170
  elementary school social studies program design
    hierarchy, 4
    typical topics, 4
  Mexico, 159–161
  rainforests, 162–164
  social studies concept, 196
  Zambia, 156–158
World War II, 54, 141, 142
Wright-Frierson, Virginia, 90
Writing activities, 35, 36, 39, 41, 42, 44, 48, 50, 53, 56, 59, 62, 67, 69, 75, 78, 81, 84, 88, 91, 95, 98, 133, 138, 139, 147, 150, 157, 166, 170. *See also* Letter-writing activities; Poetry activities; Prequel-writing activity; Sequel-writing activities; Song-writing activities; Story-writing activities

Yellow pages activities, 79, 84, 98
Yorinks, Adrienne, 124

Zambia, 156–158. *See also* Africa

About the Author

Anthony (Tony) D. Fredericks (afredericks60@comcast.net) is a nationally recognized children's literature expert well known for his energetic, humorous, and highly informative school visits throughout North America. His dynamic author presentations have captivated thousands of students in Canada, Mexico, and across the United States—all with rave reviews!

Tony is a former elementary teacher and reading specialist. He is the author of more than 100 books, including over 65 teacher resource books and more than three dozen award-winning children's books. His education titles include the best-selling *Science Fair Handbook* (3d ed.), which he co-authored with Isaac Asimov (Goodyear), the hugely popular *Frantic Frogs and Other Frankly Fractured Folktales for Readers Theatre* (Teacher Ideas Press), the highly praised *Guided Reading in Grades 3–6* (Harcourt Achieve), and the celebrated *More Social Studies Through Children's Literature* (Teacher Ideas Press).

His award-winning children's titles include *Under One Rock* (2002 Nature and Ecology Award); *Slugs* (2000 Outstanding Science Trade Book), *Around One Cactus* (2004 Teacher's Choice Award), *Near One Cattail* (2006 Green Earth Book Award), and *The Tsunami Quilt: Grandfather's Story,* among others.

Fredericks is the author of several trade books including the perennial favorite *The Complete Idiot's Guide to Success as a Teacher* (Alpha) and the acclaimed *The Complete Idiot's Guide to Teaching College* (Alpha). Tony currently teaches elementary methods courses and children's literature at York College in York, Pennsylvania.